The Unexpected Storm: The Gulf War Legacy

Hellgate Press
a division of PSI Research
P.O. Box 3727
Central Point, OR 97502-0032

(541) 245-6502
(541) 245-6505 *fax*
info@psi-research.com *e-mail*
www.psi-research.com/hellgate.htm

Editor: Kathy Marshbank
Book designer: Constance C. Dickinson
Compositor: Jan O. Olsson
Cover designer: J. C. Young

Library of Congress Cataloging-in-Publication Data
Manchester, Steven, 1967–
    The unexpected storm : the Gulf War legacy / Steven Manchester.
        p. cm.
    ISBN 1-55571-542-7 (cloth)
    1. Persian Gulf War, 1991—Veterans. 2. Persian Gulf War, 1991. I. Title.

PS3558.E6516 U54 2000
813'.54—dc21

                                                                            00-044986

Printed and bound in the United States of America
First edition 10 9 8 7 6 5 4 3 2 1

 Printed on recycled paper when available.

For any man or woman who has ever experienced war, especially those who have made the ultimate sacrifice, and never got the chance to tell their own story. And for Wil Souza — may you rest in the Lord's peace for eternity.

Contents

Foreword

The conceptual definition of war has run the gamut from the elevation of one's honor to the physical decimation of mankind. Theories pile one atop another from the gathering of historical scholars, to the summer barbecues where veterans and patriotism abound. The only pure strain of thought that crosses all these defined barriers is the truth that war is solely a distinctive "state of mind." I'm not referring here to a momentary burst of heroism or cowardice, but to a lifelong altered state which veterans either embrace, flee from, or form a livable truce with. Burdened with its superficial perceptions of war, society thereby dubs them either heroes, cowards, or "adjusted" civilians. The cold fact remains however, that this state of mind cannot be discarded from a veteran's life as a civilian might a pair of worn shoes. Here lies the innately true dichotomy: civilians must try to understand that this altered mindset is etched on the veteran until death. Only through a purely firsthand confessional, such as this, will everyone's inner-peace be attained.

American society and its leaders during Operation Desert Storm demanded our men and women in uniform what all wars do: to seek out and kill the maximum number of the enemy against whom they have no personal hatred. Desert Storm, like Vietnam, demanded that Americans enter a conflict against an armed force, which presented no physical dangers within the borders of the United States. In clearer terms, our Persian

Gulf vets were asked to kill for the ideals of fairness and honor. This reality forced every one of the 600,000 Americans involved in this conflict to deal with their own personal unexpected storm.

Steven Manchester has definitively and quite emotionally taken the concept of war to a deeply inward and higher level. Few pieces of factual literature in recent decades have ventured into this raging state of mind.

This is not merely a factually reported document, but an eerily inspiring journey through Manchester's maddening escape from civilian innocence, fluctuating alteration of personal values and fruition of nightmarish courage. His suicidal disappointment in some of his fellow men, God-questioning soulful descent upon his return to married civilian life and the seemingly raised-eyebrow treatment of his Gulf War Syndrome by our politically correct government binds him irrevocably to the reader's heart.

Manchester completely bares all of his personal dysfunctions, soulful triumphs, and America's ills, which tweak, turn and grind into the readers' psyche throughout. He constantly delves into areas where veterans and civilians alike may find it impossible to safely return mentally unscathed. *The Unexpected Storm* is not simply a war novel, but a personal search for understanding and redemption by the author on behalf of all veterans regardless of their eras.

In the eye-level section of my personal library, I have for decades reserved an area for several dozen books of varying genre which invariably "call" to me on an annual basis. The common thread tying this category together is the pieces' ability to constantly take me on a personal value-questioning journey, or to honor me with a momentary sweat-filled insight into an altered state of mind. *The Unexpected Storm* has remarkably attained both of these criteria and will always be at arm's length when I become too stoic or pompous to grow personally.

Surely, Manchester will be heard from through his literary projects over the next several decades. As in *The Unexpected Storm,* I'm sure his works will always call to and give the seeking reader their needed personal grace.

These are words of faith in a higher being, of personal betrayal, and the harsh reality of truth that literally bleeds. Most of all, these are words of the courage needed for spiritual triumph and its unending toll on America.

This book is our brothers and sisters, fathers and daughters, husbands and wives who entered their own unexpected storm.

J. M. Frost
Cpl. U.S.M.C.

Acknowledgments

First and forever, Jesus Christ — my Lord and Savior.
With Him, all things are possible.

My sons, Evan and Jacob, who share the best part of my heart. Mom and Dad, Billy, Randy, Darlene and Jenny — who walked with me all the way.

The Dream Team of the 661st M.P. Company. By choice, you will always be my brothers. All military personnel that served in Operation Desert Storm. It was an honor to serve with you. I hope this first-hand account brings awareness to the price you paid for freedom; the price many of you continue to pay.

My agent, Michael Valentino, who believed in the message of this book and saw to its publication. Emmett Ramey and Kathy Marshbank who were gracious enough to offer the world an opportunity to form its own opinion about the "Mystery Illness."

In no particular order: Jenn, Taylor and Hannah Hollinrake, Rob and Julie Letendre, Danny and Carol Calis, Nelson and Tina Julius, Jack and Karen Frost, Patrick J. Barry, Celia, Colleen and Brittney, Mark and Katja Grocholski, Lou Matos, Matt and Cheryl Olivier, Melissa Bethoney, Helen LaChance, Barry M. McKee, Ken Weiss, Garth Patterson, Charles Turek Robinson, Rene Charest, Mike Scanlon, George Cournoyer, Lynn Stanton,

Dennis Butler, Robert Couture, Lisa Ahaesy, Maureen Estes, Jan Olsson and all those my poor memory has failed.

My life has been richly blessed for having known each one of you!

Mr. Gary Mauk for being kind enough to provide some of the book's photos.

And Russell N. McCarthy — an angel sent to help me spread the word about the aftermath of Operation Desert Storm. His support and encouragement are evidence that compassion remains alive and well.

Introduction

After the tragic suicide of his best friend, Steve Manchester struggles to find the free-spirited fun of a childhood lost. Surrounded by a platoon of comical friends, the sweetest laughter begins to beat in his heart. Before long, however, a madman known as Saddam Hussein replaces that echo with the haunting screams of war.

The notorious Iraqi dictator invades Kuwait with his henchmen, compiling the fourth largest army in the world. The atrocities and inhumane acts committed toward Kuwait prompt support from around the globe. War is declared. The world calls it Operation Desert Storm and soldiers are called to serve their countries. But who would have guessed? It was always a slim possibility, but in the National Guard, nobody ever thought they'd be sent to war. It is a storm Sergeant Steven Manchester never expected to weather.

Carrying his family's heavy bag of pain, at only 23, Steve sets a shaky foot on the shifting sands of the Arabian Desert. Through the exploring eyes of a child, he discovers a world filled with intrigue, raw excitement and paralyzing fear. It's obvious. America has arrived to defend Saudi Arabia, liberate Kuwait and embarrass the biggest bully of the post cold war era. America's sons and daughters have come to exact justice. The responsibilities brought to bear are immense, as there is so much at stake. Politically, there's America's leadership of the free world. Economically one tenth of the world's oil resources. Morally, the protection of human life. But silently, there is a rebirth of America's spirit. Steve and his comrades have come to heal their nation from a ghost that has haunted them for two decades; the poltergeist of Vietnam.

While Hussein threatens America with the mother of all battles, President George Bush draws a line in the sand. That line is quickly wrapped around Iraq and used to choke the life out of thousands. On February 23, 1991, danger stows away in the shadows, while death is less patient. The Grim Reaper waits to claim the hardened and tormented souls of fighting men. It is the eve of the ground war.

Saddam Hussein swears it will take the Americans months to cross the breach; a tall berm of sand. It takes hours and it only takes that long because the 1st Infantry utilizes armored bulldozers to lead the attack. The Iraqis carefully arrange rows of lethal obstacles. These prove no match for good old-fashioned American ingenuity. The large, bulky machines bury every barrier within their path. The fields of barbed and razor wire are easily trampled. The land mines, which litter the desert, explode within the steel buckets of the dozers. The Allied Forces move fast, crushing the first of three Iraqi lines of defense. The enemy has been dug in for weeks and now sits totally entrenched within their fighting positions. As if they aren't even there, the American war machine rolls right over them. Relatively unopposed, the U.S. Army storms in, discovering that they have overestimated the enemy. Even the dreaded oil trenches are quickly plowed over with tons of sand. This creates a hellish grave of man-made quicksand for those caught beneath. Many Iraqi soldiers drown at the bottom of those greasy pits. Soon after, The Dream Team of the 661st M.P. Company is called forward.

Stealing away the last remnants of innocence, Steve and his friends witness the after-effects of 41 days of uninterrupted bombing. They quickly discover that the pictures, once created by the mind's eye, are far less devastating. It is as if someone raises the curtain to hell, permitting everyone a free show. It is literally hell on earth.

The land is strewn with unexploded bombs. The ones, that did hit their targets, leave hundreds of destroyed tanks and artillery pieces lying about. As far as the eye can see, tons of scrap metal are torn from the war machines and catapulted into the open desert. It is clear. The Arabian Desert has been used as a testing ground for every new weapon in the American arsenal.

While Hussein chooses to sit out the air campaign, his people are annihilated in masses. The Iraqi people bear the brunt for their ruthless dictator and like all victims of war; they pay with gallons upon gallons of their own blood. There is a massacre. The amount of casualties left behind is catastrophic. In such a time and place, it doesn't matter. They're wearing uniforms. It's war.

It takes four days, or a mere 100 hours, before the ground war is ceased. History is made. In triumph, Kuwait is liberated, while Hussein is humiliated before the whole world. An unconditional withdrawal is ordered. This time, the governing monster isn't in the position to ignore the instructions. Politically, the sadistic demon is slain. In reality, unlike thousands of his own people, he still lives.

America's moral crusade, however, is complete. On February 28, 1991, Iraq surrenders. The rest is damage control. The only thing left is to pick up the pieces. It is then that Steve and the boys are truly called upon. While the world celebrates euphorically, The Dream Team's work has just begun.

While America's technology continues to erase the poltergeist of Vietnam, Steve's body is invaded with its own ghost of torment. Amidst the daily chaos, he witnesses the senseless death of innocent children, the frailties of his own mortality and unlike CNN's version of the desert clash — the realization that there is no glory in war. Then, as a lasting memento, he is brutally introduced to "The Mystery Illness." Strangely enough, this only adds up to half of his inner-struggles.

From Steve's perspective, Operation Desert Storm becomes a war of anxiety and rage. He and his comrades never meet the real enemy face-to-face. Instead, the enemy remains invisible — planting their land mines, murdering sinless children and vanishing into the shadows of the shifting sands. No threat is seen, yet still felt deep within. The constant anticipation is like speeding 200 miles per hour, only to smash into a brick wall each time. Like a man restrained, Steve witnesses the slaughter of pure innocence, while being forced to helplessly stand back and watch. There are no means to displace the anger, nor any outlet for the aggression. There is only the frustration of seeing constant victimization, while being able to do relatively nothing about it. Operation Desert Storm proves to be a war like no others. Soldiers are trained to fight, sent to strike, yet watch as technology does the job. In a sick sense, had Steve been shot at, then returned fire, all of the hatred and horrifying death would have made better sense. All the rage, which was always fueled by fear, would have been unleashed and not been stored deep within, where it multiplied and silently destroyed.

Returning, visibly whole, to a proud and grateful nation, Steve reports being violently ill with flu-like symptoms. The cruel game is sinful. After the meticulous pre-war exam, the veterans of Operation Desert Storm aren't even given a token physical examination. The army doesn't even pretend to care. Like their predecessors of Vietnam, Uncle Sam just wants them off his menial payroll. After months of selfless service to their country, Steve and his friends are dismissed without so much as a proper medical screening. Only months earlier, America's defenders of democracy proudly answered their country's call. With honor, they helped free Kuwait from the forces of oppression. Now, suffering from a wide variety of debilitating symptoms, they are never diagnosed or treated for any.

Together, they must fight again. This new battle, however, proves far fierce and their invisible enemy better prepared to fight. The veterans of Operation Desert Storm must fight for the truth; the truth about what the government quickly labels the "Persian Gulf Syndrome," or "Mystery Illness."

Steve eventually determines that there are three very likely causes for the crippling ailments. They were exposed to radioactive depleted uranium used by the Allied Forces. There were preventive, or experimental, vaccines administered to all American troops. There was also the possibility that chemical agents were used in the many Iraqi Scud attacks. The government offers other potential causes. They claim that the puzzling illnesses could have been caused by microwave radiation, petrochemicals, insect bites, parasites, contamination from oil well fires, even the Allied bombing of specific bunkers storing Iraqi chemical agents. The list grows by the month. They point fingers in every direction but their own. Ironically, the causes of the physical illnesses don't really matter. That answer can only come from the same government that always realized some truths are just too big, or too expensive, to tell. The real concerns become treatment and compensation.

Steve learns that all war wounds aren't suffered on the battlefield. The government, however, is generous enough to hand him another dark, little secret. Not all war wounds are visible either. For many Desert Storm Veterans, although the yellow ribbons and flags are taken down, the shiny medals lose their gleam and the euphoria of victory subsides, the war is far from over!

For the second time in his life, the army has broken Steve down. This time, however, the damage reaches the four deepest levels of his inner being. He is affected physically, mentally, emotionally and even spiritually. Left shattered, the burden of putting the pieces back together lie in his desire to reclaim his life. It's like starting over, only now he is starting in a hole; a deep dark hole.

Operation Desert Storm is complete, but Steve embarks on a more painful mission. He is carried away in the eye of his own storm. It is a storm that rages out of control deep inside of him, tearing at his spirit, his whole being. There are two enemies to fight this time. The first is the U.S. government. The second battlefront, and one far more ferocious, rages within his heart and mind. He helped to win the war, now he only needs to win the peace. Sergeant Steven Manchester arrives at the unexpected storm . . . .

Chapter 1

Marching into Manhood

Like the wife who waited behind, the ignition of the enormous turbine engines screamed out one last goodbye. It was a C-5A Galaxy; the second largest aircraft in the world. Containing four levels, the bottom deck alone, was capable of transporting 18 Greyhound busses. Instead, several dozen Humvees, the U.S. Army's replacement for the Jeep, were chained to the floor. Both the nose and tail of the aircraft opened, allowing the armed Humvees to drive directly out of its belly. They were combat ready. Peacefully sitting idle, they waited to roll out onto the largest sand trap in the world.

The members of the 661st M.P. Company; a Massachusetts Army National Guard unit destined for the Middle East, were located on the upper deck. The seats, in tightly spaced rows, were filled with more than 120 men and women, all of them part-time soldiers or Weekend Warriors, as they were labeled. Their initial destination: The Kingdom of Saudi Arabia. Their mission: Unknown!

A madman known as Saddam Hussein, the notorious Iraqi dictator, invaded Kuwait with his henchmen, compiling the fourth largest army in the world. The atrocities and inhumane acts committed toward Kuwait prompted support from around the globe. War was declared. The world called it Operation Desert Storm, and soldiers were called to serve their countries. It was always a slim possibility, but nobody in the National

1

Guard ever thought they'd be sent to war. It was a storm the 661st never expected to have to weather.

There was a buzz throughout the cabin; nervous chatter caused by horrible anticipation. Some faces displayed fear, while others remained blank from either shock or denial. Sergeant Steven Manchester sat in the very last row of the cabin. Extinguishing a cigarette, per order of the C-5A's crew chief, he conducted one last head count of his people. There were seven men and two women. His squad was all accounted for. The crew chief politely called for everyone's attention.

Clearing his throat, he began, "The estimated time of arrival is 17 hours, but there will be a short lay-over in Europe in order to re-fuel. For safety's sake during the flight, will all squad leaders please insure that every weapon is unloaded."

Sergeant Manchester and the two other squad leaders stood and acknowledged the chief's request.

The crew chief nodded. "Get some rest people, it's a long trip." He quickly exited the cabin.

For a moment there was silence. Then, the anxious whispers of conversation continued.

Sergeant Manchester had already double-checked his squad's weaponry. He was confident there would be no accidents, at least not on the aircraft. He sat back, lit another cigarette and tried to relax. Physically, he felt exhausted. Yet, it was his mind that carried the greater burden. To him, the weight of the world rested upon his shoulders. At only 23, he was responsible for a squad of ten who were being sent to war. He left behind an injured wife to contend with their financial difficulties, so he carried that baggage as well. In such a short period of time, life had taken a brutal turn. Everything now lay in the hands of the United States Army. He knew he couldn't control his future. It was that loss of control he hated most.

Finishing his smoke, he noticed Johnny Tripp staring at him. Private Tripp, the squad's 18-year-old machine gunner, looked terrified. Putting on his most comforting smile, he shot the boy a wink. Johnny smiled back, but the look of gripping fear remained. Steve closed his eyes in search of peace. There was none to be found. There were just too many questions that needed answers.

He wondered if they were prepared. Was the brief training sufficient? What if? There were so many what ifs! He wasn't sure he wanted to know the answers. Breathing deeply, his mind began to wander. As his thoughts dove deeper, he asked himself how in the hell he'd ever gotten himself into this one? And then it came back to him; all of it. He began to remember . . . .

The year was 1984 and summer had quickly turned to autumn in Massachusetts. For most people, the foliage and gorgeous sunset were absolutely breathtaking, but not for Steve Manchester. He was born in New England, raised just 14 miles from the sandy beaches of the Atlantic.

The summer said goodbye and he was sorry to see it go. What a summer it had been! A season full of firsts; his first car, his first girlfriend and his first experience with love. He had entered into manhood at the ripe old age of 16. At least that's what he thought.

Along with the nice weather, Steve's first love headed south. He still had the car though; the car that cost him three years of tips peddling newspapers and two years of a dishwasher's wages. It was a 1965 Buick Special convertible — The Old Special. Its faded paint was powder blue with a worn interior to match. The Special was a definite eye-catcher. More than anything, he loved the car for the freedom he felt when driving. With the open skies above and the wind swirling all around him, there was no better feeling. No matter the weather, the top was down and the stereo turned up loud. Young Mr. Manchester was a free-spirit who loved life.

As he drove his rag-top up the winding road, the air felt colder. In his rear-view mirror, he glanced down at the image of the back seat and smiled. Daydreaming about his first sexual encounter, he nearly missed the driveway leading to his friend's house.

Wil Souza, Steve's best friend, was waiting on the front porch. He laughed and shook his head. He knew Steve better than anyone. His head was always in the clouds. Steve was a dreamer, the very reason he was so fun to be around. Before the car completely stopped, Wil dove head-first over the passenger side door. He landed on the front seat, his head almost in Steve's lap. They both laughed.

"Where we going, buddy?" Wil asked.

"Who cares. I still got beers left over from the drive-in!"

"Well then, if you want, we can hang out here. It's Friday night and my parents will be gone 'til late."

"Sounds good to me. The gas tank's on E anyway."

Steve jumped out from behind the wheel and unlocked the trunk. Searching hard, he finally reached in for an old styrofoam cooler. It contained a six pack and a half of Budweisers. It was the remainder of a case he had convinced some college kid to buy for him.

Remembering the long wait, he reminded Wil, "Enjoy, 'cause God only knows when we'll get more."

Twisting off the cap, Wil took a swig and raised his eyebrows in acknowledgment.

They sat parked in the driveway for hours, listening to rock and roll and drinking. The more the alcohol took effect, the more they talked. The conversation was lighthearted at first, but before long, it got serious. They talked about everything and the night reached a whole new depth. Steve realized he and Wil had never shared their feelings before.

Steven Manchester and William Souza; childhood pals from the same neighborhood. They shared the same age and both possessed a sense of humor unmatched by most. Besides these similarities, however, they had very little in common.

Steve had a baby face with blue eyes and sandy blond hair. Standing six feet tall, he was slightly overweight. The middle son of three boys, he was fortunate to have strict parents, a mother and father who instilled respect, integrity and the importance of love. Raised in a working class family, his dad was a truck driver; his mom, a full-time homemaker. He was a big kid, who grew up fighting with his brothers, Bill and Randy. He hated every confrontation. Though he did his best to conceal it, he was extremely sensitive. He absolutely detested conflict and preferred to help people when the opportunity arose. With a smile plastered on his face, he learned very young that his greatest joy was making people laugh. He even repeated the first grade for clowning around, but later told everybody it was because he flunked coloring. He was a dreamer. On the outside, his quick wit masked all of his fears and doubts. Except for his love for family and friends, he concealed most of his feelings. Growing up with more love than money, he was lucky enough to learn the truly important things in life. He was blessed.

Wil, on the other hand, was darker-complected, with brown hair and eyes. He stood taller than six feet on a wiry frame. His face appeared old and weathered. He was the youngest child of eight brothers and sisters. Born late in his mother's life, his siblings had already moved out. The family wasn't very close. His parents spent little time or attention on him. The Souza family had money, but not much else. His mom was a dental assistant and was quite submissive to his overbearing father, a Korean War veteran. The mean old coot collected a disability pension, but acted as if he were still in the service. He was a strange man at best.

Armed with a quick wit, Wil held the title as the Senior Class Clown. He made others laugh while he was dying inside. With many obstacles in his way, he wanted to do the right thing. He was scared, but hoped Steve would help him. He never doubted that Steve would.

The darkness of the night crept in, a blanket of stars covered the sky, and the beer was gone. Lounging in the front seat, Steve attempted to lighten the conversation by telling jokes. Wil cut him off.

With his famous smile, he asked, "What do you think about joining the Marines together?"

"Are you serious?"

"Yeah! What do you think?"

"Wow!" Buzzing from the beer, Steve tried to clear his fogged head. "I just started my Junior year," he slurred, "I wanna finish school, then maybe go to college for Law Enforcement. I'm pretty sure I wanna be a cop. I've always wanted to help people."

As a kid, Steve watched a police officer pull a lady from a burning automobile wreck. The man was a hero, but more importantly, he was respected. From that day on, he had wanted respect more than anything.

Wil leaned forward until he was inches from Steve's face. "Let's do it! The buddy system. We can go part time, maybe the reserves. It'll give us time to finish school. If it's good, we'll go full time later!"

As a result of the booze, Steve giggled, but his friend was dead serious. "I'll do it, buddy, but to hell with the Marine Corps. I wanna use my brain. Let's go Army — Military Police. It'll give me the edge over my future competition."

Wil smiled and nodded in agreement. "We'll go see the recruiter on Monday after school."

They shook hands. It was a done deal, if Steve's parents would sign the papers. Wil's parents, however, would be delighted. Out of eight children, only his sister, the family outcast, never joined.

Wil jumped out of the Special, giving Steve a thumbs-up.

As he backed out of the driveway, Wil yelled, "I love ya, brother!"

He smiled, returned the thumbs-up and started home. Living only two streets over, he took it slow. His head was spinning, and it wasn't only from the alcohol. As he pulled into his driveway, he secured the top onto the car. He sat back in silence for a long time. He thought about Wil and the serious pact that was just made. He put very little thought into the decision and knew there was no turning back now. No matter what, he gave Wil his word. Locking the car door, he walked toward the house. With each step, he tried convincing himself that he had made the right choice. He knew Wil. Whether drunk or sober, Wil wanted this in a bad way. His friend needed to escape.

Raising his hands toward the sky, he said aloud, "Who knows, it'll probably be a good experience for both of us." Though he never doubted that their reasons for joining were different. He would finally prove to himself that he was tough, while Wil could prove it to everybody else; especially his cruel father.

Steve was the clown of the Junior class. He made everyone laugh, even most teachers. The irony was that he was no dummy. He took all pre-college courses and earned good grades. He also prided himself on never taking home a book. His motto was: If you can't learn it in the classroom, then it can't be learned. This long-standing attitude had cost him an extra year in school. As a result, he and Wil wouldn't graduate together.

On Monday afternoon, the buzzer sounded the end of the school day. Steve put the top down on the Special and headed home. Climbing the stairs to his family's apartment, he heard his mother humming a tune in the kitchen. It was the right time. She was in a good mood. Opening the door, he noticed her standing over a large pot. Something smelled good. As he walked past her, he stopped just long enough to kiss her cheek. She smiled, but immediately noticed that her happy clown wasn't doing the same. "How was school today?" she asked.

With a devilish smirk, he yelled from his bedroom, "Same old stuff, Ma. But I think Mr. Stanley, my biology teacher, wants to adopt me!"

She chuckled at his wit, but still sensed that something was bothering him. Calling him out of the room, she raised her eyebrows. "What's on your mind?"

Without awaiting the answer, she lit a cigarette and sat down at the kitchen table. She gestured for him to sit. He anxiously joined her.

She was a good mother; the best. Nancy Manchester was a short woman, with brown hair and a pair of knowing brown eyes. She grew up the hard way, but her heart was full of love, especially for her boys. No matter the subject, she could never be fooled, and always took the time to talk. Whether it was trouble in school or conversations about sex, openness and honesty were rule number one in the Manchester family. Some things were still difficult to explain, though. He looked into his mother's penetrating stare and knew it was time to talk.

Hesitantly, he started, "I've been thinking, Ma. I wanna join the Army Reserves with Wil." The rest spilled out in one quick blurt. "They'll pay for college and I can get training as an M.P."

Her stare became deeper. "Are you sure this is what you want? Have you really thought about it?"

"It's definitely what I want, and I have thought about it, Ma. I can't go wrong!" He spoke in the most convincing voice he could muster.

"As long as your sure, I'll sign," she said, "but this is the first time you've ever mentioned the service."

He felt relieved. It was easier than he expected. He kissed her again, whispering, "Thanks, Ma."

Before long, he excused himself from the table, but his mother remained. Taking a long drag on the cigarette, she shook her head. She wanted the best for her sons and didn't like his new idea, but she would sign. It was his life and he was determined.

During supper, Steve's dad and brothers were let in on his newest brainstorm. Billy had nothing but words of encouragement. Randy kept repeating, "Air Force. Go Air Force."

His dad listened patiently while the boys talked, then strongly advised him, "If your heart tells you to go, then go, but give it all you've got!"

Bill Manchester Sr. was a great provider who expected his sons to give their best in whatever they chose. With a heavy hand and stern voice, he taught his boys the hard lessons of life. He winked. "Just remember to work smart, not hard."

Supper had just ended when a car horn honked twice under the kitchen window. It was Wil. He was in a hurry to take the plunge.

The recruiter's office was located two cities over. During the trip, both boys remained silent. Steve was deep in thought and Wil kept smiling from ear-to-ear. Minutes later, they were sitting outside a National Guard armory, while their destiny awaited them within.

The recruiter, a young Oriental built like a fireplug, greeted them with a smile. He introduced himself as Sergeant Chen, and bought them each a Pepsi from the office vending machine. As he talked, he reminded Steve of a used car salesman.

"Can you guys do eleven push-ups?" he asked.

They both laughed. "No problem!" replied Wil.

"I can already tell. You guys will have no problem."

For the next hour, the U.S. Army's top salesman talked about the benefits of joining. He played a seven-minute video tape on Army life, then made the easiest sale of his career: Two brand new recruits. Their final decision was the U.S. Army National Guard for a six-year enlistment. They were entitled to free tuition to any state college, all for only one weekend a month and two weeks out of every summer. It wasn't a bad deal. Of course, there was one final catch: Potential activation for state emergencies, or in the event of war.

"But what's the chances?" quipped the recruiter.

"With our luck, real good," replied Steve sarcastically.

Within three days, the two passed the written and physical exams. They were immediately assigned to the 636th M.P. Company, Camp Edwards, Cape Cod, Massachusetts.

"Do or die," said Wil, "we're in it together!"

Basic training was postponed until they finished the school year, so for six months, they reported for weekend drills in civilian clothes. They lacked training and weren't required to keep their hair as short as the other troops. As a result, they felt incredibly ignorant. They quickly became outcasts assigned to a unit full of fat, sloppy drunks. Though it wasn't the true impression of the National Guard, it was miserable from the start. It got worse with each passing month.

The unit contained cliques of older men. Neither Steve nor Wil were accepted into any of them. For the first time in their lives, they didn't fit in. As these men, who were anything but soldiers, laughed and played their games, the two looked on in silence. Steve couldn't believe that he and Wil had been assigned to the worse M.P. unit in the state. The 636th failed every annual training, and prided themselves on avoiding most duties. The real tragedy, however, was that the misery he and Wil felt, eventually became a wedge between them. Rather than make the most of it, they endured the grief individually. Their confidence was shaken and their friendship was being torn apart.

On several occasions, Steve tried to talk to Wil about the lousy unit. "Screw it, Wil. It sucks, but it doesn't have to change us!"

Wil hissed, "I've wanted this all my life, and when I finally get it, it's bullshit. All bullshit!" He didn't even look at Steve's face when he said it.

Steve sensed that his friend felt guilty, but there was something more that was eating at him; something much worse. As hard as he tried, he just couldn't figure out what it was. Alas, summer was approaching and he hoped that boot camp would change things. He wanted his friend back; the friend who once opened up to him. He longed for the same friend who had even said he loved him.

It was late May, 1985. Steve and Wil boarded a plane destined for Fort McClellan, Alabama. A nervous apprehension set in, and they talked openly on the flight. Each knew he was facing a rocky road ahead. It was a tremendous challenge. They were young and scared, but promised they'd stick together. It was the first time Steve had ever left home. He was determined not to return until he graduated. Looking to his right, he saw Wil's face glow with excitement. His best friend was coming back to life and he couldn't have been happier because of it. As the plane made its final descent, they shook hands. It was the same handshake they shared in Wil's driveway on the night they had decided to join. Steve truly felt he had made the right decision. He was ready to give it his all and Wil was right there with him.

Exiting the plane, he yelled, "Let the games begin!"

Pumped up with adrenaline, Wil echoed, "Yeah!" And it began.

The hot Southern air was suffocating. It was sure to melt away pounds of sweat in the weeks to follow. They were herded into a cattle car, designed to transport hundreds. Packed like sardines, everybody had the same look of horror in their eyes. Nobody knew what to expect and everybody was breathing heavy. It was a combination of the dreadful heat and thick tension. As the tractor trailer came to a stop, Steve waited for the worst. The side doors opened and the Army's newest property was unloaded, but there was no screaming or cursing. There wasn't even a hint of harassment or intimidation. There was only silence. A young Army clerk, standing alone on a high wooden platform, yelled, "Welcome to Fort McClellan, home of the U.S. Military Police Corps!" Steve looked over at Wil and smiled.

The first stop was the Reception Station. It was where all heads were shaved and numbers of bodies were slotted for the different training companies. During the processing, they enjoyed two days of the wrong impression — they relaxed. One minute, they were comfortable enough, and the next, their names were announced. Privates Manchester and Souza suddenly belonged to Delta Company, one of the five companies in the Tenth M.P. Battalion. Rumors were the Tenth was the toughest at McClellan.

After receiving their assignment, they were stuffed back into the cattle car with over 100 other boys. Everyone carried heavy duffel bags stuffed with uniforms and equipment, and they were all sweating over the same predicament. For the next ten weeks, they would eat, sleep and shit together. Everything would be shared, to include the good times and bad. There would be friendships made to last a lifetime.

The brakes on the cattle car let out a shriek, throwing everybody to the front. It was intentional. While each private scrambled to his feet, the doors opened. The real U.S. Army waited just outside. There were nearly a dozen of the meanest looking men Steve had ever seen, each one ready to play with his new toy soldiers.

The stifling air exploded with screaming insults. "You fuckin' maggots, why ain't you off my truck yet?" barked one Drill Instructor.

Other D.I.s paced back and forth, searching for the face in the crowd they didn't like. Trainees literally stepped over each other to get out of the cattle car. The D.I.s created chaos and panic. It was their job, and they did it well. Within seconds, Steve found himself standing in a formation, staring straight ahead. He felt his knees quiver, but he never moved an inch. He sensed Wil was standing on his left, but out of the corner of his eye, he spotted one of the rigid Smoky hats approaching. He was a black D.I., a monster, and he was marching straight toward him.

The D.I. bent down and stared Steve right in the eyes. He screamed, "What's the matter ass-wipe, you don't wanna look at me? It must be 'cause I'm ugly like your Mamma, huh?"

Steve stared straight through him. No eye contact, he kept telling himself, no eye contact.

Steve didn't bite, so the D.I. moved down the line. He came nose-to-nose with each of them. All the D.I.s were doing the same. They circled through the crowd like vultures, each waiting for one of the scared rabbits to flinch. Then it happened. The same D.I. who left spit on Steve's face finally got one.

He roared, "You like eye-balling me boy? You must be a tough bastard, huh boy?"

In a loud, but squeaky voice, the trainee answered, "No, sir!" It was Wil.

Oh God, not Wil, thought Steve. But the wheels of torture were already in motion.

The dark giant called everyone's attention to Wil. He screeched, "This here is a punk with an attitude problem."

Wil stood erect, as the entire staff of Drill Instructors went up one side of him and down the other. They reached decibel levels barely possible.

"Watch and learn how bad attitudes are re-adjusted in Delta Company!" Wil Souza was made the first example of many. It was anything but nice.

The D.I. graphically instructed him. "Pick up your duffel bag and double time it to the third floor!"

Wil ran the heavy bag up the stairs. He secured it in a wall locker, ran back down and reported to the smirking giant. The problem was that there were six flights to climb and he was being timed. Steve and the others watched with both fear and sympathy, as he never made it in time. He was forced to perform the duffel shuffle a half dozen times before collapsing. As the painful charade came to an end, the intended message was received loud and clear. They were now at the mercy of the drill sergeants, every second of every day.

Steve and Wil were assigned to the Fourth Platoon. Luckily, they grabbed their own bunk bed at the front of the barracks. Steve slept on the top bunk, Wil on the bottom. One was not to go anywhere, or do anything, without the other. Bunkmates were automatically buddies. It was a good deal. The Fourth Platoon, or Smoke Platoon, was run by D.I.s Vega and Spagnola, two highly disciplined soldiers. They accepted nothing less than what they could do themselves. This proved no easy task for any private.

Drill Sergeant Spagnola's upper body formed a perfect V. He was in phenomenal shape and his answer to everything was push-ups. From day one, when he thought one of his privates had screwed up, he whistled the theme song from Hawaii 5-0. As fate would have it, Steve was one of his first victims. He scratched his leg in formation one morning and found himself diving to the ground, giving Spagnola 50 push-ups. Straining to stand, he looked at Wil and rolled his eyes. He remembered the recruiter's question. Can you do eleven push-ups?

Then there was Drill Sergeant Vega. He was the shortest, most feared D.I. in the Company. With a nasty wad of chewing tobacco protruding from his bottom lip, the mean S.O.B. constantly threatened to re-cycle any private back to day one. He had that option and nobody ever doubted he'd use it.

The first few weeks were a hellish kind of culture shock. Steve soon discovered what being homesick meant. He missed his family dearly, but the unending days were filled with other things to think about. As Vega put it, "You need to keep your head out of your ass!"

The physical conditioning was intense, but nothing compared to the brutal head games being played day and night. Rudely awaken at 4:00 A.M., the torment didn't end until 10:00 P.M., which was lights out.

During one afternoon formation, Drill Sergeant Spagnola asked, "How many volunteers do I have that can run heavy machinery?"

Three privates raised their hands. Spagnola handed them each a shovel, instructing them to move a pile of crushed stone from one area to another. Several privates, standing in the rear of the formation, laughed at the fools. For their compassion, Spagnola handed them each a tablespoon and ordered them to assist. Volunteers were scarce from then on. Every private gave serious thought to each action taken. It was no joke, not a minute of it.

Right from the start, Steve and Wil made friends with their training comrades. Joking with Wil one night, Steve said, "It's no wonder the Army gets more done before 9:00 A.M. than most people do all day. We're up five frigin' hours earlier." The barracks filled with laughter.

The Fourth came from all corners of the country. Most enjoyed the Massachusetts' accents of Steve and Wil, but it was their uplifting humor that earned them friends. It made the hard times more tolerable, though it was those difficult times that fostered teamwork and camaraderie — a major training objective. As one day led into the next, the Fourth Platoon learned discipline, endurance and the importance of a positive attitude. The drill sergeants broke them down and were molding them the Army way.

For ten long, cruel weeks, Privates Manchester and Souza learned the art of exterminating human lives, while also learning to preserve their own. From rifles and hand grenades to various land mines, the training objective always remained the same: Kill or be killed. It was a simple motto and the training staff constantly imbedded it into the minds of all. During the five-mile morning runs, the Smoke Platoon echoed D.I. Vega's cadence, "Kill a Commie for your Mommy." Some labeled it brainwashing, but to the impressionable mind of a 17-year-old, it was merely preparing for the ultimate task — war.

During the last week of boot camp, Wil was dropped by Spagnola. The D.I. wanted 50 good ones. Something very different happened. Steve dropped with Wil and prepared to do the 50 with him. When Steve dropped, the ten-man squad dropped. Gradually, the entire 40-man platoon gave Spagnola 50 strict push-ups. Upon completion, the monster ordered his platoon to attention.

In his strongest voice of the summer, he roared, "It took all this fuckin' time, but I finally got myself one fighting machine. Each individual part thinks alike, works together and is willing to make the sacrifice. You boys are now soldiers and there isn't one of you I wouldn't fight alongside!"

It was a great compliment coming from Sergeant Spagnola. He was a Vietnam veteran. The Smoke Platoon exploded into cheers. Wil yelled the loudest. Steve couldn't help but think that Wil had finally gotten the approval and recognition his father never gave him. He was elated for Wil. In some strange way, Spagnola's few words made it all worthwhile. Though Steve made it too, he didn't feel any tougher, like he had expected. More importantly, he felt a great sense of achievement and pride, as though he was just a little older than 17.

Ten weeks to the day after they had trampled off the cattle car, each boy graduated a soldier. During the ceremony, Sergeant Spagnola beamed with pride, while handing out the graduation certificates. D.I. Vega stood off to the side. The cynical man just kept shaking his head. Steve knew that the son of a bitch didn't want it to end. He grinned at him with disrespect, but Vega stood stone-faced, crossing his arms.

The morning they were scheduled to leave finally came. Steve and Wil, dressed in Class-A uniforms, traded telephone numbers and addresses with their boot camp brothers. It was time to say goodbye. It wasn't easy. Most of the Smoke Platoon stayed for M.P. School and were shipped off to their regular Army duty assignments throughout the world. Like Steve and Wil, the others would return in a year to complete the school. But, most would never see each other again.

To go through so much with people, then say goodbye forever, was sad, thought Steve. For him, it was over as fast as it had started. He just couldn't smile like Wil did, but he sorrowfully managed his goodbyes.

Solemnly marching to the bus stop, he noticed Drill Sergeant Vega waiting for the small group. Vega took one look at Steve and screeched, "I'll be here next year, asshole. In the meantime, why don't you do push-ups until I get tired!"

In his dress uniform, he dropped to the Alabama clay for the last time that summer. Dropping with Steve, Wil and the rest of them did push-ups until the bus arrived. They were under total control right up until the very last minute. There were no passes or free time, just harassment, grief and thousands of push-ups. Eventually called to attention, the group filed onto the bus. Steve and Wil sat in the rear and loosened their ties. As the bus pulled away from the curb, Drill Sergeant Vega waved goodbye. He wasn't smiling.

Wil turned to Steve. "What in the hell did you do to him?"

Steve giggled. "I just smiled at him during graduation. Screw'm, if he can't take a joke!"

"No, Steve, it's more like screw us if we end up in Delta next summer!" barked Wil. Steve merely shrugged in his old carefree manner. Two seconds later, Wil laughed out loud. "You're right, buddy. Screw Vega!"

As the bus drove through the base, everybody got one last look at their summer. For the first time, the steep green mountains, which they had trampled over for weeks, looked absolutely beautiful. Even the hot, red clay, that they were forced to taste while doing push-ups, left a fond memory in their minds. Then they observed the clincher. New recruits ran in a tight formation, their cleanly shaven heads reflecting the relentless sun. Their drill sergeant was screaming his degrading vulgarities at them. Wil turned to Steve.

"Poor bastards!" he said.

No sooner had the words left his chapped lips, than the bus excited the front gates of Fort McClellan. Everyone aboard let out a sigh of relief. It was finally over, at least for another year.

The plane arrived one hour late, but it didn't make much difference. Privates Manchester and Souza were finally free and home at last. Landing at Logan Airport in Boston, the dirty harbor never looked better. Walking through Gate 16, Steve saw his family standing in a tight huddle. They were searching the crowd, carefully scanning for their soldier. His own mother looked right past him. He smiled, remembering that he was 30 pounds lighter. As he walked toward them, their faces lit up. They finally recognized him. With goose bumps, he hugged his dad and brothers. There were tears of pride and relief. It was glorious.

Nancy Manchester walked over to Wil first. She wrapped her arms around him. They both cried.

"Welcome home, Wil. We're so proud of you. Steve wrote that you did great, but we never doubted you would. We love you Wil. Always remember that!"

Wil hugged her even tighter.

Thank God for Ma, Steve thought, noticing that there was nobody waiting to greet Wil. Wil's family cared even less than Steve had thought.

Grabbing their duffel bags, they walked with authority through the terminal. The new green uniforms had that effect. The Old Special was parked right outside the airport doors. Steve's eyes lit up when he saw it. Like a kid at Christmas, he sprinted toward the car.

While driving home, Steve realized that he and Wil had endured a season of experiences neither would forget. It was a part of both of them now, something that could never be taken away.

After dropping off the Manchester clan, they pulled into Wil's driveway. There was no one there to greet him.

Putting on his best face, Wil grinned. "Where you heading?"

"Probably for a quick ride to the beach. You wanna come?"

"Thanks anyway. I'm beat." Broadening his smile, he asked, "It was fun while it lasted though, wasn't it?"

"Yeah right, Wil," laughed Steve. "What are you gonna do?"

"I'm gonna get the hell away from you for starters. Then I'm gonna find myself a party with plenty of women!"

Steve agreed. Two people could only spend so much time together before it got old. It was time they took a break from each other. They shook hands. Wil walked toward the front door of the huge house and quickly disappeared behind it.

After returning from the beach, Steve spent hours telling his family about his summer adventure. It was the first time he shared a beer with his dad. It was the best brew he had ever tasted. The night grew late and everybody finally went to bed, except for Steve and his mom. They sat alone at the kitchen table, as they had done so many times before. Looking into his eyes, she knew, as she had known for hours.

In a gentle voice, she asked, "What is it, Steve? Tell me."

He didn't answer, but his mother knew. Some innocence was lost.

At 17, her son had returned home a man, a sensitive man, but a man no less.

Chapter 2

The Tragic Death
of Innocence

While Wil began the fall semester at a local community college, Steve started his senior year of high school. He found that his reputation for being a tough guy, had grown dramatically due to his Army training. Very few high school students attended boot camp before they graduated. To the under-classmen, he was larger than life. To his peers, he was respected. He enjoyed that respect the most.

Before long, he met Monica Rinaldi. She had brown eyes, dark hair and a smile which made him fall head over heels. They quickly became an item. The other guys in school knew it was hands off, as the young lovers spent every weekend at the beach or the drive-in theater. His love for Monica grew quickly. She was different from the other girls in school and he knew it. They became inseparable. His high school buddies didn't care for it, and Wil liked it even less. He called Steve at home one night.

"Buddy, I don't think Monica's good for you!"

"You don't even know her, Wil," he snapped. "Besides, you've been so busy hanging around with your new friends." There was a pause. "From what I hear, they're into drugs pretty heavy?"

Wil had no reply. He just hung up the phone, leaving Steve cursing his name. Returning the telephone receiver to its cradle, he thought about Wil's new friends. Wil was hanging around the wrong crowd and should've known better.

From that brief phone call on, they only saw each other on weekend drills. Both acted as though there was no problem between them. Actually, they had no choice. They were forced to share one weekend a month in a situation they both despised. The unit was as bad as ever, but after seeing the real Army, they tolerated the weekend masquerades. Neither of them cared if they fit in. Instead, they rudely avoided most conversation with the others. It just didn't matter any more.

While carpooling to Camp Edwards every month, they laughed at each other's humor the entire way. It was the same during the drills. Everything was a joke. Nothing was serious. It was a turn for the worse. There were no more long talks. There was either laughter or silence.

As in the case of most high school seniors, Steve had the year of his life. The fun and games never ended. From the classrooms to their after school follies, he and his classmates lived each day to the fullest. He was on top of the world. He had the best bunch of friends; Scott, Matt and George. He had The Old Special and, of course, there was Monica. God, did he love her.

But there was something missing. It was Wil. He really missed Wil. His oldest friend was lost in a crowd of drug-using losers. Steve knew they were still obligated to face one more summer of hell together. Military Police School was coming quick. The thought of it hung over his head for the entire year. Remembering Drill Sergeant Vega's promise, he put the thought out of his head. He hoped though, that the struggles of the Alabama trip would make things right.

The year ended with a bang. The prom was unforgettable, and the parties were great. During the graduation ceremony, the class of 1986 threw their caps into the rafters of the gymnasium. Their diplomas were tickets out of childhood — free passes into the real world. Most of the Seniors were going on to college, others into the military. They all had one last summer — all of them but Steve. The U.S. Army had other plans for him.

The reality of it hit him during his going away party. The whole Manchester clan threw a cookout in the backyard, with a keg of beer included. He and Monica held hands under an ancient weeping willow tree. It was the same tree that had been used as a swing set, a fortress and anything else he and his brothers had imagined during their younger days. Monica got up to get more food and returned with Darlene, his one-year-old sister. The baby was a beautiful surprise for the Manchester boys. Their parents had decided to have a second family, 14 years after their youngest, Randy.

He and Monica played with Darlene under the shade of the old fortress. Holding the baby in his arms, he wondered if it was a vision of things to come. Then a loud noise interrupted his pleasant thoughts. Looking up, he watched as a beat-up Ford Torino rumbled up the driveway. It was Wil.

The old Ford was in rough shape. Wil parked the clunker and shut off the ignition. The car continued to run, sputtering and choking itself to death.

Walking toward the tree, he laughed. "Must be cheap gas."

Everyone laughed, especially Steve. There was excitement on his face. The love he felt for his family and friends was the only feeling he couldn't hide, and he loved Wil.

He jumped up and shook Wil's hand.

"Glad you made it brother," he yelped.

Wil was invited, but wasn't expected to show. Things still weren't right between them.

"I wouldn't have missed this for the world," he replied. "Hello Monica."

She cordially returned the gesture. Smiling, he sauntered over to Steve's mother, who was standing over the hot grill. They hugged and his eyes swelled with tears.

"We've missed you around here, Wil," she said, "it hasn't been the same without you and Steve's comedy routine."

Wil looked over at Steve and winked. "I've missed you, too. All of you!"

Steve got the message and his spine tingled. He was overjoyed. Wil was back again, and just in time.

The afternoon was filled with good food, cold beer and lots of laughter. It was like the old days. Steve and Wil took turns telling jokes and hilarious stories. It was a day that would not soon be forgotten.

Once the mosquitoes arrived, the party ended and Wil headed for his car. Rolling down the window, he screamed, "I'll see you tomorrow, Steve, bright and early. We'll finally get to show Sergeant Vega what we've got!"

Steve shook his head. "Don't even joke like that. If we get him, it'll be a bitch." There was a comical pause. "Then again, it really doesn't matter, does it?"

Wil threw out his signature thumbs-up and barely steered the tired Torino out of the driveway. Steve took that very opportunity to escape with Monica. There wasn't much time left.

The young lovers parked at their favorite spot — the beach. They kissed, and the passionate kisses quickly turned to heavy petting. Caught up in the moment, he forgot he had a surprise for her until a song on the radio reminded him. He climbed out of the back seat, leaving her frustrated and half-naked. Returning from the messy trunk, he carried a bottle of champagne, two glasses and a long stemmed rose. He jumped back into the Special, threw in a cassette of Lionel Richie and secured the top onto the car for privacy. For most of the evening, the windows remained steamed. They made love as if neither wanted the other to forget. As time passed, they held each other, made love and cried. They were facing an entire summer apart, with only hours before his departure. As he drove her home, he vowed, "I love you so much, Monica, that it hurts. I'm not sure I say it enough, but I really do love you with everything inside of me."

She wept so mournfully that she couldn't reply. Arriving at her house, he walked her to the front door and kissed her one last time. The salt from her tears tasted so strong that he held back his own. "I love you, too, Steve," she muttered, "and I know I always will." In those few minutes, they had spent an eternity saying goodbye. It was the toughest thing he had ever done. They had become so close. With an aching heart, he finally drove away, leaving her crying on her doorstep. Turning up the stereo, he took the long way home.

Nancy Manchester, dressed in an old housecoat, was waiting at the kitchen table. She looked exhausted. "You okay? Do you want to talk?"

"To be honest, Ma, I'm ready this time! I know what to expect and things are good between me and Wil again. I'll miss you all, of course, but I'm ready."

She kissed him goodnight and whispered, "We'll say so long in the morning then. Now, get some sleep."

The morning finally came and Steve made the goodbyes as brief as possible. He hated goodbyes. Picking up Wil before the sun peeked over the east horizon, Bill Sr. drove the boys to Logan Airport.

After handing Steve his duffel bag from the trunk, he slipped his son a 50-dollar bill, along with a wink. "Hopefully you get to spend it this year."

Their hug was cut short. It was time to go. Waving back, Steve hobbled through the doors leading to the Delta Airline terminal. In a year's time, he had grown out of his shiny black army shoes. They were so tight, he could hardly walk.

Dressed in uniform, he and Wil sat in the terminal near Gate Eleven. There was an hour's wait ahead. Two guys sat across from them. They could have easily passed for brothers. They wore the same haircuts, same uniforms and were obviously heading for the same Alabama vacation.

Steve looked over and said, "Hi."

Neither returned the friendly gesture. Instead, he swore that the two clowns were talking about he and Wil. He quietly revealed his suspicions.

Wil yawned. "Forget'em, Steve, let it go. We have other things to think about."

Wil was right, but for the next hour, he and the smaller of the two, a man his own size, exchanged many dirty looks. It turned into a stupid game. He didn't even know the guy, and already, he felt a deep dislike. Soon after, all four soldiers boarded the plane, with Steve limping behind.

Exhausted, he dozed off and slept during the entire flight. He was finally awaken by Wil's elbow buried in his side.

"Wake up, Steve. It's that time again." His voice was excited.

He wiped the sleep from his eyes. Smiling, he asked, "Time to go to work, huh?"

Wil stared straight ahead, never answering. He was excited, but focused on the weeks ahead.

"It's like déjà vu," Steve said. He looked behind him and saw the snickering face he had grown to dislike, hours before in Boston's airport. With a yawn, he turned back. "I hope Smiley's assigned to a different company!"

A bus, destined for Fort McClellan, picked them up at the airport. The ride was short. They drove right past the Reception Station and, before they knew it, they were parked in front of Bravo Company, Eleventh M.P. Battalion. Unloading their duffel bags, all four reported to the drill sergeant on duty. This time was different. The area was deserted. There were no screaming D.I.s and no privates doing push-ups.

D.I. Godfrey's face appeared weary. There was no hiding it. He was burned out. Sizing up the new stock, he laughed and grabbed Wil by the arm, placing him near his assigned buddy. It was the one Steve didn't like. The jerk smiled. The feelings were obviously mutual. Godfrey let out a cynical laugh. He knew he had split up two pairs of friends. It was no careless act. Steve cursed under his breath. D.I. Vega was nowhere to be found, but he and Wil were separated. It wasn't going to be like boot camp.

The four unpacked their gear and it was time to get acquainted. Steve introduced Wil to Pat O'Malley, his new partner. Grinning, Wil introduced Steve to Ryan White. Then it started.

Ryan asked, "Have you always had a bad attitude?"

"Just toward whimps!" responded Steve, with confidence.

For the next hour, witty insults and harsh words were exchanged between the two. Wil and Pat were quite entertained by the show.

Aiming for each other's throats, Steve finally hit a nerve. "I noticed your girlfriend leaving the airport. She jumped into some dude's car. I imagine she'll be playing the flute all summer while you sweat your ass off!"

There was silence. Everybody waited for punches to be thrown. Even Steve knew the comment was a low blow. Ryan sat with his mouth half-open. He had no comeback. A few tense seconds passed before he began giggling and couldn't stop. Steve and the other two joined in. The ice was broken. It took some nasty words, but at that moment, they had gained respect for each other. That respect became the foundation of a true friendship. Pat, Ryan's best friend, stood and shook Steve's hand.

"You beat him, buddy! Since we've been kids, I've never met a cockier bastard able to put his ass in check. It was great!"

Pat O'Malley stood six-feet, four-inches tall on an incredibly large frame, with light hair and eyes. Coming from a tight knit Irish family, he had one sister, but had figuratively adopted Ryan as his little brother. He and Ryan grew up together and were as close as Steve and Wil. They played high school football on the same team, and liked to party as much as anyone. The strongest trait Pat possessed, though, was his quick temper and rare fighting abilities. For those few he considered real friends, he gave the world, but for those who disrespected him, he was merciless. He was a tough kid who refused to lose. Thankfully, he was ordinarily in a good mood and his mere presence intimidated most enemies.

Ryan White, not quite so large, also had light hair and eyes. He was a big kid with a passive temperament. The product of divorced parents, Ryan's family consisted of mostly friends. Once he felt comfortable enough to open up, his personality was absolutely magnetic. He was a clown, attracting him many friends. It was anything for a laugh, no matter the price. His pranks normally landed him into trouble. Though he wanted to be a cop, for the time being, he enjoyed a child's view of life. But Ryan was also a bit of an instigator. More than anything, he loved to watch his giant friend fight.

Toward the end of those first few days, Steve discovered that Pat and Ryan had been laughing at the way he walked in the airport. The thought of a soldier limping from airport to airport, in shoes that no longer fit, even made Steve laugh. Through all the laughter, the four became the best of friends. It didn't take long. The blood blisters the shoes had caused, however, made Steve do anything but laugh over the next few weeks. Phase Two of Military Police School began.

The beginning proved even more difficult than boot camp. The runs started at five miles and the physical training was intense. The drill sergeants' names and faces changed, but the attitudes were the same. Every private was pushed to the very edge — the game to find each man's limit. For the four new guys, there was a lot of catching up. They were out of shape from a year of gluttonous home life. Bravo Company's First Platoon had already bonded through the hardships of boot camp, so there wasn't much room for outsiders. Displayed by the majority, this attitude forced the four friends to become even closer. With their distinct accents and ability to laugh in any situation, they stuck together from morning until night. Eventually accepted into the platoon, the new friends chose to keep things as they were. All four stood together as one.

Military Police School brought long days, and proved academically boring. Taught at a third grade level, for some it was still too fast. This frustrated the Massachusetts' boys. The head games had tapered off slightly from boot camp, but still were a major factor. The intimidation wasn't as hard to take. The experiences of the previous summer had built so much confidence that the boys were no longer as scared or impressionable. However, there was an incentive for behaving this time. It was the weekend passes. If all tests were passed and nobody screwed up royally, they were released from training on Friday afternoons.

The foursome normally went into Anniston or the next town over, Oxford, and rented a motel room. The sinks were always filled with crushed ice and beer. Partying all weekend became a ritual. It was their way of blowing off steam, while trying to capture a small piece of summer. Returning to the base for Sunday afternoon formations usually meant vomiting and severe hangovers. The drill sergeants had their share of fun at the expense of the suffering drunks. Sunday afternoon's physical training was brutal. It was never a pretty sight, but it didn't stop any one of the privates from drinking to excess, especially the Boston Crew.

The weeks flew by and Boston's Awesome Foursome — a label given by Drill Sergeant Godfrey — did more push-ups than any of the other privates. Godfrey never dropped just one for punishment. It was always all four, and not one of them had a problem with it. Sharing the grief was a morale builder. It actually became fun. Their stamina was building, but not as fast as their confidence. Nothing could stop them. One time, Steve even asked D.I. Godfrey to borrow his car. The platoon held back the laughs, as he and the boys nearly pushed Alabama off the map.

Midway through the cycle, the boys decided to switch the platoon's gruesome motto with their own twisted version. They sang, "Ginger bread, ginger bread, peppermint stick. We're not gay, but we suck *#@%!"

Everyone laughed but Godfrey. He was furious. "Platoon dismissed — except the Boston Crew." He barked. The laughs ended up costing the crew three days of extra duty in the kitchen, two nights loss of sleep and one weekend pass. In the long run, however, the prank sealed their reputation as being the laugh-makers.

Toward the end of M.P. School, Bravo Company was sent into the field for two weeks. They slept in tents, ate dehydrated food and played war games from dawn until deep into the nights. For the short hours of rest, Steve and Pat slept with the tent flaps open. They talked in whispers, with the stars as their cover. They roughed it, and were never overly concerned with hygiene. Wil and Ryan, on the other hand, acted like two old ladies. They took sponge baths, kept their area neat and fought off the insects attracted by the sweet smelling soap. Steve and Pat sat back and laughed at the two. The insects were having a feeding frenzy on the clean, tender skin of Wil and his partner.

Before turning in on the last night, Steve and Pat shared a cigarette. It had been a tough day of running, hiding and killing invisible enemies. The red glow from the cigarette lit up their small area of the black forest. There was a welcome serenity in the night. Yelling and slapping sounds quickly drifted over from the tent next door.

Pat joked, "We've gotta borrow some of that soap, Steve! They must be runnin' out of blood!"

Steve laughed and waited for Ryan's response. It didn't take long.

"Big joke, you stinky bastards!" he yelled, "at least we can sleep near each other without puking!"

"Is that live bait talking?" asked Steve, "I thought he'd be dead by now?"

They all laughed until the subtle sounds of the Southern forest sang them to sleep.

The next morning, Steve and Pat packed up their field gear. The training exercise was over. It was time to return to civilization. They met Wil and Ryan at the Jeep and filed into the convoy heading home — home to the Eleventh Battalion's hot showers, edible meals and warm beds. They couldn't wait. Steve and Pat stunk like pigs. Wil and Ryan were swollen from head to toe.

On the ride back, Ryan screamed, "Steve, don't move!" There was no humor in his voice. For once, Steve sensed he was serious. Ryan slowly reached over and flicked a baby scorpion off his shoulder. It was only inches from his neck.

"I owe you my life!" Steve joked. There was a nervousness in his voice.

"No," said Ryan, "but definitely a beer!"

First Platoon was released for their last weekend pass. As usual, Steve phoned Monica, then the foursome headed straight for their favorite motel. They purchased more beer than ten men could drink, and partied through the night.

Reminiscing about their summer together, Steve suggested, "What do you guys think about getting a souvenir to commemorate our vacation together?"

"What?" the other three asked in chorus.

"Something different. Something that'll last a lifetime!"

Caught up in the moment, Steve called a taxi. Within a half hour, the four staggering friends were standing in a tattoo parlor. Pat went first, then Wil, then Ryan, while Steve was the last to be branded. The three stood by, admiring their new tattoos, as Steve got a scorpion carved into his shoulder. It seemed suitable, though he knew Monica wouldn't care for it.

They returned to the motel to drink more, only to find that their eyes were much bigger than their stomachs. They didn't even put a dent in the beer.

Ryan, who was capable of pulling any prank without notice, stripped naked and jumped into the pool. The other three quickly followed. While swimming nude under a full Alabama moon, the giggles eventually turned to sentimental talk. Pat started. "It would be a frigin' shame to go though all of this and not stay in touch."

They all agreed.

"You're not lying," Steve added, "nothing sucks worse than getting close to someone and not being able to see them again." Taking a swig of beer, he stood. "Most people spend a lifetime calling someone their friend, and never get as close as we've gotten in two months!" He felt as close to Wil, Pat and Ryan as he did with his own brothers.

"We'll stay in touch," Ryan promised, but everyone knew it was going to take more effort than that. Steve remembered taking part in similar intoxicated conversations before, but even through the alcohol, there was a serious sincerity. They all knew that they found something special that summer. Nobody wanted to lose it.

Pat finally asked Steve, "Why don't you and Wil transfer into our unit when we get home? It's gotta be better than the 636th?"

Steve looked at Wil, who merely shrugged.

"That's the best offer we've had all night!" Steve joked, but it was no joke. It was the solution to keeping everybody together. He was ecstatic.

Wil agreed, but he was quiet. It was no longer just he and Steve.

Steve squealed with joy, "I love it! We can prolong this summer for at least four more years!" It was settled. "The awesome foursome will be together forever!"

As they flailed around in the pool, someone yelled from the balcony. It was the motel manager. "If you boys don't get outta my pool," he screeched, "I'm gonna call the cops!"

Ryan wasn't only the first one in, he was the first one out. As he dried himself, he was happy to show his friends a full moon. The sight was nothing new.

Giggling like an uncontrollable child, he eventually slurred, "Well boys, it looks like this summer's mission is over!" He was right. The graduation was in two days, then it was home, sweet home.

The flight home was similar to the year before. The same anticipation and excitement beamed from their young faces. Steve and Pat sat together, while Wil and Ryan reclined in front of them. While on the plane, they stripped out of their rigid uniforms and put on civilian clothes. The novelty of the dark green suits had worn off. Landing at Logan, Steve met Monica and his family with joy. After melting into his girlfriend's arms, he noticed there was nobody waiting for Wil again. He shook his head in disgust, but Wil only mumbled, "Some things never change." He quickly joined in the Manchester's warm welcome.

Pat and Ryan were introduced to the family. They returned the gesture. Before going their separate ways, the foursome celebrated their latest achievement with a toast. Every patron in the pub joined in. The training was over, no more Alabama. From then on, it was just one weekend a month and two weeks out of every summer. It was a time for celebration.

After a quick four days with Monica and his family, Steve started community college. It was the same school Wil had attended, though Wil had transferred to a university at the end of his Freshman year. Tied down with studies in Criminal Justice, Steve was also appointed a reserve police officer, and began the academy at once. It was a hectic time. When he wasn't bogged down in the books, he was working details for the police department. Whatever free time he could find was spent with Monica. There was also one weekend drill a month. He began to feel the weight of his responsibilities.

Wil found a college girlfriend named Sheila, and before long, they moved into an apartment. He was finally free from his father's torment, or at least that's what Steve hoped. They stayed in touch, but eventually Wil hooked up with the bad crowd again, and they gradually drifted apart.

Steve was unwilling to give up on the old friendship and called him one night.

"You ready to put in your transfer papers, brother?"

"I'm ready," said Wil. "Why don't you put in yours right away, and I'll go down next week."

Steve sensed there was something wrong. "We'll do it together, Wil, like always."

Wil snapped, "I said I'll do it when I'm ready, okay?"

"No problem, brother. It's no big deal." Steve stayed as calm as possible. There was no doubt about it anymore. Something was definitely wrong.

They said goodbye, but Steve held the receiver to his ear. Wil hung up, leaving him dazed. "It must be those damn drugs!" he said aloud.

Steve put in the transfer right away. He had to get out of the terrible unit. It was M.P.s like those in the 636th that gave the National Guard a bad name. He no longer wanted any part of it. Pat and Ryan belonged to the best unit in the state. The average age in the 661st was 20. The unit was filled with clowns, but they also possessed pride. When the state needed a job done, the 661st was the first to be called. Steve prayed that Wil would keep his summer promise and join their friends.

But Wil never put in for his. Things between them got worse. They didn't even speak, never mind confide in each other. And there were no more tough summers to bring them together again.

It was Steve's last drill with the 636th. There was no big party given, no wishes of luck or even a goodbye. It was as if he never existed. He expected it from the unit, but not from Wil. Steve grabbed his check from the unit's clerk. The last formation was called and the unit was dismissed. As he walked out of the armory for the last time, he looked over his shoulder and saw Wil staring at him.

He stopped and pleaded, "I wish you would reconsider the transfer, Wil?"

"Maybe some day." His head was down.

Steve shrugged. "Well then, I guess it's so long for now, buddy."

Wil looked up and for a second, their eyes met. In an unusually firm tone, he said, "Goodbye, Steve," then walked away.

Two weeks later, Steve and Monica pulled into the front parking lot of the police station. He jumped out of an orange colored Ford Pinto — a car that looked like a huge tangerine on wheels. Months before, The Old Special was totaled in a freak car accident. He hated to let it go, but there was no choice. The damage was too extensive. His old friend was way beyond repair. Besides, he got more than his money's worth from the car. The memories it made were priceless.

He yelled to Monica, "I'll only be a minute, Babe. I just need to check my schedule for the week." She smiled, then turned up the radio. Attempting to dart falling raindrops, he sprinted toward the station. Once inside, he waved to the desk sergeant on duty. Sergeant Simpski didn't return the courtesy. He was busy on the telephone. Grabbing the clipboard from its peg, Steve searched for his name in a list of many. He had picked up two details for the week. One was a nightclub job, the other, a cruiser shift. Writing the dates and times in his small note pad, he started for the door.

Sergeant Simpski stood and extended his index finger for Steve to hold on. His face was troubled.

Steve took a seat and expected to be assigned another detail, but he quickly realized that Simpski was talking to the coroner's office.

Simpski reclaimed his seat. "It's crazy, Don," he rambled, "the guy's seven-year-old nephew found him stiff as a board." Pausing, he answered, "The deceased party is 19 years old, and Andy said he left a note. It seems he no longer lived there. From what I understand, he did it in his parents' house, but they're somewhere in Europe. The Red Cross has been contacted. Hopefully, they'll get in touch with them soon."

Again, Simpski stood. This time, he placed his hand over the telephone's mouthpiece. Changing his tone from professional to compassionate, he directed his last statement right at Steve. "It's Wil Souza."

Steve's body froze and his breathing became shallow. His face went white and his mind began to race. As he ran out of the station, everything moved in slow motion. Jumping into the Pinto, he squealed the tires out of the lot.

Monica saw the look of panic in his face. "What is it, Steve? Tell me — you're scaring me!"

He didn't answer. He was in shock and didn't even hear the question. While they raced toward Wil's house, Monica grabbed his arm and tried to bring him back. His knuckles, wrapped around the steering wheel, turned white. The wheel cracked under the pressure.

He finally looked over at her. His eyes were glassy and distant, but he managed, "It's Wil — I think he's dead!"

Monica wrapped her arms around him and began to cry, screaming, "Oh, my God! What happened?" Speeding through the pouring rain, he turned back and stared straight ahead. "I have to get to Wil," he mumbled, "he needs me!"

Skidding across the Souza's front lawn, he saw the police cars and ambulance parked in the driveway — the same driveway that hosted so many good times. He sprinted toward the house and was nearly tackled by a young cop who didn't recognize him. The cop's actions never phased him. He had tunnel vision and didn't even see the patrolman. His mind continued to race. He couldn't separate his thoughts and, without realizing it, he kept repeating, "My God, not Wil ... please God, not Wil ...."

Andy LaVoie, the police officer on the scene, stood in the threshold of the Souza's front entrance. Seeing Steve rush toward the house, he placed his arm across the door, blocking the entrance. Andy knew that he and Wil were as close as brothers. He yelled into Steve's ear, "You don't wanna go in there, Steve. Wil's been dead for a few hours."

As though he weren't even there, Steve pushed past the older officer. Running up the stairs to his friend's old bedroom, he shoved past the cops and E.M.T.s standing in the doorway. Breaking through the crowd, his worst nightmare became reality. It was true. Wil was dead. Wil's lifeless body lay in a puddle of vomit. Steve stopped breathing and for a split second, his heart stopped beating. He stared down at his best friend, his mind freezing on the gruesome picture that he would keep for life. At that moment, a part of him died with Wil. Unable to handle anymore, he ran out of the house as fast as he could.

Andy caught up with him outside. "I'm sorry kid. I tried to warn you."

Steve shook his head, though he didn't remember hearing or seeing Andy before this. His broken heart was in his throat, but he finally asked his older friend, "Tell me, Andy, how did he die?"

Andy smiled compassionately. "Steve, we can talk about this later. Go home for now."

Peering hard into the man's eyes, he cried, "No Andy. I need to know. He was my best friend!" He could no longer hold back the tears. Andy knew that there was no other choice. He took Steve by the arm and explained to his young friend everything he knew. As they walked, he spoke slowly.

"It was a suicide, Steve, a well-planned suicide, with only one snag. Wil obviously didn't plan on Joey, his seven-year-old nephew, finding his corpse. By talking to the neighbors, we estimate that he arrived at this house at approximately three in the morning. Evidently, he watched television and got drunk on whiskey. After consuming almost half a quart, he took a bottle of Valium. The name on the bottle's label was scratched off. There's also a suicide note, Steve. Wil left the note in sloppy, almost illegible handwriting. It basically says that he loves everyone, but can't take it anymore. He must have already been sedated when he wrote it. He then lied down on the bedroom floor and went to sleep." Andy's eyes watered. "I'm sorry, Steve. There was nothing anybody could do. Wil knew no one would be around. He had to really want this."

Steve said goodbye. Monica helped him into the car and drove the ugly Pinto away from the flashing lights of the crime scene. Not 40 yards from the Souza's house, Steve watched as a hearse passed by them. He closed his eyes tight and felt Monica's hand intermingle with his. She was crying. He just sat back in shock, picturing Wil's lifeless body. Feeling buzzed from the adrenaline, he informed her, "Wil overdosed. He's dead! Wil's dead!" His body shook at the truth of it. "My God, Wil. Why?" he screamed.

His chest began heaving. His lungs struggled for air. Once they reached Monica's house, she led him upstairs. In her darkened bedroom, he sat in the corner. Quite naturally, his body rolled itself into the fetal position. He wept uncontrollably, his body convulsing from nerves. It came out of him — all of it — and he wailed for hours.

Monica matched every tear and held him. As he regained some composure, he said, "Please don't ever leave me, Babe."

She tightened her embrace. "I'll never leave you. I swear it. We'll be together forever!"

He believed her and felt better for it, but he also needed solitude. He needed to sort out his jumbled thoughts. He drove to the beach alone.

Turning off the ignition, he stared at the raging sea. The harsh winds tossed the waves into the jagged rocks. The ocean was in turmoil and so was he. The numbness was wearing off. As his emotions ran wild, his insides violently churned.

He felt overwhelmed with guilt and screamed, "I should have seen it. I knew there was something wrong, something very wrong with Wil. I should have been there for him. If I was, maybe he'd still be alive." Then he felt anger. He screamed louder, "If I could have him back for one minute, I'd slap him silly. How could Wil do this to me?" He felt every emotion, but as they drained out of him, he eventually felt only one. It was grief.

He finally understood the degree of Wil's intense pain. His search for peace ended; his escape from his uncaring father, complete. A tormented soul since Steve met him, Wil could finally rest in peace. For the rest of the night, the rain pounded off the Pinto's roof, while inside, Steve mourned the death of his best friend. They had gone through so much together, good times and bad. For Wil, there was no other option. He had tried his best. On that very night, however, Steve vowed that he'd never contemplate taking his own life. No matter the circumstances, suicide was a permanent solution to a temporary problem. Besides, he'd never put his family and friends through the same ordeal. Suicide just wasn't an option.

After two bitter weeks, the Red Cross located Wil's parents and the funeral ceremony was held. The casket was closed, but a picture of Wil's contagious smile sat in a frame on top. There were hundreds of people in attendance to show their respect. There were members of the 636th, each one a hypocrite. Then, Pat and Ryan walked in.

They rushed over and hugged Steve. Pat said, "We're here for you, brother." Ryan nodded. "We'll always be here."

Steve returned the smile, knowing that they meant it. Together, they sat in the rear of the church, grieving the loss of a brother. Painfully, it was still sinking in. The awesome foursome was cut down to a saddened trio.

As the priest spoke about the tragedy of a young life lost, he prayed that Wil would find eternal rest. Steve shared his wishes, but also prayed that the Lord would understand and forgive his friend. Throughout the ceremony, people whispered rumors of the reason for the suicide. Some believed it was because of drug problems. Others assumed it was girl problems. Steve leaned forward and stared at Wil's father. They both knew the reason. Tragically, it no longer mattered. It was too late. He and Wil were no longer in it together. Wil was gone and the reality of it felt like a piercing sword. To some, Wil became nothing more than a statistic. But to Steve, as long as he had a breath in his body, William Souza would live in his heart.

Ironically, as the ceremony came to a close, Wil's father approached Steve.

"Can we talk a moment?"

Steve rudely obliged.

Mr. Souza's eyes were red and swollen from crying. Sucking in a deep breath, he asked, "Steve, you knew him better than anyone. Why did he take his own life?"

He responded in cold blood. "Well Mr. Souza, the answer is really not that difficult. Anytime you walk by a mirror, just look in it and you'll know. You'll always know!"

The man stood speechless. With great cruelty, Steve patted him on the shoulder, turned and walked away.

Stopping at his car, he told Pat and Ryan, "In a strange way, Wil has finally gotten his father back for all the years of pain. He killed himself under his dad's roof and that's gonna haunt Mr. Souza for the rest of his life."

Pat smirked. "Too bad for Mr. Souza."

Steve opened the bright orange door of the beat up Pinto and remembered his old friend. He had to smile, picturing the funny bastard giving him the thumbs-up.

As he crept out of the lot, a small bird circled the church's steeple. He stopped the car to watch. It was a turtledove. The dove hovered, then finally perched itself on top of the steeple's cross. Steve felt a warmth that filled his soul.

He screamed aloud, "I never said it brother, but I love you, too. God bless you, Wil!"

Continuing out of the parking lot, although his cheeks were streaming with tears, his heart was at peace. Wil would live inside of him for the rest of his days. Spiritually, they were still in it together.

Chapter 3

The Few, the Hard – the National Guard

S teve's life moved on, though he felt an unfillable void inside. Never being able to see Wil hurt deeply. He carried a vivid picture of his best friend's death, but he kept his eyes focused on the future. Wil would have wanted it that way.

Two painful weeks after Wil's funeral service, he stepped into the armory of the 661st M.P. Company. There were at least 50 strange faces milling around, all of them waiting for the morning formation. Pat and Ryan, standing in the middle of the mob, eventually noticed him. It didn't matter who was there. His friends gave him a hug, welcoming him to his new home. Everybody looked on curiously at first, but when Pat and Ryan openly displayed their affections for the new guy, the faces instantly changed. He felt it. He was accepted as one of the boys. It was a good feeling. He had spent two years in the 636th and there was never so much as a smile offered by any of them. Here, he was surrounded by strangers dressed in camouflage uniforms, each of them extending their hands in friendship. He felt the warmth of being home. His face shined. It was definitely going to be different in the 661st.

As he joined in the small talk, First Sergeant Kline, a tiny man with wire rimmed glasses, walked out of his office. In a surprisingly deep voice, he ordered, "Formation!" Soldiers hurried to their assigned positions within the squads. Steve stood back, lost in the stampede.

Ryan ran over, laughing. "You're with me. First Platoon, Second Squad. I had to pull some strings. You owe me another beer, buddy!"

Steve remembered the scorpion and chuckled. Running to catch up, he yelled, "Thanks Ryan." They were the last soldiers to file into Second Squad. Snapping to Attention, they stood shoulder to shoulder.

First Sergeant Kline started roll call. He called out each name alphabetically, waiting to hear the same response, "Here, first sergeant." One man after another responded loudly, until Kline called the name of a soldier who was absent. He looked up and waited, but heard nothing. Shaking his head from side to side, he wrote a quick note on his big clipboard. Ryan giggled.

Getting to the bottom of the list, he called, "Private Manchester?"

Steve responded, "Here, first sergeant." For the second time during roll call, Kline looked up from his roster.

"Welcome to the 661st, son," he said, "I'm sure you'll find a difference."

He returned a blushing smile and nodded his head in appreciation.

Ryan whispered, "Don't let the little guy fool you. He's a real hard-ass!" Other squad members overheard Ryan and tried to muffle their laughter. Kline's head flew up.

"Something funny, First Platoon?" he roared. There was no answer. Ryan just glanced over at Steve and smiled.

When roll call was complete, a woman at least six feet tall, weighing well over 250 pounds, stood before the formation. She requested Private Manchester's presence in the orderly room.

The formation was dismissed and he reported directly to the orderly room.

Staff Sergeant Volmer stood up from behind the desk and introduced herself. Up close, she was massive. Steve couldn't help but to think that in a fair fight, she might even give Pat a run for his money.

She welcomed him to the company, adding, "You're way overdue for your promotion to Private First Class. I'll put in the paperwork right away." He couldn't believe it. The first half-hour of the day was too good to be true. He thanked her and they talked for a brief time.

Ryan and Pat were waiting. Pat asked, "Did the Amazon Woman show you how she can tie a cherry stem into a knot with her tongue?"

Steve giggled. "Next time I go in there, one of you guys are coming with me."

The three friends laughed and so did the rest of the squad. As the laughter subsided, Pat introduced Steve to the others.

He sat back and took it all in. It was one great big happy group of young men. The entire company was made up of young soldiers. Most wore pressed uniforms with creases and spit-shined boots. They were all in fairly good shape and their laughter engulfed the armory. What a difference, thought Steve. With the exception of Wil not being there, it was a fantastic change. He knew right away that he'd fit in. Over the remainder of the weekend, he met the rest of the First Platoon. They were a bunch of guys with the reputation of being the life of the party. Pat and Ryan wasted no time describing each character within the 30-man unit. There were a few idiots, but for the most part, they were tight. The majority were friends during the monthly drills, and even outside of the National Guard.

The chain of command was also introduced. There were the squad leaders, all sergeants. They hung with each other and rarely mingled with the commoners. His squad leader was Sergeant Veronica Tate, a quiet lady, with a smug look about her. She was described to Steve in one word, incompetent. Sergeant Tate avoided most responsibilities and after morning formations, she literally disappeared.

Then, there was Platoon Sergeant Frank Smith. He was a small-framed man who stood stiffer than any person Steve ever met. His uniform was impeccable and he even shaved his mustache to meet Army regulations. His profile was similar to Adolf Hitler's. The man was by the book and, unfortunately for him, he never swayed. He had very little authority in his voice, but tried desperately to control his merry band of free spirits. It was impossible. Steve felt sorry for him at first. The man received very little respect from his own platoon. As time elapsed, Steve decided he didn't deserve much. It seemed Smith couldn't have cared less for his troops. He never displayed any compassion or common sense. His head was stuck in thick Army manuals, and his mind on his own future promotions. He was one dimensional, caring about only himself. As old D.I. Vega put it, "His head was buried up his Smith." The man's futile attempts to show off to the upper echelon fueled a resentment from within his own platoon. As a result, he always looked bad. There were so many crazy jokers working against him, each of them plotting and sabotaging, anything to break him.

By the end of the weekend, Steve was escorted into the Commanders office. Captain Jeffrey Lyons sat behind an antique oak desk. His eyes were glued to the pages of a sail boating magazine. First Sergeant Kline and Lieutenant Rodney Myers, the leader of the First Platoon, were sitting across from him. Kline and Myers talked about a party they attended the night before. Steve stood at attention, waiting to be acknowledged. It took a few minutes. Eventually, Kline made a half-hearted introduction. Myers started to get up, but decided against it. He extended his hand, offering a weak handshake. Captain Lyons looked up from his magazine. He nodded his head and gave a half-hearted smile. There was an uncomfortable silence. Steve sensed that his presence wasn't wanted. With a simple wave of Kline's tiny hand, he was dismissed.

The first drill came to an end. On the ride home, he reflected back on the 661st. The morale of the unit was extremely high. People were happy and the camaraderie was due to the fun-spirited friends who filled the ranks. There was no doubt he had made the right choice. He thought about the new friends he had made and smiled. The first impressions were very good.

The following drill, a three-day excursion, was spent in the woods of Camp Edwards. The 661st trained in U.S. Army Infantry tactics. With their faces painted green and black and their M-16 rifles loaded with blank bullets, the wild animals of the First Platoon were set loose. Steve was fortunate for the field exercise time. Within those three hilarious days, he became closely acquainted with the dominant personalities in the platoon. He also found that, as a result of his twisted humor and sarcastic wit, he soon fit into that category. First Platoon consisted of small groups of friends. Collectively, they formed a tight clique. Bouncing from group to group, he quickly got to know the others.

At the break of dawn, they set up camp. Steve dug perimeter foxholes with Greg Medeiros and Dennis Ahern. Scooping dry dirt with small shovels, they talked for hours. Greg was a lanky private, with bleached blond hair and a mustache to match. His appearance gained him the nickname, The Aryan Nightmare. He possessed the energy of a child. It was funny to watch him run around, trying to accomplish everything by himself, then collapse from exhaustion. When he slept, the guys joked that he was recharging his battery. Greg was also the closest thing to a genius Steve ever met. He had set out to become an officer and knew more about Army training than anyone. After a few drills in the 661st, however, he had changed his mind.

His partner, Dennis, wasn't well liked by most of the platoon. He was tall, dark complected and one good looking son of a bitch. The problem was that he knew it, and never kept it to himself. Dennis loved to talk and constantly complained about his girlfriend. He bounced from job to job, waiting for a shot at a police position. After talking, Steve decided he liked him. His inflated ego was just a front for hiding his true insecurities. Dennis was a good-hearted guy. It didn't matter what the others said.

It took hours of sweat before the three men sat in their deep, dark fox-holes. The walls of earth were damp, but comfortable. Then, someone tram-pled through the woods toward them. It was Sergeant Tate. She called out their names and got angrier with each summons. As the woman searched, they laughed into the sleeves of their jackets. She kept calling, but it was going to take some time to find her lost sheep. They camouflaged their afternoon hideouts with branches of leaves and netting. Winking at each other through the small cracks between the leaves, they remained silent. The rest was up to her. It was a game of hide and seek and Steve loved the irony. It was normally Sergeant Tate who found a hole to hide in. Besides, the relaxation was well deserved.

As the evening rolled in, Steve woke up from a nap. He scanned the other foxholes. There was no movement. His friends were still sleeping. He chuckled. Peeking over the rim, he watched Sergeant Tate and another squad leader kicking up leaves. Tired of the silly game, he threw a pebble that landed at her feet. She started in the other direction. Six tiny rocks later, she was only two feet away. It was amazing. He was staring right at her frowning face, but she still didn't see him.

He finally stood up and said, "There you are, Sergeant Tate. The perimeter's secure!"

She was outraged. Steve heard the giggles of his neighboring ground dwellers. As he toyed with their squad leader, Greg and Dennis were watching.

Tate screamed, "Well, Manchester, it didn't take you long to become a fuck-off like these two!"

"I'm trying my hardest to fit in Sarge," he replied, pissing her off even more.

"Just what I need. Another dummy."

Steve knew he was many things, but stupid was not one of them. The comment was unacceptable.

In a very serious manner, he responded, "That's not funny, Sergeant Tate. It's not my fault I have a plate in my head."

"You what?" she asked, her face turning red from embarrassment.

Steve's pout turned into a devilish smirk. "Don't worry, Sarge. It's only a paper plate. My parents couldn't afford metal."

Greg and Dennis ran into the woods. Their laughter faded away with each step.

"Okay, smart-ass. I've got a perfect job for you," she hissed, "for the rest of the night, you're assigned to communications. You can wake me at 0500!"

Steve smiled. He got under her skin. Saluting, he said, "You got it Sarge, 5:00 A.M."

It was his second drill and he was already being punished. It felt just like M.P. School.

The night dragged on, as soldiers from each perimeter foxhole checked in every hour. A choir of crickets chirped throughout the dark hours, while Steve and Doug Donnely endured the loss of sleep together. Smoking one cigarette after another, they talked quietly.

Private First Class Donnely was a true comedian. He found humor in everything, the very reason for his after hours duty. Steve laid in his warm sleeping bag, listening to him tell detailed stories of his greatest pranks. Occasionally interrupted by the squelch of the old army radio, they laughed all night. At 2:00 A.M., Dennis Ahern called in for Greg and him.

Steve advised, "Go to sleep, buddy. We've got you guys covered."

The radio crackled and Dennis responded, "I appreciate it, but I can't sleep. I guess I caught too many Zs this afternoon!"

Dennis' laughter faded off, as the radio went silent. Steve noticed the crickets stopped singing. The snores of the nearby tents became louder. It was aggravating to listen to the squad leaders sleeping peacefully.

Fed up, Doug asked, "Wanna have some fun?"

Without answering, Steve jumped out of his sleeping bag and followed. Doug crawled on his belly toward a row of Jeeps. He lifted the squeaky hood of Platoon Sergeant Smith's Jeep as slowly as possible. Within seconds, he closed the hood, but was holding something in his right hand. Sneaking back to the commo tent, he revealed the coil wire that he had stolen. Steve busted out laughing. Smith wouldn't be driving anywhere in the morning. While Doug dug a hole and buried the evidence, Steve's belly ached from laughter.

The night was stolen away by the glow of an early sunrise. The new friends sat exhausted. There were many hours left before they'd sleep. Steve looked at Doug and remembered Wil. They were so much alike. They both needed to be the center of attention for the same painful reasons. Both of them were true clowns, forever making others happy, while they suffered alone. He missed Wil.

They completed their assigned duties by waking up the sleeping company. Steve insured that Sergeant Tate was the last to rise. He tapped on the tent's door flap at 6:15 A.M., yelling, "Sergeant Tate, are you gonna get up. This is the third time I've tried to wake you. Let's go, it's getting late!"

He heard her grumble something profane, but her complaints only broadened his weary smile.

Turning to Doug, he yelled, "She's got alot of nerve. I keep trying my best, but I guess it's never gonna be good enough?"

They walked away from the tent giggling.

"You're gonna fit in well," Doug said, "You're probably a bigger ball-buster than anyone."

Not two seconds later, Platoon Sergeant Smith screamed for the Motor Pool. He was frantically trying to start his Jeep and was already late for the early morning briefing. First Sergeant Kline wasn't going to be impressed. The late night mission was complete.

Steve put his arm around Doug. "I guess I'm not the biggest ball-buster around here. Not yet, anyway!"

First Platoon was briefed on the morning's mission. They were shoved into a deuce and a half, a two-and-a-half-ton truck. The bulky diesel rumbled down an old tank trail, stopping four miles into the north end of the woods. The boys leaped out of the back and rushed into the tree line. Within minutes, they were set into a half-moon ambush. Concealed behind trees and rocks, they camouflaged their positions and waited. They waited for Third Platoon's convoy to pass. Once the first three Jeeps passed by, they were supposed to attack. The First Platoon played the enemy, while the Third's reaction was evaluated. They sat in the wood line for hours and waited. It was a typical Army exercise: Hurry up and wait. Steve lit a cigarette and offered one to Specialist Tom Kigley. Tom accepted the smoke and they sat together. Steve was far beyond exhaustion, but he managed to keep his eyes open. He struggled to listen, as Tom gave him the real deal on the platoon.

Tom Kigley was the oldest in the First. He was 28, and his hairline was creeping up his forehead. From his appearance, he was considered the most mature person in the platoon. It was only an appearance. Tom was usually the mastermind of the better pranks during drills. His target never changed, and Smith always wished it would. With a talent for incredibly good impressions and foreign accents, he was the funniest person Steve had ever met. One of his stories actually started on a serious note, as he explained he was going through a nasty divorce. Midway through the sad tale, he grinned. He caught his wife messing around, but never let on that he knew. Instead, he punctured a whole in her diaphragm and waited. Within two months, she was pregnant. They weren't sleeping together, so he got the last laugh. He always got the last laugh. Steve was getting giddy when Tom's partner, Specialist Chuck Emond, came rustling through the woods.

Chuck was a regular Army M.P. for three years before joining the group. He was short, stocky and always looked ready for a fight. With a fat cigar sticking out of his mouth, he shook Steve's hand. Steve had met him earlier and found Chuck to be intense. The man possessed a strong conviction, though nobody knew why. And he loved to fight. Besides Pat, Chuck was definitely the toughest guy in the unit. He and Tom talked, while Steve's eyes grew heavy. Before dozing off, Steve remembered laughing hysterically at something Tom had said.

Steve awoke to the sound of gunfire. Scurrying behind a tree, he peeked out onto the road. Through all the commotion, he could still hear Tom and Chuck's laughter. Confused, he turned around and saw Doug shooting his rifle toward the road. But there was nobody there. He looked over at Tom, who continued to laugh hysterically. It registered. There was nobody there! Third Platoon never showed up. Instead, Doug decided to break up the boredom by starting his own war. The platoon went ballistic. Everybody began firing and moving through the woods. It was wonderful chaos. Platoon Sergeant Smith crawled to the edge of the wood line and shouldered his rifle.

Appearing troubled, he scanned the deserted road. Doug screamed, "Sergeant Smith, I saw four of them. They were trying to sneak up on us, the no-good bastards!"

Smith tried to yell over the pounding of the machine gun, but everybody ignored him. He rolled over to Tom's position.

"Did you see ..." but before he even finished asking the question, Tom was screaming in his ear.

"They're over there. I just saw them running!" Tom fired his clip of blank ammunition. Before emptying it, Smith was firing along with him. It was hilarious. Smith didn't see anything, but was completely convinced that the Third was trying to make him look bad. He barked, "Troops, move out!" Each one of them ran, holding their sides from laughter. Lagging behind, Ryan even wet himself.

After one good hour of searching, Smith rounded up his crew. He was enraged, but not at the First Platoon. The paranoid man was convinced that the Third was out to get him. As he de-briefed with his squad leaders, a convoy of Jeeps drove straight at him. The Third Platoon finally arrived. Smith screamed, "Fire! Fire!", but heard nothing. His platoon was out of ammunition.

Instead, the boys yelled, "Bang! Bang!" As though nobody was there, the convoy drove right through. It was perfect. Platoon Sergeant Smith would have to explain to Kline why he couldn't stop the small convoy. Everybody doubted Kline was going to be as naive. The laughter continued.

It only took two drills before Steve found that for the boys in the First Platoon of the 661st, the laughter was continual. They played the silly training games until they were tired of it. At that point, one of them always changed the rules. The insanity was non-stop. Just when they thought they had seen it all, one of them would top it. Steve got to know each of them well. He grew to love them like brothers. They were close, all of them.

When they got into trouble, they all took the heat. Each year, the 661st was required to provide security at the West Point Military Academy's football game. Steve's first year was quite the experience. The boys started drinking beer on the long bus ride to New York. They were singing and laughing when Captain Lyons nearly tripped over a bag of empty cans. The Commander never said a word, but looked at Ryan, who was downing a cold one. Upon arrival, they staggered off the bus and tried to line up into a straight formation. Platoon Sergeant Smith asked Ryan to stand before the platoon. Giggling, he did as he was told. Smith then advised his men, "Private First Class White is being busted for drinking alcohol while on duty."

The boys screamed in rage. Greg Medeiros stepped forward. "You can't do that. You knew we were all drinking and nobody stopped it. Besides, we're not on duty until tomorrow morning!"

Smith smiled arrogantly. "Well then, if anyone else would like to open his mouth, he can forfeit a stripe too!"

Without hesitation, 14 of them stepped forward.

Tom yelled, "You can have two of my stripes. I have plenty!"

There was an outburst of laughter, though their faces showed no happiness. They were angry and for the first time, Steve actually saw fear in Smith's face. It was real fear. He was close to experiencing a mutiny, so he scurried off. Half the platoon — 16 soldiers — lost rank. In the long run, it was worth it. It was a true display of solidarity. If you screwed one, you screwed them all.

Steve had never seen such chemistry between so many people. They all came from different backgrounds. Each one possessed his own distinct personality, but when brought together, it was magic. For one reason or another, they shared the same need for laughter. The only time they took anything serious was when it needed to be. Those times were few and far between. On one September morning, however, they received such a call.

The unit was activated for a state emergency. It was a hurricane unlike anything New Englanders had experienced in decades. The unit was trucked to Cape Cod where they eventually stopped in Hyannis, Massachusetts. The high gusting winds were devastating. Vehicles were tipped over in the flooded streets. Homes along the coast collapsed, while most others were severely damaged. There was debris of every sort flying around. The storm reeked havoc and the results were disastrous. When Mother Nature finally calmed herself down, the unit was dispersed into the streets to assist. Half of them were stationed at shopping centers for preventive purposes. The aftershock brought looters. The other half randomly helped people in need. While cleaning debris from the streets, they frequently transported victims to a nearby shelter. It was no joke and everybody knew it. Steve loved the teamwork, as well as the opportunity to lend a hand. It took four long days, but when it was over, First Platoon proved that humor was not their only skill.

Outside of the National Guard, Steve's life was speeding along. Into his second year of college, he withdrew from his studies to attend the Massachusetts Correctional Academy. The experience of walking a beat behind the giant walls of concrete, bricks and steel would prepare him for his police career. The seven-week academy was relatively painless. Soon enough, he found himself working in the most dangerous, negative and erratic environment he had ever imagined. It was a place where nightmares came to life. Hidden from society with killers and rapists, he waited for a police position. For political reasons, his name was never called. Neither he, nor his family, knew the right people.

His career in police work was finished. Another hard lesson was learned. No matter how good the plan was, sometimes life traveled the road that it pleased. Shaking off the disappointment, he became the best correction officer he possibly could. By doing that, he changed. It was inevitable. Day after day, he provided care and custody for society's vermin. The job was depressing, but the money and benefits made it too difficult to leave. He was locked in. As time went on, he grew a hard shell and learned to conceal his feelings more than ever. It was necessary for survival. He learned about racial prejudice and bigotry. The unpredictable and violent inmates who overcrowded the tiers caused him to hate all races equally. He was blinded to what was happening. Gradually, he was losing his love for humanity — a caustic result of spending each day with misfits and cold-blooded men. Ryan White and Chuck Emond worked in the same concrete jungle. At least he wasn't alone.

After years of dating, the day arrived when Steve told Monica on bended knee, "I never imagined loving someone as much as I love you. What's more, I also need you. I need to share my life with you ... the rest of my life ...."

Her eyes filled with joyful tears.

Grabbing her hand, he asked, "Will you be my wife?"

Through the tears, she managed, "Yes!"

It was a Cinderella wedding, everything Monica had always wanted. Steve stared into her beautiful eyes and repeated the priest's words. "For better or for worse. For richer or for poorer. In sickness and in health ...." He never felt stronger about any promise he had made. Monica was everything.

She vowed the same, and through it all, they never once broke eye contact.

The priest said, "I now pronounce you man and wife." Steve kissed his wife. The two were finally one. Applause echoed through the church. Steve never heard it. He was too busy listening to his wife whisper, "I love you."

At the reception, most of the First Platoon sat up front and danced the night away. During the second slow song, the boys coupled up and danced with each other. The Manchester family laughed hysterically, while the Rinaldi's looked on in horror. The twisted humor took some time to get used to, but by the end of that glorious night, the alcohol threw everyone into the spirit. Proudly, Steve asked the D.J. for the microphone. The music stopped. Everybody waited for the unexpected. He called for the boys of the First. They formed a tight circle and sang the anthem that Tom Kigley had composed years earlier. The song had been practiced a thousand times during weekend drills. Its original intent was to infuriate people. When all else failed, the song always worked. Later, the humor of the lyrics became their trademark. The deep voices actually created a wonderful harmony. Arm in arm, they sang:

"We're the men of the National Guard,
Fighting wars in our backyard.
If a hundred men went to war today,
Ninety nine would run away.

Drunken soldiers, from the sky,
Rather drink, than fight and die.
Once a month, two weeks a year,
We consume alot of beer.

They paid for school, that's why we're here,
So disregard what you might hear.
If our state, got attacked today,
We'd just turn and walk away!"

The boys burst into laughter. The audience, however, gave a standing ovation. Overcome with happiness, they sang an encore. It was a strong rendition of the *Star Spangled Banner*. Everybody stood to listen. At the end, there wasn't a laugh to be heard. The applause only grew louder. On that very night, those songs became a tradition for future weddings and just about every function the boys attended.

Returning from a gorgeous honeymoon in Cancun, Mexico, all too soon Steve was back at the prison. He and Monica purchased an overpriced house, so he put in the long hours. The responsibilities of being a new husband and homeowner weighed him down. At 21 years old, his days of careless fun were cut short. He looked forward to the weekend getaways with his buddies. The need for laughs became more intense, and the boys played their games even harder.

Steve stood rigid in his sharp Class A uniform. The sun gleamed off of his black combat boots, and the screaming spectators made his head pound. He was excited also, but retained a professional gaze. Standing on Heartbreak Hill, the 25-mile mark of the Boston Marathon, a lump formed in his throat. The first competitor, a man strapped to a wheelchair, pumped his arms like lightning. He moved up the hill at a rapid pace. Sweat covered his body and a look of sheer determination sparkled from his eyes. The man had heart, it would take a steeper hill to break it. Not 30 seconds behind, the other wheelchairs followed. The crowd roared in support and admiration. Steve pushed them back on the sidewalk. It was essential that the course remain clear. It was no easy task, but with a polite smile, he performed his assigned duty.

There was a brief lull between the wheelchairs and world class runners. First Sergeant Kline approached Ryan who was standing on Steve's right.

"Where's your squad leader?" he asked.

"Who knows?" replied Ryan, in his ordinary sarcastic tone.

Kline furiously shook his head and stormed off.

The crowd grew louder. Steve watched the front runner, an anorexic looking man, come speeding past. He was cursing the media truck that was driving a short distance in front of him. The exhaust fumes were cutting down his oxygen, but the news people continued to ignore his pleas to leave. To them, the runner's finish time was trivial. It was the news footage that mattered most. The other runners were closely trailing behind and finally, Steve couldn't help himself. As they passed, he cheered along with the crowd. Some people offered the runners cups of water. Others handed out orange slices. He spotted Doug extend an open pack of cigarettes to the tired sprinters. He yelled over, "Donnely, you really are a sick man!"

As the middle of the pack of runners passed, he choked back the tears. An older, stocky man pushed his paraplegic son. The boy was strapped into a special wheelchair, with a plexi-glass shield covering his upper body. The crowd went crazy. People were crying and running beside the pair. The man paid no attention. He kept his eyes fixed on his son — eyes that were filled with love. Steve had never seen anything so unbelievable. The man had already finished 25 miles, yet he continued to push his quivering legs. He was an inspiration.

Returning to the bus, First Platoon removed their jackets and ties. First Sergeant Kline boarded, whispered something into Smith's ear and left. Smith stood and faced his men. He announced, "Sergeant Emond is now the leader of the First Squad. Sergeant Medeiros will be his assistant. Sergeant Kigley will take over the Second, with Corporal Manchester as his assistant. Third Squad will remain as is!" Smith sat down with no further explanation.

Ryan slapped Steve on the back. "Finally! Now, we'll really control things!"

Sergeant Tom Kigley quickly took the lead and was great. The boys were shipped to a mountain range in Vermont. It was cold weather survival training, the most dreaded drill of the year. Second Squad set out on a land navigation course, but Tom had a different idea. Just outside the view of base camp, they found a cozy knoll in a nearby pine grove. The squad went to work. In no time, they were seated on a pile of comfortable pine boughs. The dry wood they located, crackled and popped in the camp's warm fire. The icy wind whipped through the trees, but they sat with their shirts off; their heavy boots, unlaced. Telling jokes and listening to Tom's Australian version of Platoon Sergeant Smith, they laughed the frigid afternoon away.

Hours later, Smith trudged through the deep snow and found the squad's improvised shelter. His face was frozen. His voice was even colder.

"What in the hell do you think you're doing?" he screamed.

Tom stood. "Sergeant Smith, we ended up getting lost, so before we froze to death, I decided to apply our survival training to a potential disaster!"

Steve held back the tickle in his throat. Smith stared hard at his squad leader.

"Do you realize you're only 200 yards from base camp?"

The seriousness in Tom's face almost convinced the others. "You've got to be kidding? We walked for hours, but I guess we must have walked in circles. I'll have to brush up on my map reading."

Smith shook his head. "At least you had the smarts to get your people out of this weather."

Tom smiled. "I do the best I can, Boss."

Smith never caught the wink he aimed at the others. Kigley was the best of conmen.

Marching back to base camp, Ryan took a left and climbed the face of the mountain. Nobody noticed him missing until they heard some strange laughter from above. The squad stopped and searched for the odd sound. Then they spotted him. Tom shook his head. He told Smith, "I'll take care of it."

Seated on a green trash bag, Ryan was sledding down the mountain like a child. With one arm stretched toward the sky, he resembled a cowboy, struggling to stay atop a bucking bronco. He was moving fast and almost made it to the bottom. Not 20 feet from the squad, he wiped out, spraying snow on his friends. Smith was livid. Tom approached the human snowball and whispered, "Bad boy, don't you ever do that again!" Returning to Smith, he confirmed, "Don't worry, Boss. He knows he's in big trouble. I'll handle him!"

The squad brushed the snow off the little boy and marched on.

First Sergeant Kline finally realized that the First Platoon was completely out of control. After refusing to take part in the winter training and making a mockery of their platoon sergeant, he needed to do something. He did. He dismissed Smith from his duties. The boys were ecstatic. Platoon Sergeant Smith was assigned to a recruiting job. The only fear was, who would have the backbone to take over for him.

The following drill, Platoon Sergeant Anthony Rosini flicked a cigarette butt from his mouth and cleared his raspy voice. "Do not be mistaken,

I know all about you guys! I know that I've recently inherited a motley crew of jokers. You should also know that things are gonna change in this platoon and quick!"

Rosini stared into the blank faces of his men and smiled. "I also know I'm replacing an asshole. So, I'll make a deal with you guys. When it's time to work, we work hard! But, when it's time to play, we'll play just as hard! Deal?" He lit another cigarette and waited for the answer.

On Steve's cue, the platoon quietly sang their anthem. It was Tony Rosini's welcome to the First Platoon and he knew it.

He chuckled. "I guess I'm gonna have to learn that one!"

The boys cheered. Platoon Sergeant Rosini was the leader they needed all along.

Tony was a giant of a man, standing six-feet, five-inches tall. His hands were huge, with leather-like skin. Behind a pair of thick army glasses, peered the eyes of experience. He had a slight limp in his walk, a souvenir from his second tour in Vietnam. It was his voice, though, that stood out most. He started a sentence in a raspy tone and ended it with a hoarse rumble. It was a combination of years of screaming and chain smoking. His voice was unmistakable. It commanded respect and, during his first drill, the First Platoon hung onto his every word.

As usual, the boys camped out in the woods of Camp Edwards. All day, they busted their humps in the brush in order to prove their worth to their new platoon sergeant. Somehow, the veteran soldier already knew. Greg stood back at base camp, stockpiling wood and making preparations for their traditional nightly gathering. When dusk barely passed, the training day was over. Returning to camp, the boys found a bonfire already burning. Rosini stoked the fire, as his men sat down in a circle. They removed their sweat-drenched shirts; each of them finding a tree or rock to rest against. When neither could be found, they sat back to back. Rosini knelt by the fire and revealed an open quart of brandy. He took a long swig, then passed the bottle down the line. It was time to get acquainted.

He talked about his life in the regular Army. "I served two tours in Vietnam. My second was cut short by two bullets that smashed into my right kneecap." He spoke with sincerity, pouring out his soul. First Platoon sat in silence, each face entranced by his adventurous tales. As the hours whisked by, the boys joined in. Most asked questions. Rosini answered them all — all but one.

It was a stupid question, but everybody sitting by that fire was thinking the same thing. Doug asked, "Did you ever kill anyone in Nam?"

He merely bowed his head and replied softly, "I don't know. My eyes were closed the whole time." The answer was clear. The question should've never been asked.

Breaking the tension, Rosini traded funny National Guard stories with his men. The laughter outlasted the bonfire. The fire that once blazed turned into small glowing embers. It was time to turn in for the night. The boys settled into their sleeping bags. As they laid shoulder to shoulder, the confinement of the tent made things cozy. The chatter eventually stopped and for the briefest moment, there was silence.

Steve whispered, "Goodnight, Scout Master."

In his distinctive voice, Rosini replied, "Goodnight, Stevie-boy."

Platoon Sergeant Rosini was now just Tony. He was one of the boys. They giggled themselves into dreamland.

The following month, Steve packed his gear for the annual two-week training. He met Pat and Ryan at the armory. They were destined for a place they never thought they'd see again — Fort McClellan, Alabama. Their mission was to train with a regular Army M.P. Company. In reality, it was a competition in field exercises. A neutral unit evaluated the war games and they began immediately.

With Tony at the helm, the boys entered the competition quite determined. Relying on their basic training, the experience of their civilian occupations and Tony's abnormal instructions, First Platoon quickly eliminated their enemy. After four days in the field, the training exercise was called off. The regular Army commander had seen enough. He took his ball and went home, leaving the boys of the First singing their anthem with pride. As their adversaries marched past, Tony even belted out a few lines. It was an embarrassment for the full-time M.P.s, so the 661st was punished. They were assigned to provide site support for the active base. For the next week and a half, they stood post at the front gate of McClellan. They checked I.D.s twelve hours per day. Still, the boring duty never stopped their fun.

Steve halted an old pick up truck. There were two men inside. Neither was wearing a seat belt. He advised them, "Gentlemen, you are required to fasten your seat belts while traveling on federal property."

The driver raised his hands in confusion. He stuttered, "We would, Sir, but there aren't any seat belts in this old truck."

Steve frowned. "Then I strongly suggest, for safety sake, you wrap your arms around each other."

The two men stared in disbelief. Steve's face remained serious. They didn't know what to say until giggling poured from the brick covered gatehouse. Inside, Ryan was laughing hysterically. His odd cackle contagiously rubbed off on the confused men. Steve informed them, "Have a pleasant day," then allowed them entrance. The old truck drove off, with its passengers shaking their heads.

For the remainder of the summer camp, each night was spent in search of fun. There was always a poker game to be found. The coolers were loaded with beer and everybody remained in good spirits. If anyone passed out, he found himself waking up naked under the latrine's urinal. There was always a photo taken for future reference. Steve nicknamed the platoon The Dream Team. Everybody liked it and the name stuck. On the last night, the boys went all out. They chipped in and threw a keg party. Ryan invited the girls in the unit. In awe, Steve watched as Doug and Dennis strolled out of the barracks dressed in only pantyhose. Everybody laughed. With the exception of the nylons and their green woolen socks, they were totally naked. The girls didn't mind. Everybody sang and helped empty the keg. At the end of the party, Keith took group photos. The clan stuffed themselves into the camera's view. Every young face smiled, their arms wrapped tightly around each other. It was proof that life was good.

Summer camp was over. Two months later, to everyone's dismay, so was Sergeant Tom Kigley's career in the National Guard. Tom announced he was returning to school, in order to pursue a career in nursing. The one weekend a month would take time away from being with his son. He was a clown, but his priorities were in order. Steve was the sorriest to see him leave. He loved Tom. They had become the best of friends, not to mention, he was going to have to pick up where Tom left off.

Dismissed from the last formation, the boys paid tribute to him with a strong version of the infamous anthem he had created. He solemnly chuckled. Lightening the mood, Steve offered to buy him one last drink. They entered a local convenience store. Steve headed for the soda coolers, while Tom stood by the register.

With a strong feminine tone in his voice, Tom asked the clerk, "Do you have any of those chocolate flavored condoms? You know, the edible kind?"

The girl shook her head. She didn't dare open her mouth, fearing she would laugh at the serious question. Steve placed two Pepsi's on the counter and, from the smirk on the young girl's face, he knew something was up.

Tom asked, "What is the date on that *Playgirl* magazine?"

She giggled. "August 1990."

Tom gasped for air. Excitedly, he said, "We'll take one!"

Without another word, he walked out, leaving Steve to deal with the situation. Steve could feel the blush of his embarrassed face. He quickly purchased the soft drinks and magazine, then noticed the disturbing headline of the daily Boston Herald. In big, bold letters, it read: IRAQ INVADES KUWAIT! He was sure that through his tears of laughter, Tom had missed it. He decided not to mention it. He met his friend outside and they laughed. It was like always. Tom got the last one in. Steve handed him the magazine. "Here, fruitcake. Enjoy! And let's stay in touch, okay?"

Tom agreed, though they both knew that no matter how close they became, people lost touch. Life was funny like that.

Tom drove away laughing, and Steve returned to the store. The giddy cashier was still grinning from ear to ear when he purchased the newspaper. He was anxious to read the details. Saddam Hussein and his powerful army overran Kuwait before dawn. President Bush ordered an immediate U.S. economic embargo against Iraq. After reading the lengthy article, Steve sensed that all hell was about to break loose in the Middle East.

Corporal Steve Manchester was now the leader of the Second Squad. His assistant was Pat O'Malley. They did their best to carry on tradition. For the most part, things stayed the same. For the next few drills, he learned the responsibilities of taking the heat for his squad. He didn't mind. He knew he deserved it.

During those long months, however, Steve monitored the newspapers and media coverage of the inevitable road to war. Hussein's merciless acts on the citizens of Kuwait included everything from random slayings to the removal of premature babies from their life-sustaining incubators. Then the lunatic quickly announced a new military government for Iraqi-occupied Kuwait, declaring that Kuwait was part of Iraq. In no time, the shock was wearing off. A good part of the civilized world became enraged.

For the remainder of 1990, Steve became engulfed in the incredible events that unfolded before the eyes of the world. Deep down, he knew that those outrageous events would eventually affect him personally.

For the remainder of August, a worldwide economic embargo was imposed against Iraq, while President Bush ordered a deployment of U.S. combat troops and warplanes to Saudi Arabia. Most countries agreed to join the multinational force. Iraq closed its borders to foreigners, trapping thousands of Americans and other Westerners in Iraq and Kuwait. The Western hostages were moved to vital military installations to be used as human shields. President Bush signed an order, calling up reservists to bolster the U.S. military buildup in the Gulf. Steve cringed at the news, though it didn't truly surprise him. It was easy to see where things were heading. Toward the end of the month, Iraqi television broadcasted Hussein talking to a group of terrified Western children in his office.

He told them, "Your presence here and other places is meant to prevent ... war!" Steve watched the telecast with his heart in his throat. He felt sympathy for the children, but it was his anger that began to block out most other emotions.

September found the countries of Russia and Jordan attempting to mediate the U.S.-Iraq confrontation. It didn't look good. A diplomatic approach was emphasized, but Bush stood by the U.S. military commitment. Iranian leader, Ayatollah Khamenei declared the struggle against the U.S. presence in the Gulf a holy war! Iran and Iraq, long-standing enemies, were strengthening their relations.

Hussein formally stated, "Iraq will fight to the finish in a war with the United States," adding that he'd destroy Israel and launch an all-out war before allowing the U.N. embargo to strangle Iraq. The month ended as poorly as it started. Iraq ordered Kuwaitis to apply for Iraqi citizenship, while threatening to hang any diplomats sheltering Westerners in their embassy compounds.

The beautiful month of October revealed that Iraq developed Scud Missiles capable of hitting targets in Saudi Arabia. Diplomatic relations were renewed between Iraq and Iran after a decade of hostility. The remainder of the month, however, was spent in futile attempts at peace negotiations and strong concerns over the price of oil.

At the beginning of November, President Bush, commenting on the Middle East situation, said, "They have committed outrageous acts of barbarism. Brutality ... I don't believe that Adolf Hitler ever participated in anything of that nature." Steve questioned whether Hitler was any better, but for the most part, Bush summed it up. If not stopped, there was no telling what destruction Saddam Hussein could wreak. The world's largest oil supplies were at stake, which could create a devastating economic crisis. Yet, there were other things much more valuable that needed to be protected and preserved. For starters, the helpless babies left to die on the floors of Kuwaiti hospitals. No matter what any of the so-called experts said, there was more to it than oil. There were human lives being exterminated.

November was spent amassing troops and the numbers being sent over were staggering. Hussein continued to move his troops as though he were playing a twisted chess game. The weeks to follow quickly proved that he was playing against a master, General Norman Schwarzkopf. At the very end of the long month, the U.N. Security Council voted 12–2 to give Iraq six weeks to pull out of Kuwait before the U.S. and its allies were free to launch a military strike. One last ditch effort was made on behalf of the U.S. to discuss ending the Gulf crisis. It proved hopeless.

The rumors of war floated around the armory for months, but everybody was too busy screwing around to take them serious. Labeled Operation Desert Shield, a final deadline was set for Hussein to pull his troops out. He wasn't going anywhere. To Steve and the rest of the country, it was clear. Preparations were made and the decision was all but carved in stone. The U.S. was going to war with Iraq. For the rest of the country, the only question was when. For Steve, there were a thousand and one other questions that needed to be answered.

It was December and the easiest drill of the year rolled around. The boys sat down in the chow hall located in the basement of the armory. While eating turkey with all the fixin's, the rumors of being activated for war were the only topic of conversation. Steve sat with his squad. They were joking as always, but he felt troubled. He looked at the laughing faces of his friends and thought about the possibility of war. Remembering his recruiter, Sergeant Chen, he asked himself what the chances were.

Finishing his lunch, he called Tony to the side. "Hey Boss, with all the trouble in Kuwait, what's the chances of us getting sent over?"

Tony laughed. "Don't worry about anything. It'll have to get pretty bad over there before we get the call!"

Steve left the armory feeling confident there was no reason for concern. If anyone had any idea what was going to happen, it was Tony. He had seen it all before.

The Christmas Tree was cluttered with unwrapped presents. The festive voice of Bing Crosby filled the candlelit room. Steve and Monica, finishing their eggnog, snuggled on the couch. Savoring the last minutes of a magical holiday, they started kissing. The spirit of the moment was rudely interrupted. It was the telephone.

Excusing himself, he complained, "Who in the hell can this be at 10:30?" He picked it up. "Hello."

"Hello Stevie-boy." The raspy voice was unmistakable. Steve thought it odd that Tony would call so late.

"What's up, Tony?"

"I've got good news and bad news, Steve. Which do you want first?"

"Too much holiday cheer, huh, big boy?"

Tony laughed. "Okay, the good news is that you've been promoted to sergeant, effective tomorrow! The bad news is that I just got the call, Steve. We've been activated for Operation Desert Shield ... for one year. I need you to contact your people and make sure they report to the armory on Monday, 0700 hours."

Steve laughed. "Cut the shit, Tony!"

"I wish it was a joke, buddy, but this one's for real!" Steve knew Tony wasn't kidding. But it was just too large to grasp.

"Okay, Tony, I'll make the calls," whispered Steve.

"Oh Steve, by the way, merry Christmas." The line went dead, and along with it, Steve's smile.

He hung up the phone and looked at Monica. Without saying a word, her tears told him that she knew. Their worse fears were coming true.

He held her. "Don't worry, Babe, everything's gonna be fine." He heard his words, but didn't feel them. Staring out of the frost covered window, he felt a shiver travel up his spine. It wasn't the frigid wind beating off the glass that made him cold, it was the pictures of war running through his mind. As he kissed his trembling wife, his body went numb. He braced himself. It wasn't the time to reveal his thoughts, or his feelings. It was time to be strong, at least for Monica and the Second Squad.

Chapter 4

A Family's Burden

Steve couldn't sleep. He tossed and turned. His mind wouldn't allow him to rest. There were just too many things to think about. He lay awake for hours, holding Monica in his arms. Throughout the endless Christmas night, he watched as her tears soak the pillowcase. She was distraught over the dreaded phone call. Yet, it was her physical pain that made her cry and moan. It was nothing new.

Five months earlier, Monica was seriously injured at work. Employed as a merchandiser for a large bakery, she was lifting a heavy tray of bread over her head when something snapped in her neck. The sharp pain caused her to drop the tray in the middle of the store's aisle. She suffered two herniated discs and some substantial nerve damage. The bakery was less than sympathetic. They stopped workers' compensation payments after the first month. She spent her days in physical therapy, while her nights were spent in pain and worry. The bills piled up. Even the mortgage to the house fell behind. The bank was threatening foreclosure. The young couple tried to explain their dilemma, but business was business. That lack of compassion and understanding forced them to seek legal assistance. As the lawyer tried to reinstate compensation benefits, they prepared to lose everything they had worked so hard for. The trying time brought them closer. Now, even that was being taken away. Steve thought things couldn't get any worse.

He helplessly watched, as she suffered every night for months. He held her tighter, knowing he'd be sent away soon. Though it was out of his control, he couldn't help but feel guilty about leaving her. She would be left to suffer alone. His eyes filled with tears and he gently caressed her back until she fell into a sound sleep.

The following day, he sat in his basement, as far away from Monica's ears as he could get. He made the most difficult telephone calls he had ever made. Dreading his friends' reactions, he finally picked up the receiver and dialed. With a full pack of cigarettes sitting on the list of numbers in front of him, he called the O'Malley's.

Three rings later, Pat picked up. "Hello."

"What's up, buddy? How was your Christmas?"

"Good brother, and yours?"

Steve decided that the longer he waited, the harder it would be. He came right out with the shocking news.

"Pat, we've been activated for Desert Shield. It looks like a one-year deal. First formation is 7:00 A.M., Monday morning." He expected silence.

Instead, Pat yelped with excitement. "I knew it, Steve! It'll be the experience of a lifetime! Do you need me to make any calls?"

Steve couldn't believe Pat's joyful response. "No, buddy. I appreciate it, but I think I should make the calls."

"I understand. Well, I guess I'll see you on Monday morning." On an extremely happy note, Pat hung up the phone.

Lighting another smoke, Steve sat dumbfounded. Pat made the first call easy on him, but he felt strange about his friend's reaction. Hoping that Pat's enthusiastic attitude would rub off on him, he dialed the number belonging to the Ahern residence. Dennis' father picked up. Steve asked for Dennis.

The older man politely said, "My son's not in at the moment. May I ask what this is about?"

Steve understood the concern. He never called Dennis at home. "Actually sir, I'd rather speak to Dennis first."

Mr. Ahern's cordial voice changed instantly. He barked, "I'm Dennis' father. I think that I have a right to know!"

The man obviously assumed the worse, or in this case, the truth. Steve politely asked that Dennis call him, then hung up, leaving Mr. Ahern quite upset. He was sure he made the right decision. It was better for Dennis to

hear the news from somebody who was thinking rationally. That somebody had to be him.

Seven phone calls later, he finished a half of a pack of cigarettes. Each
call proved to be a new experience. Some cried. Others put on a good front,
but he still sensed their fear. It was the same fear he already carried for
hours. No matter what the future brought, do or die, The Dream Team was
now in it together!

Later that afternoon, Steve met Ryan White at the prison. With orders
for a one-year activation, they delivered the paperwork to personnel. The
friends spent the next hour saying their goodbyes. Everyone said they'd be
missed, but that the desert couldn't be any worse than the Big House. Steve
laughed. Walking out, the two were attracted by the loud mouth of an older
black inmate, a convict who Steve despised.

The cynical man quipped, "Hey boys, try not to get yourselves killed
over there!"

It never ceased to amaze him just how fast the word spread throughout the joint.

"I'll tell you what, convict," Steve snickered, "why don't you stay here
where it's safe. We'll be home to tuck you in before you know it!" The old
con strutted away, laughing. Ryan shared the inmate's laughter.

Steve turned to his giggling friend. "I hate this frigin' place. I hope I
never come back!"

Ryan shrugged. "You better watch what you hope for. It might come true."

Monday morning rolled around and Steve reported to the armory earlier than required. On the ride in, he took his time on the slippery, snow
covered roads. The six inches of white powder was beautiful, but white
was not the color that caught his eye. It was yellow, hundreds of yellow
ribbons tied onto trees and the front doors of neighborhood houses. He also
noticed more American flags flying in the front yards than he ever saw
before. The support for Operation Desert Shield was phenomenal.
Everybody wanted to display their patriotism. Chills traveled up and down
his spine. America had finally wised up. Regardless of the outcome, this
war was going to be very different from Vietnam. At least this time, the
love and support of a nation was being sent over with the men and women
called to serve.

He pulled into the empty parking lot. Sitting in the car, he watched as
a civilian volunteer hung a banner over the armory's front doors. It read:
GOOD LUCK 661st M.P. COMPANY. Tied to each side were enormous

yellow ribbons. Staff Sergeant Volmer walked out of the building with another soldier. Together, they slowly raised the American flag. Inch by inch, the symbol of freedom reached toward the morning sky. Steve stared in amazement. Until that very moment, he never saw the American flag for what it was. Many brave men sacrificed their lives defending the freedom of others. The torch was now being passed on to a new generation. With great confidence, he stepped out of the car, prepared to carry that torch.

He stood at the head of Second Squad. Looking to his left, he noticed that the faces had already changed. There was no smiling. He turned to Pat. "Well, buddy, this is it!"

Pat grinned from ear to ear. "You know it, baby! Operation Panty Shield. We'll make history!"

Interrupting, First Sergeant Kline called the company to Attention. Before starting roll call, he announced, "Captain Lyons has recently transferred to Battalion."

The entire company snickered. "What convenient timing," Steve whispered, "Battalion's staying home." Kline screamed for silence. He introduced Lyons' replacement, Captain Lois Wall.

Captain Wall strutted to her place before the large formation. She was a tough looking woman, with the swagger of a man. She was short and pudgy, and wore thick glasses. It was the black leather motorcycle gloves, though, that made the soldiers mumble. She introduced herself. As soon as her mouth opened, her deep voice caused laughter. Ryan turned around from his new position in First Squad. He whispered, "At least we got another man to take over."

Kline screamed in rage. He turned to Captain Wall to apologize, but she just stared up and down the ranks. She was tough.

"We have about ten days before we ship off to Fort Devens," she continued, "In the meantime, I expect all equipment and weapons to be functional and packed. There won't be time at Devens. Also, there will be people coming in to assist you in getting your personal affairs in order. This means finances, insurance, even your last wills and testaments. Bottom line, people, if the worst does occur, we all need to provide for our families."

Steve looked at the faces of his friends. Captain Wall had hammered reality home.

She finished her dry speech. "I expect that we'll be training at Fort Devens for a short period. However, at this time, I'm not at liberty to divulge our destination or the mission we'll be tasked with." Without another word, she stomped off, causing the whispers to begin again.

Steve grabbed Chuck. "She's full of shit. I don't think even she knows where we're going yet."

Chuck snickered, "I was thinking the same thing. But I think any unit being activated now, will be heading for the Middle East!"

Tony called the platoon into a huddle. He explained his expectations. They were the same as Chuck and Steve's. He knew that six years were spent screwing around, so he grumbled, "We have very little time to prepare, so it's crucial that we make every minute count. You people call yourselves The Dream Team. Now, it's time to prove it!" Nobody cheered after the pep talk, but they all agreed. He was right. The next few weeks could make the difference between life and death. The joking had to be replaced by discipline, teamwork and a positive attitude. First Platoon was determined to give 100 percent.

For the next nine days, from 7:00 A.M. to 5:00 P.M., the boys listened to one briefing after another. Steve signed over his power of attorney to Monica. Before his last will and testament was completed, he took out a life insurance policy worth $100,000. The insurance was offered to any soldier being sent overseas. Some insurance company gambled that most would return safely. Between briefings, weapons were cleaned and tents were folded. All equipment was packed and made ready for shipment. The Dream Team stole anything that wasn't nailed down. With a simple spray of paint and a stencil, everything that they re-allocated became their property.

Two of Steve's scroungers carried a footlocker out of the supply room. Another soldier was diverting the supply sergeant. Steve stopped them and opened the heavy steel box. There were hundreds of Vietnam-issue bayonets inside. He laughed. "And what are we supposed to do with these knives?"

The young soldier shrugged his shoulders. Like a child who got caught by his father, his face turned red. He squeaked, "I don't know, Sarge, but we figured we could trade them off later for something we might need?"

Steve patted him on the back. "Smart thinking, Tripp." The rules changed. All was fair in war.

Each night after 5:00 P.M., Steve found himself surrounded by family and friends. There was no solitude, not a moment of privacy to think things through. Everybody needed time with him. They all hoped for the best, but each anticipated the worst. Every second was precious but, as most felt it could be the last moments spent with him, it was anything but enjoyable. Steve's mask was held firmly in place. He continued to smile, while reassuring his family of his confidence. Even then, he was determined to be their strength and put their minds at rest. He convinced his friends, but his family saw straight through it.

It was a crisp Saturday afternoon, the start of Steve's last weekend before shipping off to Fort Devens. The weekend was booked solid. The night was going to be consumed by visiting friends and family, and the following day, Ryan and Pat's double wedding. On Monday morning, they were scheduled to march from the armory to the bus station. He resented the lack of time with Monica.

Billy, Steve's older brother, pulled into the icy driveway and honked the horn in two, short blasts. Jumping into the cab of the pine scented truck, Steve asked, "Before we head to dad's, can you stop at the store for a pack of smokes?"

Billy laughed. "When are you gonna quit those things?"

"Just as soon as I get back."

Billy realized he had chosen a stupid time to preach. He quietly pulled out of the driveway.

Steve quickly broke the silence. "Brother, it's okay. To be honest with you, I'll be glad when we finally ship out. It's been a bitch on everyone, and the sooner we start kicking Saddam's ass, the sooner we can get our own asses home!"

On the ride, the brothers reminisced about their days of carefree youth. One started a funny story, but before finishing, the other excitedly interrupted, "That's nothing! Do you remember when . . . ?" Steve and Bill, born one year apart, were always close. Both men were happy it never changed.

Several miles down the snow plowed road, they passed Steve's old college. He wiped the fog from the passenger's side window. Gazing through the streaks in the glass, he noticed a large group of students huddled in a tight pack. Most were waving picket signs and screaming at the passing vehicles. He wiped the steamed window again and read the largest of the signs. As if it were meant for him personally, it jumped right out at him. It read: MURDER FOR OIL. His joyous mood came to a screeching halt.

"Stop the damn truck!" he screamed.

Billy smiled compassionately and calmly asked, "Why, Steve?"

He never answered. His heart was sick and his mind filled with rage.

Billy placed his hand on his brother's shoulder. He said, "I don't agree with it either, but, Steve, think about it. It's one of the very reasons you're going away. It's always been like that — men like you defending the fundamental rights of people like them! Right or wrong, they have the right to voice their opinions, and you're job is to defend that right. The problem is maybe they've never taken the time to understand or appreciate those who fought for such freedoms, or those who continue to protect and defend them?"

The truth and wisdom of his brother's words came as a complete shock. They hit as hard as the giant letters of the offensive sign.

Passing the last of the protesters, Steve rolled down the window. "You cowards!" he yelled.

One young man attempted a mean look, but was no match for his penetrating stare. The sign bearer quickly looked away. They all did. He rolled the window back up and glanced over at Billy. They burst into laughter.

"I know you're right, Billy, but I just had to!"

Billy continued to laugh. "I expected nothing less and I don't blame you, but it sure beats getting arrested for hitting a man who obviously isn't ready to fight."

As they continued to drive along, the cab of the truck bottled the heavy laughter within. Steve loved his brother's sarcasm, but felt confused about the brief experience. His mind told him that Billy was right, but his heart felt troubled. His thoughts quickly flashed to Tony Rosini and his comrades who had shipped off to Vietnam two decades earlier. In a small way, he had just experienced the slightest burden of their pain. Like them, he was only called to serve his country. He didn't start the war, nor would he be the one to finish it.

He sat thinking, while Billy gave him the silence to do it. He stared out the window. The huge mountains of snow piled up on the side of the road were already turning a dreary gray and black from the exhaust of the traffic. Looking up, the overcast sky mirrored the same depressing colors. It was a dark day. Within minutes, they pulled into their dad's driveway.

Bill Sr. and Randy were waiting outside. It was late afternoon and though the sun had reached its peak, the air temperature remained frigid. Both men were bundled up in heavy jackets and oversized boots. When they talked, billowy clouds of steam escaped their mouths. Billy parked the truck, while Steve noticed that the Christmas decorations on the house had already been removed. They were replaced by even more yellow ribbons. Bill Sr. hurriedly approached the truck. "Steve, why don't you jump in with me. Randy can ride with Billy. I've been craving a Hawaiian pizza. Lorenzos makes the best!"

It was a good try, but all three brothers saw straight through it. Lorenzos served the most horrendous pizza and it just happened to be a half-hour ride. The old-man wanted some time alone with Steve. It was time for one of those famous father-son talks. Steve wasn't sure he wanted to hear it, but he never denied his father anything. He switched vehicles and off they drove.

Before the car reached the end of the driveway, Bill Sr.'s face was beet red, and his eyes were swollen with tears. Out of respect, Steve waited for his father to speak. The middle-aged man looked at his son with incredible torment in his puffy eyes. He finally coaxed the words from his mouth. It sounded like he was speaking through a wad of cotton. "I love you, Steve, and I'm afraid. Hussein's threatening the war of all wars. I don't want to lose a son!" No sooner did the words leave his lips, than the tortured man broke down and cried freely.

Steve was taken back a bit. He had only seen his father cry once. It was at his grandfather's funeral. Even then, his dad wept quietly. Steve realized that he had inherited the trait of bottling up emotions from his father.

For the entire journey, the two men covered many topics of conversation regarding the war. His father questioned whether or not he was prepared to kill even a woman or child if necessary. He assured his dad that he'd do anything he had to in order to return home safely. Self-preservation and survival was the name of the game. Concluding the deep conversation, he told his father, "Believe in me, Dad, because I believe in myself. I'll come home. I promise!"

His father's eyes finally showed a bit of relief. Minutes later, they arrived in Lorenzos parking lot. Steve and his dad hugged. It was a long hug, the kind where nothing more needs to be said. The two met Billy and Randy inside.

The four Manchester men sat down to indulge in the greasiest pizza ever cooked. Lightening the mood, Randy joked, "Great pizza, Dad! Even without a beer chaser, it slides down nice."

The three brothers laughed. Bill Sr. only smiled, but it was a peaceful smile, and it made Steve happy.

Wiping his mouth, Billy stood. "Let's get out of here and go for a quick drink."

Nearly 40 minutes later, they ended up in a small tavern in Newport, Rhode Island. Scott, Steve's best friend, was sitting at the bar. Something was up.

As Bill Sr. ordered the first round of drinks, Steve turned to his older brother, "Long trip for a quick drink, isn't it?"

Billy laughed, but as he started to explain, he was cut off by their father's heart-felt toast. "To Steve, the first Manchester to go to war! I'm proud of you son and I know there isn't a man sitting at this table who wouldn't go with you! Do what you have to do, then get your ass home in one piece!" The last few words drifted off in a struggle for air. The men raised their glasses and washed back the lumps in their throats. Steve looked in each of their faces. His father was right. Billy had wanted to serve in the Marine Corps, but was denied. Randy was serving in the Air Force National Guard, but never got the call. Scott, an army reservist, was assigned to an incompetent infantry unit. Everybody knew he wasn't going anywhere. Then Steve looked at his father. If his dad had to, he would walk through hell with him, no questions asked.

Two patrons at the bar overheard the toast and joined in. The waitress rushed over and advised Bill Sr., "The two gentlemen at the bar have offered to pay for the next round. They said they won't take no for an answer."

Steve looked over to find the men still holding up their glasses to him. One even shot him a thumbs-up and yelled, "We're behind you all the way, buddy!"

He nodded his head in appreciation, but feared opening his mouth. He felt overwhelmed with emotion. The pride and patriotism that filled the tavern was heart-warming. From that moment on, the beer poured freely, while everybody joined in the Manchester party.

Billy slapped Steve on the back. In between sips, he joked, "We took a collection and you have a choice. You can either get a T-shirt or a tattoo?"

Steve chuckled. The T-shirt was sure to fade away, but the tattoo would commemorate the night forever. He realized why his brothers chose the old tavern. It was only two doors down from the tattoo parlor.

Steve and his older brother excused themselves and headed for the shop. Walking along the narrow cobble stone street, the two passed a couple of souvenir stores. Like most seasonal businesses in Newport, they were closed.

The parlor was packed with men; mostly biker-types. Billy headed straight for the artist to find out how long the wait would be. Steve scanned the cluttered walls of colorful prints. He was looking for the right tattoo. It took less than a minute before the perfect one caught his eye.

One hour and $200 later, they staggered back into the tavern. Bill Sr. slurred, "Well, let's see it." Steve removed his shirt, then the blood-stained gauze. Every drunken man at the table stared in awe. Through their blood-shot eyes, he saw the beginning of more tears.

Finally, Randy stuttered, "It's perfect!"

Steve's upper arm was completely covered in red, white and blue. There was a bald eagle, in flight, in the center of the arm. In the eagle's sharp claws, the bird of freedom carried the American flag. The flag appeared to be waving in the wind, while the staff stood rigid. At the top of the flag's staff, there was a spearhead, used only during war. In the background, the artist placed a shooting star. Above it all, a large banner read: U.S.A. The tattoo was beautifully detailed and summed up the feelings of every man in the tavern. Without another word, they filed out of the crowded bar. Patrons patted Steve on the back as he headed for the door.

He whispered to Scott, "At least if the bastards do kill me, they'll know where I came from!"

Scott threw his arm around his friend. It was time to go home. His going away party was about to begin.

As Billy made a left into Steve's long driveway, everyone came to life. The place was packed with cars. The Manchester and Rinaldi families were waiting. Steve never doubted they would, but hoped that a few had already left.

Billy was searching for a parking spot when Steve snapped, "Just put it on the lawn!" His change in mood took everyone by surprise. He apologized, jumped out and walked toward his front stairs. Looking up, he saw a homemade banner. It read: GOOD LUCK STEVE! He drew in a deep breath. He was dreading this moment and expected a horror show inside. The fiasco was unavoidable, so he calmly walked in.

As he ascended the stairs, he peered through the cracks in the banister. It was as he expected. The chairs were assembled in a circular fashion with the Rinaldi's on one side and the Manchester's on the other. It was always that way. Except for the marriage of their children, the two families shared nothing in common. There were cultural, social and economic barriers separating the two. Monica hated it, but Steve never pushed the sensitive issue. It just wasn't that important.

The living room looked like a small amphitheater where a horrible play was about to unfold. The characters were all in place, with the leading man making his grand entrance. Within seconds, he felt sober again, though he wished he didn't. He made his respective rounds with kisses and hand-shakes. Everybody was overjoyed to see him. Amidst a chorus of different conversations, he displayed his tattoo for all. The Manchester's loved it. The Rinaldi's were less impressed. Monica smiled, though he was sure she didn't care for it either.

Steve, his brothers and Scott grabbed their plates of food and took their seats within the circle. Once the meal was devoured, there was a bombardment of questions. Everyone's attention was focused on Steve.

As if rehearsed, one after the other took their shot for his attention. There were apologies for disagreements long forgotten. There were wishes of luck and promises of daily prayers. As the circle closed in, his old friend George got his turn.

Innocently enough, he commented, "It's a damn shame you have to get sent thousands of miles away to fight for oil."

Impulsively, Steve exploded in anger. "I'm not stupid enough to think this has nothing to do with oil, but I know in my heart that there are more noble reasons. I'm not about to risk my life, or take the lives of others over crude oil. There are innocent people, many of them children, dying in masses at the hands of a madman. Trust me, George, you can believe what you want, but I've already justified the cause in my own mind!"

The room went silent.

Eventually, the natural ripple in the circle continued, producing a heated argument between Steve and the Rinaldi's. Mr. Rinaldi, the family spokesman, passionately expressed his concerns about his daughter. He felt she should abandon the house and move back with her parents. Monica went ballistic. She adamantly refused to leave her life, adding, "I'm waiting for my husband right here!" The harsh words continued.

In a commanding voice, Steve said, "If that's what she wants, that's the way it will be!" It was obvious to him that a previous discussion between his father-in-law and wife had already taken place. He didn't like it.

The bickering only ended when Steve's Uncle Brian chimed in. He hated the whole charade as much as Steve.

Brian Vallee, Nancy Manchester's brother, served in Vietnam, but rarely spoke about it. When questioned years earlier about the experience, he humbly responded, "When your best friend's head rolls between your legs, how do you talk about it?" Uncle Brian had self-medicated ever since. This night was no different.

He was drunk, but spoke with authority. "Steve, there is no way to prepare yourself for the things you're about to see or experience over there. It'll change your life forever. The only thing you can do is to cover your ass, get home, then deal with it later!" He cracked open another beer and swallowed most of it in one gulp. Steve could easily see how his bitter uncle was still dealing with it.

Steve repressed every emotion that churned inside of him. For the next hour, the mood of the room darkened even more. Everybody said good-bye — everybody but Nancy. She smothered him in hugs and kisses. Then she held him in her arms and whispered, "Keep the faith."

Steve caught the penetrating stare of his Aunt Margaret. "Tell us, Steve, what is it that you fear most?" It was the only question of the night concerning his own feelings. All eyes were fixed on him.

The room felt like a vacuum with no noise and little oxygen. He knew the answer, but waited to speak. He desperately tried to conceal his feelings. So far, he had done quite well. No matter how he felt, he wanted to be the rock that his family could lean upon. This question, however, proved to be too much.

To everyone's surprise, he bowed his head and his body began to tremble. He placed his face in his hands and for the longest time, said nothing. Lifting his weary head, he spoke slowly. "I fear for the lives of the friends who fill my squad. For six years, I've done nothing but screw around, but now my job isn't to make people laugh. My job is to keep each one of them alive. I know in the bottom of my heart that if any one of my friends die, it'll be like tying a cement albatross around my neck for the rest of my life!" Looking at Monica, he added, "And God forbid anything happens to me . . . ."

He couldn't finish. He bowed his head again and wept like a child. Days of mental anguish came pouring out. The family began crying uncontrollably. As he had feared, everyone in the room adopted his pain.

It was approaching three in the morning when the gathering finally broke up. Steve's immediate family promised they'd see him off on Monday morning and left in a drunken stupor. Uncle Brian and Scott were the last to leave.

Brian placed his arm around Steve. "Sorry about tonight. And to think I've complained for years about not having a decent send-off to Vietnam!" As the door slammed shut behind the staggering man, his hearty laughter stayed behind for a few seconds.

Steve led Scott downstairs. Reaching behind his bar, he retrieved an old bottle of vodka and handed it to his best friend. Confused, Scott just shrugged.

He explained, "I want you to hold on to this for me. When I get home, we'll share it. If I don't make it, you and the boys have one last drink on me."

Scott hugged him. Walking toward the door, he looked back. "Don't worry, Steve. I'll keep it safe. Before you know it, we'll be wrestling with this bottle together!" Scott vanished into the night and the house was quiet.

Steve plopped down on the top step and lit a cigarette. As his mind bounced from one negative thought to the next, Monica stepped out of the bathroom wearing a sexy negligee. She whistled, calling his distant mind to her. He spun around and, seeing the soft light of the room highlight the contours of her body, his mood instantly changed.

She joked, "Hey, soldier, goin' my way?" Steve chuckled. He was exhausted, but needed love so much more than sleep. She took his hand. As they walked toward the bedroom, with a serious face, she joked again, "Great party, huh?"

They both burst into laughter and closed the door behind them, closing out the world for a few precious hours. Steve asked, "What would I ever do without you?"

She never hesitated answering. "You'll never have to know!"

Due to sheer physical exhaustion, foreplay was cut short. Steve reached into the nightstand for a condom. Monica grabbed his arm. "Are you sure you want to use that?" she asked. He sat up puzzled. She explained her feelings. For a half hour, they talked about the good and bad points of Monica getting pregnant.

Pulling no punches, he explained, "Monica, God forbid I do get killed over there, a baby won't make me immortal. Besides, I would never want to leave you with that burden. I want children, but there are enough in this world without fathers. When I get back, we'll start our family!"

He knew his wife wasn't ready for kids. There were still too many problems. He held her tight. It was the kindest, most thoughtful gesture anyone had ever offered him. Putting on the condom, he made sweet, gentle love to his injured wife. The alarm clock read 4:45 A.M. before the lovers dozed off. They only had five hours to sleep. The double wedding was at noon.

As usual, they were fashionably late. It wasn't planned that way, but the alarm clock just couldn't scream loud enough. At breakneck speed, they made the long trip in less than an hour. Turning into the American Legion's parking lot, Steve found an empty space in the rear. While Monica put on the finishing touches of make-up, he adjusted his tie in the rear-view mirror. They were finally ready. Hand in hand, they entered the enormous hall.

It was obvious that it wasn't going to be a traditional wedding. The decorations consisted of American flags and yellow ribbons. Walking through the threshold, he heard the rowdy screams of The Dream Team. Several of them summoned he and Monica to their table. While the Justice of the Peace took her place before Pat and his fiancee, Kerry, Steve said his brief hellos to his Army comrades. They took up five tables in all. Everybody was in exceptionally good spirits, everybody but Tom Kigley.

Steve took the seat near Tom. Sensing his friend's sorrow, he whispered, "Everybody knows that if they let you go, then you'd be there. Personally, I don't think we need ya!" He finished with a devilish smirk.

Tom said nothing, but leaned over and hugged him. The loud bunch of tables simmered down to listen to the nuptials.

Before the Justice of the Peace ever opened her mouth, the crying began. It started toward the front of the hall and within seconds, spread to the tables surrounding Steve. Pat and Kerry exchanged their simple vows, but it was sad. They planned a large wedding for the spring, but Saddam Hussein couldn't wait. So, with the sincerest intentions, they became husband and wife. Though the ceremony was brief, Steve watched through tearing eyes. It was like watching a scene out of a WWII movie, where the young couple rushes to get married, only for the husband to march off to war the following day. Steve scanned the room. Every woman was openly weeping, while most of the men bowed their heads. After the married couple's long kiss, Pat yelled, "Let's get rocked!"

The hall echoed with applause, with the boys of The Dream Team clapping the loudest. The line at the bar was long and the boys waited together. Dennis Ahern asked, "Steve, how was your going away party?"

He rolled his eyes. "Ever been to your own funeral?"

Without thinking, Dennis responded, "Yeah, last night! Everything was there but the casket!"

The friends laughed. Steve imagined that most of the boys must have experienced the same nightmare. As they bellied up to the bar, he offered to buy the first round of many. While giving the bartender his order, the hall erupted into cheers. He spun around. Ryan, Lori and their small wedding party entered the double reception.

Like Pat, Ryan had also decided to get hitched. This entitled their wives to all military benefits during the one-year activation. Though it was true love that brought them all together, it was a noble gesture to make the commitments before being sent away. Ryan and Lori decided on a private wedding at home, but upon their arrival, the party was in full swing. Late into the night, everybody partied hard. In a way, it was like their real going away party.

Ryan eventually made an announcement. He informed his guests that he and Lori were leaving. Steve rushed out the front door to help decorate their car. In shaving cream, he drew a heart on the back window and noticed Ryan's duffel bags on the back seat. The starch-pressed uniform was hanging stiffly, proof that the time was drawing near. Ryan and Lori scrambled out the front door and ran toward their car. Steve stood at a distance, smiling. He loved Ryan and remembered when they first met. He made fun of Lori just to piss his friend off. Now, they were all friends. It was one big, happy family. The boys of The Dream Team, as well as their wives and girlfriends.

Steve found Monica, grabbed his jacket and told the boys, "I'll see you all bright and early!" Everybody said they'd be there and started to get up one by one. It was a glorious night, the perfect send-off party, but there was an early wake-up call ahead. The next day was going to be a milestone in each of their lives. Couple by couple, they filed out of the hall.

Steve awoke well before the sun. His head was heavy from the night's alcohol, but his thoughts were focused. He turned to his sleeping wife. She looked so peaceful. As gently as possible, he ran his fingers through her dark hair. Whether she was dreaming or felt his soft touch, she smiled sweetly. He kissed the back of her neck. Staring at her, he whispered, "Dear God, am I going to miss this woman." Ever so quietly, he slipped out of the warmth of their bed and walked toward the kitchen. Starting a pot of coffee, he lit the day's first cigarette, then peered out of the frost-covered window. For ten minutes, he sat in complete solitude. His mind was blank, and his body, relaxed. There would be plenty of time to think later.

Monica was up, though barely awake from the look of her squinted eyes. As he offered her a mug of steaming coffee, her eyes widened. She pushed it away. Instead, she accepted a hug. It was a long hug, without a word being spoken.

She finally dragged herself into the shower, while he removed his camouflaged battle dress uniform from the closet. He put it on. Walking past the hallway mirror, he caught his reflection and stopped. The uniform looked good. His head was cleanly shaven and his boots gleamed like black glass. He chuckled, knowing that the outfit was going to get old really quick. After securing his duffel bags in the trunk of the car, he headed for the garage. Before the huge, squeaky door was completely open, McGruff, the family's black Labrador Retriever, came sprinting out. He filled the big baby's bowls with food and water, then played fetch with his old friend. The playful dog ran back and forth, content with his master's attention. Steve suddenly noticed that the front door was open. Monica was standing there dressed and ready. She was watching as the two played in the snow like children. He looked at his watch. It was time to go.

He tied the dog onto the runner in the backyard and gave his canine friend one last hug. McGruff actually took his mind off the morning. He turned and walked away. As if he knew, the dog began to whimper. He never looked back. Monica was already in the car when he rounded the front of the house. He opened the driver's side door and paused. He stared at his house and shook his head. The house had cost so much and it wasn't only money. There was worrying, arguments and loss of sleep over the financial burden. He climbed into the front seat and smiled. He also remembered the many good times there. Besides, as long as Monica lived there, it was home. As they backed out of the driveway and started up the road, he wondered if they'd still own it when he returned.

The ride up the highway was driven in silence. They held hands firmly, while glancing over at each other every few minutes. Each knew what the other was thinking. Their feelings were identical and everything was communicated through touch. He took the exit slow and within minutes, they were driving along the parade route. Storefronts flew American flags and hundreds of yellow ribbons were tied around poles. Monica tightened her grip and her breathing became heavier.

They reached the town square, located several hundred yards from the armory. In the middle, an enormous American flag fluttered in the icy wind. Just below it, a nicely decorated reviewing stand engulfed the square. Steve turned into the armory's parking lot. Grabbing his duffel bags from the trunk, he noticed the sun barely peeking over the horizon. The day had finally arrived.

They walked into the warmth of the armory. Not two minutes later, Kline screamed for the start of the morning briefing. Steve kissed Monica and joked, "Wish me luck, it'll be hell in there!"

She chuckled, giving him a slap on the rump. "I love you," she whispered.

Steve met Chuck at the door and shut it behind them. The two friends took their seats in the rear of the room near Platoon Sergeant Tony Rosini. Standing at the podium was a full-bird Colonel. His uniform was impeccable, but his face showed several days of lost sleep. Calling the briefing to order, he began in a hoarse voice.

"Good morning, people. The day has finally arrived!" Starting with his own political views, he hissed, "We cannot allow Saddam Hussein to control this region! If we allow him to control 40 percent of the world's oil supply, we'll allow him to hold us as economic hostages!"

Steve looked at Chuck and whispered, "Maybe to him it's about oil."

The tired man continued, "You are the fifth National Guard Unit to be activated, however, your ultimate destination is unknown. It could be Europe or the States, anywhere to back fill for other units. It could also be deployment to the Persian Gulf . . . ."

The room buzzed with questions. The man was speaking in riddles. Sensing his vague and indirect instructions, the old war relic smiled.

"People, some things are still confidential, but I will say this: You are about to enter a very dangerous environment and there is a chance some of you are going to get hurt. Above all else, watch out for your people. If somebody does get hurt, don't let it be from an accident. Please keep safety in mind. I know you will do your duty!"

He cut to the chase and in his own way, told them all they needed to know. Steve looked at Chuck again. They were right.

The man rambled on while Steve scanned the room. All the heavy hitters were in attendance. The briefing lasted well over an hour.

With one last piece of advice, the Colonel called it quits. "Thousands of people are coming to see you off today. Let's look good out there, okay?"

Everybody stood, saluted and filed out of the smoke-filled room.

It hit Steve like a tidal wave. The armory was packed with hundreds of people. He walked through the crowd, making a head count of the people in his squad. All ten were accounted for. It was a relief. Rows of duffel bags lined the floor, marking each soldier's place in the company. He kept walking, amazed at the quietness of the crowded armory. With the exception of reporters and television crews running around like ferrets, people were knotted together in small groups. The O'Malleys and Whites stood together. The Donnelly and Roble families spoke amongst each other. Steve passed the Medeiros and Ahern families, only to receive a dirty look from Mr. Ahern. He grinned. As he walked, he heard the same responses to the media's questions, "I always knew it was a possibility when I signed on the dotted line! We'll do the job we've been trained to do and get home! It was a contract I signed when I got sworn in — to defend my state and my country!" He beamed with pride. His friends were all there with the right intentions. Each one was a clean-cut, red-blooded, all-American boy, the finest the country had to offer. The mood was upbeat. He knew that his friends weren't eager for a war with Iraq.

He spotted Monica standing with his family. They were huddled in a corner, watching him make his last-minute check of Second Squad. Grinning from ear to ear, he headed for them. Ten steps away, an annoying reporter stopped him.

He raised his hand before the question was even asked and said, "It's always good for adversaries to talk, but we don't expect a substantial resolution to come of it. We support the cause and we're ready to go!"

Scratching the words into her small notepad, the reporter asked, "Can I quote you on that Sergeant Manchester?"

Steve chuckled. "You already have, haven't you?"

She scribbled some more and walked over to her next victim.

Before he even reached them, the family was already in tears. He looked at his watch. There was ten minutes before the formation — ten minutes to say goodbye. It was nine minutes too long. Starting with Monica, he hugged and kissed them all.

He looked into the face of each one and vowed, "I love you!" Bending down, he picked up his three-year-old sister. He held the baby tight in his arms. Big crocodile tears streamed down her beautiful face. She was like an angel, a perfect picture of unconditional love and innocence. He froze the picture in his mind. Reaching down again, he scooped up Darlene. The two little girls smothered him with kisses. Each one was crying for a different reason. Darlene sobbed because she feared losing her older brother and Jenny, because everybody else was crying. Steve thanked God that at least the baby didn't understand what was happening.

The last to say goodbye was Nancy Manchester. She pulled him to her and swayed back and forth. Steve felt like a child being rocked in his mother's arms. As they embraced, another reporter attempted to step between them with a tape recorder. Flash bulbs were going off all around them. Steve became furious, but before he could react, Randy, his even-tempered brother stepped in and swatted the vultures away. Nancy Manchester didn't even notice the intrusion.

She grabbed her son's face and whispered, "Keep the faith. And so long for now."

Steve wept freely. He couldn't hold it back any longer. Shielding his feelings behind his mother's shoulder, he whispered back, "Thank you,

Mom. I'll come home!" Nancy Manchester was the only person who never said goodbye.

First Sergeant Kline screamed, "Formation. Let's go people!"

Steve wiped the last tear from his eyes and took his spot at the head of Second Squad. Roll call was held as normal before First Sergeant Kline put on a show for the news cameras. He spoke of pride and duty, causing yawns throughout the company.

Captain Wall called the company to attention, and marched them out of the armory. In full combat gear, under the weight of a heavy field pack, Steve shouldered his rifle and led his squad into the street. There were thousands waiting. Once outside, the company took a few minutes to line itself up perfectly. It was just enough time for the reporters to penetrate the ranks. Steve was the first to be approached. He laughed. They were a complete annoyance, but he gave them credit for their persistence.

A young man, wearing a Press card in his hat, asked, "What are your last thoughts before you march off to war?"

Steve offered his devilish smirk. Over the emotional screams of the crowd, he shouted, "Saddam Hussein is nothing but a mosquito and we've got the bug light packed!"

The reporter giggled with glee and scrambled off into the crowd. The company was moving.

The unit was halted before the large reviewing stand. There, standing at attention, the boys listened to the experienced words of military officials and the long-winded, eloquent speeches of local politicians. They stood in the cold air for two hours, listening to candidates talk in circles, trying to gain votes for the next election. As they rambled on, Steve noticed a Christmas decoration in the background. It was as big as a billboard. It read: PEACE ON EARTH. Beside the sign stood war memorials — statues of soldiers of wars long past. He smiled at the irony.

He stood rigid, listening attentively when the speakers really had something to say. To his surprise there were a few, and Captain Wall was one of them.

She compared the 661st M.P. company to the 9th Coastal Artillery, a unit nicknamed the Doughboys. They had marched off 73 years earlier to fight the battles of Europe.

"Like them, we are citizen-soldiers who left our families, friends and homes to answer the call. Now, it is our time!" Directing her next words toward the company, she added, "I know you can, and will, perform any duty required. My faith in you is great, my expectations high!" Finishing her speech, she turned toward the thousands of onlookers and barked, "We are about to enter the unknown. We will face this challenge, do our jobs as soldiers and return with pride. To these principals, we will not be compromised. I promise to take care of each and every soldier and bring them home safely!"

She did well, right up until the end. The last promise was empty, causing a giddy commotion throughout the ranks. Steve held back his own chuckle to stare down his men. With a bad look, they were quieted.

There was a loud a commotion in the crowd. Turning slightly, Steve saw a protester's sign that read: WAR IS NO SOLUTION! The sign was violently ripped from the air. A brief struggle ensued before Tom Kigley stood, raising his own sign. It read: PROTESTER'S AGAINST PROTESTER'S! As Tom melted into the crowd, Steve giggled. Tom had obviously assaulted a person with a different view, and was going on his own mission. Denied back into the unit, he would be doing his own part at home. Steve stared straight ahead again, only to find Tony wearing the biggest smile. It was the smile of irony, the irony of two decades of contrast.

Speaker after speaker lauded the U.S. effort in the Gulf. The sentiment was nice, but it was freezing and everyone was getting restless. The boys wanted to get the show on the road. The chaplain took the floor for a few brief words and a much needed prayer.

The 214th Army Band struck up John Philip Sousa's *Washington Post March*. With a crisp order to march, the 661st were on their way.

Goose bumps covered Steve's entire body. As he peered from beneath his helmet, his whole being was consumed with honor, patriotism and pride. He marched steadily ahead, with only three miles between he and an unknown future. Thousands of people lined the streets. He looked at the faces in the crowd. Sadness and worry were etched on some, but most observers were caught up in the hooting and clapping. Office workers came out to wave, while schoolgirls screamed, as if greeting rock stars. People waved signs of support. Steve's heart pounded in his ears. As was common lately, he felt overwhelmed.

One mile into the parade route, he glanced to his right to find his father matching each of his steps. On his dad's shoulders sat baby Jenny. The baby was crying and waving. Right behind them, the rest of the Manchester clan forged ahead. He turned his head. It was too much. He never doubted they would go as far as they could with him, but it was breaking his heart.

Keeping his eyes straight, he faintly heard his name being called. It was Chuck Emond.

Chuck whispered, "Don't worry, Steve, I can't look at your sister either. My God, it's fuckin' killing me."

Steve nodded. Chuck possessed the strongest character in the platoon, but baby Jenny's tears were too much for even him.

There was one last bend in the road before he spotted the buses waiting to be boarded. The parade was over. The company was halted and dismissed for ten minutes to say goodbye. Steve decided that he wasn't going through it again, nor was it fair to his family. Removing his uncomfortable helmet, he approached them. He went down the line and told each of them, "Take care and write." Reaching the end of the line, he felt a soft tug on his shirt. He turned to find his sisters' arms opened wide.

He bent down, gave them each a hug and whispered, "Every night, at 7 o'clock, I'll wish you girls a goodnight, and you do the same, okay?"

Through red, tearing eyes, they promised.

Choking back his own tears again, he grabbed Monica. "I'll see you at Fort Devens on the weekend. I love you ... and please take care of yourself."

They kissed and he vanished into the big commercial bus.

Walking to the rear, he noticed that everybody was already aboard. It was time to think differently now. His new family was now sitting on the bus. Feeling their sadness, he took it upon himself to boost morale. There was no better time to start.

In a high-pitched, feminine voice, he began, "We're the men of the National Guard. Fighting wars in our backyard ...."

It took a few seconds to spread, but he smiled when the entire bus began belting out the old favorite. The air brakes let out a sigh of relief, the diesel motor began to rumble and The Dream Team were on their way to learn the art of desert warfare.

Chapter 5

Training Behind a Desert Shield

The caravan of buses forged north, with The Dream Team appropriately taking the lead. The trip to Fort Devens should have taken no more than four hours, but the further north they traveled, the slower they drove. The highway was a mess. There had been a few bad storms just days before. Slouching back in his seat, Steve stared out the tinted window. The autumn trees were stripped of their majesty from weeks of pounding snow and rain. Their bare, frozen limbs stretched toward the gray sky like old, bony hands begging for mercy. The countryside was covered in a blanket of white. Hints of evergreen trees peeked out from under the weight of the heavy snow.

The bus suddenly slid sideways. The driver had hit a patch of black ice. He regained control within seconds. Relaxing back in his seat, Steve noticed that the evergreens weren't the only ones feeling the weight. Hours before, the singing had subsided and now his friends sat in silence. Most eyes were closed or staring off into space. Every young face reflected a broken heart. Every man was in his own world — worlds that included homes and families. Steve stared out the window. He was determined not to dwell on his family, but he wasn't ready to think about training for the war either. It was a time for peace, a brief time, but for now, he'd take what he could get.

Eight hours after they departed from the depot, the bus entered the gates of Fort Devens. The trip took twice as long as it should have. Nobody minded. It wasn't like they had anywhere to go. As the bus tried to stop in front of some dilapidated barracks, Steve stood in the aisle. The tired coach caught a strip of dry road and came to a screeching halt. Violently throwing everybody toward the front, Steve slammed into the back of Chuck Emond.

As Chuck turned around, he whispered, "Do you believe this shit? There must be two feet of snow up here and whatever isn't covered, is frozen! And this is where they've sent us to train for desert warfare?"

With a grim look, Chuck returned the whisper. "I know. We're fucked!"

Everyone filed off of the bus into bitterly cold air. Steve felt the chill right down to his bones. Drawing in a deep breath, his lungs welcomed the clean, but frozen air. The road was covered with an inch of ice. Everything was frozen, from the ground to the dark sky. The bus driver tossed the duffel bags into one big heap. The man wanted the warmth of his bus and worked in a hurry. As the boys searched for their own gear, First Sergeant Kline called for a formation. Abandoning the search, every soldier took his place.

Kline looked like a nervous wreck, but his trembling was caused by the icy wind hitting his face. Steve grinned. It wasn't going to be a long formation. Through chattering teeth, he could hardly make out what the first sergeant was saying.

In a loud clear spurt, Kline announced, "First Platoon is assigned to barracks 1262, bottom floor. Second Platoon, top floor. Third is in 1263, bottom floor, the Fourth, top. Females are in 1264. Dismissed!"

Steve found his two bags and headed for his new home. Walking toward the threshold of 1262, he hoped the inside of the building was in better shape than its exterior. It was an old WWII barracks.

The building was probably condemned at one time, but reopened to accommodate the overflow of soldiers training for the confrontation in the sand. At the head of the barracks were two rooms, each furnished with two steel beds. The urine-stained mattresses were rolled up, and the flat striped pillows were placed at the foot. He passed the rooms and entered the open bay area. There were two long rows of bunk beds lining the walls. Taking a bottom bunk toward the front, he threw his duffel bags on the floor. Unrolling the mattress, he flopped down on the bed. The springs bit through the thin mattress.

The run-down building smelled musty and probably hadn't been cleaned since the last war. Many of the floor tiles were missing. The ones that remained were either chipped or curling up. The walls, once white, were a dingy yellow. Their lead paint was peeling off, leaving large flakes on the floor. He shook his head in disbelief. Unprepared to check out the latrine, he started to unpack his gear. The distinctive rumble of Tony Rosini echoed through the large room. As if summoning a small child, he yelled, "Manchester, I want you in this room!"

Steve looked up and laughed. The funny giant was wiggling his massive finger at him. Nobody else took notice. They were all too busy claiming their new territory.

"I'm okay right here, Sarge," replied Steve, "this is where my squad is sleeping, so . . . ."

Cutting him short, Tony yelled even louder, "Stevie-boy, all squad leaders sleep up front, okay?"

Gathering his things, Steve walked into the room to find Chuck Emond getting comfortable. Tossing his heavy bags onto the floor, he joked, "Honey, I'm home." Chuck's hands were folded behind his head. His eyes were closed.

Obviously removed from some deep thinking, Chuck eventually smiled. "Well, it isn't much, but it is home for now." His new roommate was right. It was time to settle in.

The first night proved to be a lesson in teamwork as The Dream Team threw their own house-warming party. Although there was no alcohol, music or women at the spontaneous gala, mops, toilet brushes and the scent of pine oil soon replaced the musty air. The G.I. party, the Army's version of some hyperactive spring cleaning, lasted late into the night. In good spirits, the boys worked feverishly. No matter how temporary their situation, none of them wanted to live like swine. After Steve and Chuck passed their own white glove inspection, they joined their squads in scrubbing down the huge bay. Before it was over, it took five hours, the sweat of 30 men and gallons of disinfectant to make their living quarters livable. The party was a success, topped off with the Quarter Master handing out fresh linen. Feeling his own physical exhaustion, Tony wished his boys pleasant dreams and turned out the lights.

As Steve lay in his new bed, an eerie silence replaced the grunts and groans of his hard working friends. No sooner did his head hit the pillow, than he began thinking about the days to come. It was January 7th, and President Bush, along with the U.N. Security Council, had set a January 15th deadline for Iraqi forces to leave Kuwait. Iraq didn't look like they were going anywhere. The U.S. was one week away from war. He caught himself dwelling on things completely out of his control, fluffed the stiff pillow and looked out the frozen window. With the sleet and tiny hailstones pelting off the windowpane, Mother Nature finally sang him to sleep.

Steve awoke. It took a few moments to realize where he was. Reality wasn't kind. The first formation was held just outside the barracks complex. Half asleep, he took his place on the road that looked like white stained glass. First Sergeant Kline, who had already been issued his extreme cold weather clothing, was in exceptionally high spirits. It was because he and Staff Sergeant Volmer were the only two wearing the warm apparel. Smiling from ear to ear, he took his sweet time about things. The entire company suffered.

Grumbling traveled through the ranks, and it all amounted to the same thing: Kline was a no-good bastard. Steve never tried to stop the mumbled complaints. He was in total agreement.

Kline took 15 minutes to say, "This first day will be dedicated to medical screenings." Just shy of sustaining frostbite, the company was finally released to a row of old school buses. The buses were painted olive and drab green, which instantly transformed them into U.S. Army transport vehicles. They were quickly loaded with dozens of camouflaged popsicles.

Though the boys of The Dream Team were going anywhere but school, most started to learn a few lessons about the true character of their friends. Until now, they had spent one weekend a month and two hilarious weeks each summer together. No one realized it, but those drinking-buddy friendships were changing. Most of the changes were good, others shockingly bad. It was inevitable. Above all else, each man wanted to preserve his own life and his survival depended on those around him. The changes were subtle at first, but things were definitely changing. According to Tony Rosini, "Change is constant; growth, optional!"

The Dream Team pulled into an enormous, vacant parking lot. The Fort's gymnasium was recently converted into a giant medical clinic. Walking onto the gym's parquet floor, the boys were met by a large group of doctors, nurses and other medical personnel, each dressed in camouflage. Steve sensed the start of something very big. A hard smack of reality hit him square in the face. Everybody knew that there was no turning back once they were cleared medically. He summoned his squad into a huddle. Piling one hand on top of the other, the squad displayed their solidarity, then offered their bodies to the U.S. Army.

Hours passed and he couldn't believe what transpired. Herded from one station to the next, each soldier was poked, prodded and ordered to play contortionist for one doctor or another. There was blood, urine, every bodily fluid extracted for testing. Lengthy interviews were conducted, with the emphasis on gaining personal testimonies. The Army demanded personal guarantees of good physical and mental health from each soldier. Steve signed the waiver provided. After a brief lunch, the inoculations were administered. They received shots in their arms, legs and butts. Swollen and throbbing with pain, the company held an informal formation. They were addressed by the doctor in charge, a full-bird Colonel.

In a thick Southern drawl, the man started, "You people have been inoculated against every disease and virus known to man." He laughed at his own dry humor until he realized he was laughing alone. "But seriously, people, we've done all we can here. As far as protecting you from any chemical or biological agents, well, those preventive medicines will be administered in the theater of operations — the Persian Gulf." Without another word, he walked away. Though nobody realized it, the man confirmed their reservations for a long desert vacation.

Captain Wall took the floor. Wincing from the slew of shots, she barked, "Take a seat, people, and relax. We have to wait on the results of some of the tests." There was no need for coaxing. The company did just that; they relaxed.

Steve stretched out on the floor with his squad. Turning to Pat, he joked, "Damn, I wonder if they were ever this thorough at NASA?"

Pat chuckled. "I know, I thought for a minute there, I was gonna have to give up a kidney or something!"

As they joked, the twisted grapevine passed on the day's best news. First Sergeant Kline flunked the physical. He wasn't going to the Gulf. There were cheers throughout the gymnasium. Soldiers openly displayed their sincere joy about Kline's poor health.

Steve grabbed Tony. "Tony, what's this shit about Kline. The little asshole's not goin'?"

Tony tried to conceal his grin. "From what I understand, he was in a motorcycle accident years ago and lost his spleen. He has to take meds for it. I guess they gave him the option and the coward chose to stay." Raising his hands, his grin widened. On the brink of laughter, he turned and strutted away.

Steve returned to the boys with the news. As they talked, he got angrier and snapped, "You know, that's bullshit. The abusive son of a bitch practices for years, but when it comes game time, he decides he's gonna sit this one out? Screw him!"

As Steve finished his passionate spiel, First Sergeant Kline walked past. Looking directly into the coward's eyes, he snarled, "SPLEEN? I think the doctor screwed up and meant SPINE!" The cold words stopped Kline in his tracks, but just long enough to realize he had no defense. Kline knew that as long as he took his pills, he could go. He put his head down and walked outside where it was warmer for him. As the door slammed shut behind him, everybody looked disgusted, everybody but Dennis Ahern.

Returning to the barracks, Steve throbbed from every limb. The first day was long and painful, but it was over. As he smiled at the thought, the room door swung open.

It was Chuck Emond. A look of disgust covered his serious face. "Steve, it looks like we have another coward on our hands. Lucky for you, he's in your squad."

"Let me guess, Dennis Ahern?"

Surprise replaced Chuck's disgust. "How did you know? From what I hear, the mouse just told his partner, Medeiros."

"I could see it on his face today at the gym. Son of a bitch, I knew it."

Steve found Dennis lying on his bed. His face was flushed. As he approached, Greg Medeiros grabbed his arm. "Steve, he's takin' a lot of shit from the platoon. I told him that it was his decision to make."

Brushing Greg off, Steve asked Dennis to speak in private. Through a sea of bad looks in the open bay, he led Dennis into his room. As soon as they walked in, Chuck stormed out.

He cut to the chase. "Dennis, what's up?"

Through a crackling voice, Dennis explained. "Steve, I know you're not going to like this either, but I'll give it to you straight. One of my knees is shot and might need surgery. My doctor at home said it could wait, but today, the Army doctor gave me the option to have it done now. If I do, then I get to stay here, but I don't know what to do. They gave me two days to decide."

In a calm, friendly tone, Steve asked, "Dennis, do you need the surgery now or can it wait until we get back?"

Dennis' eyes swelled with tears. His face burned red with embarrassment. "It can wait, but there's more to it than that. Steve, my daughter is five years old and . . . ."

Steve could no longer contain himself. He exploded, "You bastard, we all have family and there's no guarantee that any of us will see them again. Every man in this platoon has something to lose!" Searching his friend's watering eyes, he lowered his tone. "Hey, it's your decision to make and nobody can help you, but remember this Dennis — you have to live with yourself!"

Dennis shook his head, but said nothing. He was scared, confused, but in the same boat as all of them. He wiped his eyes and walked out.

Steve followed and headed for the latrine. As he walked, the bay remained terribly quiet. All the boys were full of smiles. Everyone heard their conversation. He wasn't happy about any of it. On the contrary, he was disappointed and disgusted with his old friend. No matter what decision Dennis made, it didn't matter anymore. The Dream Team was all done with him. With the exception of Greg Medeiros, Dennis didn't have a friend in the Army. He could no longer be depended on. In one brief moment in time, Dennis Ahern lost the respect, trust and friendship of 28 men. In turn, he was given the most offensive label any man could have — he was now a coward.

Steve turned in for the night, but not before Tony called him outside. "I know it wasn't easy for you, but you did the right thing. Just keep an eye on our conscientious objector. We both know he's wrong, but believe me, war is a funny thing. It makes men do and say things they normally wouldn't. Bottom line; I don't want anyone hurting him and I don't want him hurting himself, okay?"

Steve nodded in agreement. Then, he jumped in bed for a restless night's sleep.

Morning didn't come as quickly as the one before, but the sun eventually lit up the dreary sky. The morning formation found a new first sergeant. His name was John Avery, a Massachusetts State Trooper who had volunteered to serve in his second war. He quickly proved to be a good and fair man, the complete opposite of Kline. A bit quiet, but as long as the job got done, he was happy. First Sergeant Avery was the perfect replacement for little Hitler.

The second day was spent at everyone's favorite office, the dentist's. To the surprise of all, the Army actually filled cavities and didn't pull every tooth with the smallest hint of decay. Steve sat drooling like a newborn, his mouth frozen from Novocaine. He got two temporary fillings. As the numbness was wearing off, Dennis timidly approached. "Steve, I thought about what you said. You were right. I've decided to go!"

Steve shook his head up and down, unsure if he could talk. It didn't matter anyway. There was really nothing more to say. The irreparable damage was done. The irony was that Dennis was given the choice and he still decided to go.

The following day, the actual training started. Command Task Training was basically everything a soldier needed to know. It was merely a condensed form of basic training, a refresher course in killing others while preserving one's own life. Beginning with the identification of enemy aircraft, tanks and weaponry, the instructor found it easy to keep everyone's attention. He was a Vietnam veteran. The boys soon found that though the names and faces changed, at least half the instructors were just like him.

As Vietnam veterans, they saw death and knew combat intimately. The boys listened to words of wisdom spoken from priceless experience. Steve also found, however, that beneath the professionalism lied a burning animosity. These soldiers fought a war, labeled a campaign, for an ungrateful nation. Without good wishes, they were sent into the jungle and returned to face harsh words, ignorant judgments and little support from a confused government. Now, two decades later, they stood at lecterns, teaching younger soldiers who had the love and support of the free world. They were angry, but it was directed at the wrong people. During the day's second break, Steve voiced his observations to Tony.

Tony responded in fury. "You could never understand what it was like ... to fight for a fuckin' country and its people who hated your guts! You have the support of both!" Even Tony held a deep resentment, and he was going to the desert.

Steve returned fire. "Why don't you take a good frigin' look. I wasn't there yelling or spitting at you when you came home. I was in diapers. You can't blame this generation for the mistakes of another. As a matter of fact, if I, or any of the guys in this platoon were born 20 years earlier, we would have been with you in Vietnam. Unfortunately, as working-class slugs, we got stuck with this war. Nobody gave us a choice!"

Tony stood without reaction. Steve couldn't read his face one way or the other. The older man finally shot him a wink and walked away, leaving him confused. The wink was half-hearted and meant to keep peace. Perhaps Tony was right, nobody could ever understand what it was like.

Friday rolled around and The Dream Team filed into another classroom. This day, however, was different. The instructor, a nasty man, had difficulty holding anyone's attention. He represented the other half of the instructors. They were career soldiers who never saw combat and weren't chosen for the desert battle. These men also felt a harsh resentment and were angry, but for other reasons. It was so obvious to everyone. Wars were few and far between. For career soldiers, it meant promotions, recognition and a meaning to the years of training. Ironically, they were tasked with teaching part-timers, while they became consumed with envy and bitterness. The irony amazed Steve. The Dream Team would have traded places in a second. These instructors never realized they were doing their own part.

The first training week was behind them. Steve and Chuck headed for their room. Turning out the lights, Steve could hear the whimpering of a man from behind the door. From the look on Chuck's face, he knew that he wasn't hearing things. Chuck slowly opened the door. Tony Rosini was sitting in the corner of the dark room.

Through a gurgle, Tony cried, "Leave the fuckin' lights off." The two knew it was going to be a long night and shut the door behind them. It was better that nobody else in the platoon witnessed their leader's bout with Vietnam.

Through the long hours of the dark night, Tony experienced flashbacks from the trauma he suffered in the brutal jungles of Vietnam. Steve and Chuck, unprepared for the new burden, tried everything to console their broken friend. Nothing worked. Tony continued to wail and cry out names from the past, names of men who had made the ultimate sacrifice. Steve remembered reading the last words of a dying soldier. In a final letter to his wife, the brave warrior wrote, "I have been lucky. I was with men who stood tall and proud, not in protest, but in humility, regretting they had but one life to give."

With both respect and sympathy, Steve watched as Tony came apart at the seams. Covered in sweat and mucous, the old horse refused to be taken to the hospital. The very idea made him turn on Steve and Chuck. With murder in his eyes, he roared, "You fuckin' candy asses have no idea. Before this one's over, you'll both hate God and the day you were born!" Bowing his head, the poor soul mumbled and spoke in riddles. Tony was sick and in great pain. Steve had seen enough. Knowing he could do no more, nor hide it any longer, he ran out to get help. Within minutes, he returned with First Sergeant Avery, Tony's friend from Vietnam.

Leaving the two men alone, Steve and Chuck walked toward the latrine. The bay was silent, though every man was awake. Sharing a cigarette in the shower area, they talked in whispers. "Another wonderful night," kidded Steve.

Chuck grinned, but the determined look he possessed grew stronger. Everything that needed to be said was conveyed without words. It was clear to them both. Chuck was the assistant platoon sergeant. From here on, he would be running the show. Tony would remain the figurehead, but Chuck Emond was going to take the reigns and lead The Dream Team into the desert.

As Steve poked out the cigarette, Chuck grabbed his arm.

"I'm gonna need your help with all of it, Steve. We need to stick together and keep an eye on Tony!"

The friends shook hands. It was a firm handshake, the kind that sealed a pact. Exhausted, they spoke no more and went to bed.

Saturday morning formation was a blur until First Sergeant Avery called Steve and Chuck to the side. "Guys, I appreciate what you did last night, but it's between us, okay?"

Before Chuck could open his mouth, Steve responded, "Sorry, but it's not between us. The whole platoon heard what went on last night. I'll be honest, boss. It's bad enough Tony had to go through it once, but doesn't it seem a little unfair that he has to experience another war?"

Avery stared coldly into his young eyes. "Steve, the platoon will do fine, we all know that. As far as fair, well, you'll learn soon enough that none of this is about being fair. Tony wants to go. Although it's just about pride, no one is gonna take that away from him! Do we understand each other?"

Steve dropped his gaze. "Yes, we understand each other." Patting both he and Chuck on the back, Avery marched off. He was a good man, but Steve still disagreed.

As usual, a change in plans quickly spread through the warm barracks. First Sergeant Avery announced that although weekends were scheduled for time off, the first weekend was going to be spent catching up to the other companies. He was right. Nobody knew when they were going. It made sense to train as hard and long as possible.

More bad news came through the door. It was a messenger from the medical section. Steve read the report. From the very first words, his heart sank. Greg Medeiros, the hard-working whiz kid, was diagnosed with an abnormal heartbeat. It was just an adult heart murmur, but the Army wasn't taking any chances. Greg was grounded. He would be staying back with Kline and a few others. Steve called his friend in to give him the news. As he read the report for himself, Greg began crying. Weeping openly, he finally composed himself enough to speak. "Steve, this sucks. I wanted to be with you guys, now they won't even give me the chance."

Steve stood and patted his friend's back. "Greg, you had no say in this one. Besides, you stupid bastard, who knows, you could be one of the luck-iest men alive?"

Greg shook his head. "You know what I mean brother. You wouldn't feel lucky either." Returning the pat, Greg walked out to tell his friends.

Steve watched as Greg took the letter from bunk to bunk. The boys just patted him on the back and offered their congratulations. Steve shook his head. He knew what Greg meant. They had been friends for years. The man was dedicated, loyal and one hell of a soldier. More than that, he believed in the cause and was prepared to fight. As Greg approached his best friend, Dennis, the irony became more incredibly amazing. Both men cried; one because he didn't want to go, the other because the Army wouldn't let him. Dennis looked horrified. He was definitely on his own now. If it had only been reversed, everyone would have been happy. First Sergeant Avery was right. Fairness had nothing to do with anything. Things happened without rhyme or reason. It was the luck of the draw. Steve only hoped that his friend would someday count the blessing he was given. For all anyone knew, he had been given a second life. The others would have to wait and see.

The personnel change allowed Tony to flex whatever authority he had left. Calling for an emergency meeting, he held a draft and the platoon was rearranged. It sounded good at first, but within no time, Chuck Emond stacked the deck in his own favor. Picking the more experienced soldiers, the other two squads were left unbalanced. Steve was enraged.

"What in the hell are you doing, Chuck? If you take all the stronger guys, the rest of us are walking dead!"

Chuck never backed down from a fight in his life and snapped back, "My first responsibility is to my squad!"

Nose to nose, Steve screamed, "Screw you and your squad, Overlord. We're all supposed to be friends, but if Second and Third Squads get wiped out because we don't have the right people, then that's just too bad, right?"

Chuck felt challenged. He was all done talking. Two seconds away from exchanging blows, Tony stepped in. With a simple wave of his pen, he squared the squads away and made things right again. In the end, the only change was that Ryan White was taking over for Greg, stepping up as Chuck's assistant squad leader.

Steve was almost asleep when Chuck asked, "Hey, brother, where in the hell did 'Overlord' come from?"

Steve laughed. "Chuck, you have to be the most determined, most convicted man I've ever met. You're overbearing, rash, but your intentions are usually good, so nobody ever questions you!"

Chuck giggled. "Come hard or stay home," he said. It was his motto on life. He never half-stepped anything.

Steve laughed and pulled the green woolen blanket up to his neck. The nickname, Overlord, stuck. He was sure Chuck loved it, even if the hard-ass never admitted it.

The first week of training rolled right into the second. Everybody was all business. The more they learned, the more they increased their chances of survival. From before sunrise until late into the evenings, they became sponges, absorbing every word spoken, and the words that didn't need to be said. They sat through some long, but interesting classroom lectures on Middle Eastern customs and the anticipation of nuclear, biological and chemical warfare. As a result, they learned a bizarre Iraqi weak point. Through their strict religion, the Iraqi people believed that if they weren't physically whole, they would never be permitted into Allah's paradise. Smiling, the cynical instructor finished, "That means that if you have to kill any one of them, take a finger or ear first!" He laughed, but laughed alone.

At last, Wednesday, January 15th, the date set for the deadline, arrived. It was late into the evening and, no different from any other Americans, the boys monitored the news. There was no television available.The radio reports left more to the imagination. One expert after the other offered their theories and predictions on the crisis in the Gulf. Sitting in a tight circle, The Dream Team caught up on recent events.

The Soviets were pursuing new diplomatic avenues for peace. Hearing this, Pat blurted, "No shit! That's only because the Iraqis are using all Soviet weaponry and, for once, the whole world will see that it ain't worth shit!" Everyone laughed but Pat. He was serious. The reporter continued that in an historic vote, Congress gave Bush the authority to wage war in the Gulf. The Commander-in-Chief had the green light. Saddam reiterated that his country was ready to fight to keep conquered Kuwait. Then, he attacked Mother Nature. The madman opened up a pipeline and flooded the Gulf with crude oil. After a long night, the 12th hour finally struck. The White House announced that Bush was ready to make the tough decisions. They said nothing further. No shots were fired. The anticipation of war remained, and the boys felt anything but relief. Nobody knew why, but it looked like Washington was biding their time. Exhausted from the wait-ing and worrying, the boys turned in for the night.

January 16th also passed without the inevitable occurring. The entire world sat on the edge of their seats, waiting. The Dream Team had already fallen off those seats and were anxious to get the ball rolling. The general consensus was that the anticipation of a fight was always worse than the fight itself, no matter what scale it was fought on.

On the frosty morning of January 17th, the boys found themselves stuffed into an unusually small auditorium. The instructor, a monotone, anal-retentive type, rambled on about Saddam's various land mines. The dictator had planted countless mines and the instructor quipped, "Just stay out of his gardens, people, or you'll be coming home in body bags!" The dark humor wasn't appreciated, though everyone could understand its meaning. It was crystal clear. The instructor was one soldier who would be spending an entire career talking theories, but never testing them out. Though the class was incredibly important, the boys found it difficult to stay focused. Between thinking about a wild weekend coming up and wondering when the fighting would actually break out, everyone's mind wandered.

Returning home to 1262, everyone stripped out of their layers of thick clothing and got comfortable. Into the early evening, they listened to the increasingly tense news reports and talked about the days ahead. After a late dinner, the reporter's excited voice attracted the boys to Pat's bunk like flies. Glued to the tiny transistor, the invisible man's nervous voice reported history in the making. It had started. The war had finally started. The shield was replaced by a storm — a storm that raged out of control.

While Hussein threatened America with the mother of all battles, President George Bush drew a line in the sand. That line was wrapped around Iraq and used to choke the life out of thousands. Faking out his enemy with a false amphibious assault, through Task Force Normandy, Bush finally pulled the trigger. Eight Apache Gunships, flying in the dark cover of a moonless sky, were dispatched to destroy two Iraqi radar sites, blinding them with hellfire missiles. Stealth Bombers were sent to jam radar defenses, severing enemy communications, while the USS *Wisconsin* fired its lethal cruise missiles at political and military targets in Baghdad.

From one of the many aircraft carriers stationed in the Gulf, 17 fighter jets were catapulted into the desert sky, helping to launch the heavy air campaign. Flying these first sorties, the pilots bombed strategic targets in Iraq. Along with the rest of the world, the boys held their breath and waited for the pilots' safe return to their floating air base. If he were in the cockpits with them, Steve couldn't have felt any closer to the men. That was the glory of being in the Army. It was one big team working toward accomplishing the same goal. That goal was to completely destroy the other team.

As each jet landed safely, the boys screamed with joy. Steve's body tingled with pride and the realization of his future. In between the emotional reports of another safe landing, he also felt fear. Looking in his friends' faces, he knew he wasn't alone. Everyone was acting elated at the successfully fierce air strike, but beneath, each man was trying to accept his own fate. As the last jet taxied down the air craft carrier, The Dream Team celebrated with hugs and high fives. It was an overwhelming experience, but once finished, they quietly returned to their own bunks.

The following day, the restless crew lay in the snowdrifts of the firing ranges. Qualifying with rifles and machine guns was never so painfully difficult. Before this, it was never so important.

The squad leaders filed into an abandoned Quonset hut. Their instructor was waiting. The man was a Vietnam Vet. His impeccable uniform displayed his combat infantry badge, along with his jump wings. His shiny, black forehead revealed the lines of some hard experiences. He smiled sincerely, then went straight to work. The class, though well informed, ended with a bang.

Finishing his lecture on the M203 grenade launcher — the weapon carried by all sergeants — a strange question was asked. It echoed from the back of the hut. "Sarge, in the Nam, did you ever take a gook out with the launcher?"

The older man placed the weapon on the table, jumped up and took a seat alongside it. He replied, "Son, I did engage the enemy with the weapon, but the son of a bitch never exploded." The silence droned on. Everyone waited for him to elaborate. In a serious tone, he added, "However, the grenade knocked the man to the ground, allowing me enough time to engage him with my M16-A1 rifle."

The entire class laughed. The instructor never cracked a grin. He continued, "People, war is a horrible experience. Men sometimes see and do things that just don't sit right. My only advice is that you cover your asses and take care of your brothers out there. If you see someone sitting alone or just not acting normal, talk to them, bring them back to reality. Believe me, it's not so hard to slip away." Standing erect, he placed his starched hat onto his shaven head. Without another word, he marched out into the cold.

Everyone sat dumbfounded. The man had scared the shit out of them. But it was no ghost story. He was speaking from experience. Steve stood up to leave when he caught his old friend out of the corner of his eye. It was Ryan White, sitting alone. His head was down. The instructor's words had struck like a bolt of lightning. Steve understood. Ryan had been different ever since they arrived at Fort Devens. He was unusually quiet. He stayed out of trouble and wasn't cracking jokes. Something was horribly wrong. Steve approached. "Hey, Ryan, did you get the feeling that he was talking about you?"

For the first time in two weeks, Ryan smiled. For the next three hours, the two friends talked. At the end, Steve understood. Ryan was grieving the loss of his new wife as if she had died. His love ran deep. If Steve could relate to anything, it was that. He hoped that his friend would break out of it soon.

The first weekend pass brought wives, girlfriends or both to the frozen tundra. The boys were released to the end of their brief sobriety and some marathon intercourse sessions. Steve and Monica camped out at a local motel. She tried to conceal her fears of losing the house, but it was no use. He knew her too well. They talked about it, but things were changing. He didn't care so much about the burdens of an unaffordable mortgage anymore. Instead, he worried about her physical pain, the future of his friends and the fact that precious time was being wasted worrying about a pile of shingles. Priorities were changing. Other things were more important.

Monday arrived, Monica returned to her life and Steve settled into his new routine. Each weekday started with a hearty breakfast, then training, a huge lunch, more training, an even bigger supper, the nightly de-briefing, then lights out. By the end of the second week, Steve had watched his friends grow larger and heavier right before his eyes. Looking into the mirror, he noticed that his own baby face had swelled with a second chin. None of them were overly concerned with weight control. It was no less than gluttony. It was all you could eat at the chow hall and the boys did just that. Laughing over their increasing sizes, he kidded Pat, "It has to be that dessert carousel. It's almost hypnotizing!"

Pat snorted, "That reminds me, I've only indulged in two puddings this evening. If you will excuse me, please!"

Steve sat back and looked around. It was astounding. Everyone was fat. He turned to Ryan. "This extra weight isn't gonna help in that hot desert."

Steve and Chuck's room was eventually dubbed the Amnesty Room. It was where all complaints, concerns, problems and fears were discussed and handled. They felt it was most important to be there for their squads, so they set up a relaxed atmosphere. They installed a television, and provided coffee. Many hours were spent talking there. Nobody went to Tony, and though he seemed content with the peace and quiet, Steve was sure he was burning inside.

The third week brought some desperately needed field training. Desert camouflaged Humvees were issued, three to a squad. The motor pool boasted about the bulky vehicles having wide wheelbases, making them all-terrain. Allegedly, they could go anywhere without getting stuck or tipping over. The platoon practiced on convoy escorts, ambushes and rear-area security missions. Toward mid-week, Steve turned on the television and stood in shock. Photos of three American pilots kept flashing on the screen. The Iraqis had shot them down and each was badly beaten. Obviously held against their will, one of the men recited a fabricated plea to his country. He claimed, "America's actions are killing innocent women and children." Steve thought he was going to be sick. Filled with rage, he realized that after the third time he saw the same footage, the U.S. government was using the tragedy to their advantage. The propaganda was intended to fire the country up. It was working quite well. Though he understood the game, he remained outraged and wanted the taste of blood.

Playing Rat Patrol in the winter wonderland made for a fun week, and the boys started to remember the old days. Nicknames were given to the vehicles, as well as each soldier in the platoon. Steve's call sign became Swamp Yankee, after his grandfather, while his vehicle was affectionately named Bug Light. Everyone followed, and chose whatever names suited them.

At the end of the week, fantastic news came from the White family. During the extremely short honeymoon of Mr. and Mrs. Ryan White, the troops hit the beach and a baby was conceived. Beaming with pride, Ryan broke the news to the team. He was instantly proclaimed Papa White and the boys understood the silent message. Ryan was to be looked after; his unborn child, adopted as a sign of hope. The baby was another reason for a safe and speedy homecoming. Ryan's attitude changed. With the miraculous news, he was born again. Steve secretly shared his joy.

As usual, the weekend was spent at restaurants and hotels, but the time was drawing near. There were so many telltale signs. For Steve, the clincher was when Senator Ted Kennedy showed up.

Drifting in from a snowstorm that refused to quit, Senator Kennedy was followed by his entourage, several yes-men and a slew of news media. Shaking off the snow, the silver-haired legislator set up for his audience — the news cameras. Planting a smile on his enormous red face, old Ted approached Keith Robles and extended his hand. Keith offered his own and was immediately blinded by the lights of the rolling cameras. Kennedy started with words that were obviously practiced. He assured Keith that while America's youth faced another war, he would take care of the families back home. The words sounded sincere, but as the man spoke to Keith, he never once looked at him. Ted Kennedy just smiled into the cameras and recited his speech. Steve stood amazed. His speech was anti-war in the

Gulf. To the joy of the media, Kennedy received a frigid welcome. Each pair of young eyes met him coldly.

The media ate it up. Jumping from soldier to soldier, interviews were taken right in the presence of the honorable Senator. Reaching Doug Donnelly, a television reporter asked, "What if the Senator is right? What if this war proves tragic for you and your friends?"

Without hesitation, Doug proudly answered, "We'll drive off that bridge when we get to it!" Everybody stood frozen in place. Even time stood still. Doug hit a nerve, referring to Kennedy's accident of years ago when his car drove off a bridge, killing his girlfriend and leaving him unscathed. Kennedy left the scene and was never charged with the crime. The scandal rocked Massachusetts for some time.

The piercing words revealed everyone's true feelings and the old politician had heard enough. As his face turned a brighter shade of red, he stormed out of the bay.

First Sergeant Avery attempted to salvage a little respect for Kennedy and ordered a formation outside. The boys took their places. In a furious voice, Avery yelled, "Present Arms." Each man saluted Kennedy, as he and his puppies walked past. Steve watched him closely, realizing that Senator Ted Kennedy never had a chance. Any peace-loving person would have been done before they ever got started. Mentally, the boys couldn't live in two worlds at one time. Their mind-set had changed. They were being removed from peace and thrown into war. It was too bad, but 30 angry young men stood shoulder to shoulder in the frozen afternoon. They were prepared to fight, not listen to the eloquent, but empty words of a white dove.

The snow crunched under the weight of the car's tires and before long, Senator Kennedy was a safe distance from The Dream Team. Steve stood, remembering the same man's voice from early childhood, probably since the days of potty-training. It was the most inspirational quote he ever heard.

It was an old 45 record that Nancy Manchester played on Saturday mornings while housecleaning, a song about the '60s and the assassinations of that generation's greatest men. At the end, Ted Kennedy was recorded offering the eulogy at his brother Bobby's funeral. Remembering the heart-felt words, Steve got goose bumps.

In the Kennedy's strong Bostonian accent, Ted stated, "Like it or not, we live in times of danger and uncertainty. That is the way he lived. That is what he leaves us. My brother need not be idolized or enlarged in death more than what he was in life. Be remembered simply as a good and decent man, who saw wrong and tried to right it, saw suffering and tried to heal it . . . saw war and tried to stop it. Those of us who loved him and take him to his rest today, pray that what he was to us, what he wished for others, will someday come to pass for all the world."

Ted's quivering voice, betraying the tremendous grief he felt, finished by quoting his late brother. "Some men see things as they are and say why. I dream things that never were and say why not."

They were words to live by and, though Steve never idolized any man, Robert Kennedy was considered the greatest American in his book. They were the words of an idealist, though, and not a realist. It was over two decades later and America was returning to war. History spoke for itself. Men didn't want peace. They hungered for war. Peace-loving men, such as John and Robert Kennedy, were murdered in cold blood.

First Sergeant Avery called for another formation. He looked unusually distressed. Steve could sense it. It was show time. Avery announced, "Okay people, the fat lady has started singing!"

"I know it's short notice," Avery continued, "but call your people and tell them to get up here. We ship out at 1200 hours tomorrow, Westover Air Force Base. The rest of the day is yours. Have fun, but please be careful. Dismissed!"

Nobody moved. Then, it sunk in. There was a race to the pay phones. Within the hour, everyone was contacted. Steve hung up the receiver, leaving Monica a wreck. Billy would be driving her up.

The second, and last, barracks party was even more successful than the day they arrived. The Amnesty Room was converted into a coatroom, while the bunk beds in the open bay were placed flush against the walls, turning the sleeping quarters into a huge dance hall. Billy and Monica arrived shortly after the keg of beer. The boys quenched their thirst for one last night of raising hell. Everyone knew it was the last taste of beer for one year, so the cold brew poured freely.

Hours flew by like minutes, and Tony made the dreaded announcement. "People, you have 15 minutes to say your goodbyes, then I want all civilians out and all members of the First Platoon in bed. We have a big day ahead of us tomorrow!"

Billy wrapped his strong arms around Steve. They said goodbye. With the numbing help of Mr. Jack Daniels, it was easier than they expected. Steve kissed his brother's cheek and assisted him out the door. Billy looked a little pasty. Steve wasn't sure if it was because he was so upset, or needed to puke his guts up. Billy stumbled toward the nearest snow bank and gave him his answer.

Turning around, Steve saw Monica standing alone. He held her close and together, they watched as the open bay turned into an ocean of tears. He whispered, "I love you Monica and, I promise, I'll come home!"

She broke eye contact and her body violently shook. She cried hard. With a hand on each side of her soft face, Steve positioned her head so that they were staring into each other's eyes again. His words repeated the promise, but it was his eyes that told her the words were true. Somehow, he knew. Her body went limp and she melted into his arms. She believed her husband, and kissed him for his tender reassurance. Gently pushing him away, she ran out the door. For one precious moment, she looked over her shoulder and yelled, "Go to work Sergeant Manchester, but remember, I'll be waiting!"

Standing in the doorway, he watched as the dark night slowly swallowed her up. She was gone and, in the giant room filled with people, he felt alone.

Drunk and overwhelmed with emotion, he retired to the Amnesty Room. Collapsing onto his bed, he started to worry about who would be driving the car home. Billy was hammered. Monica was a bundle of nerves. He also wondered if things would be the same when he returned, or if there would even be a return. As a hundred questions flooded his anxious mind, the room spun several times and stopped. Thanks to the excessive drinking, he passed out, joining the rest of his drunken friends.

The morning formation looked no different from any other day, but the differences were undeniably immense. Steve watched as his friends shuffled their feet. This time, it wasn't only to retain body heat. Everyone was nervous. Off to one side, the same buses that had transported the company to Fort Devens were patiently idling. There was a nice prayer held by the Chaplain, then Captain Wall ordered First Platoon to file onto their bus.

Steve couldn't believe it. For a split-second, his legs refused to budge. He was frozen and, while gasping for the breath he had lost, he remembered the marathon runner who inspired him years ago. He told his paralyzed legs to move. They did, but it certainly wasn't a voluntary action. He looked back to see if anyone had noticed. Nobody had. It didn't matter. It was enough to shake his confidence and fill his tired mind with doubts he didn't need. It scared the life out of him. Walking past Kline, Medeiros and a handful of others who would be left behind, he felt like he was taking the final stroll. He forged on, knowing that if he could convince his heart to do something, then his body would follow.

Like everything else that happens in the military, the bus ride dragged on. The convoy coasted into Westover Air Force Base way behind schedule.

As the platoon passed time with light-hearted conversation, an Air Force lieutenant boarded and lit up the interior with her smile. She was beautiful. The only thing missing was the halo. The Air Force was so different from the Army. They actually treated their people like people. Then again, their only warriors were the pilots. The remainder of the force was support personnel. Compared to what they were used to, The Dream Team was about to be treated like royalty.

A formation was held, the equipment unloaded and the boys were led into a pair of handball courts. The lieutenant joked, "Sorry about the accommodations people, but this is where you'll be sleeping. With the war running full-steam, the inn is booked up." The courts echoed with laughter. She really wasn't that funny, but all the boys were in love with her.

Steve awoke without ever realizing he had slept. Raising his heavy head, he looked up at Tony and said, "I hardly slept last night. I kept having nightmares of a small blue ball flying past my head."

Tony held his side, laughing. "You're too much, Stevie-boy. And, you look like shit!"

First Platoon was transported to a desolate hangar located off of the main flight line. Scheduled to fly out in three hours, the boys stacked their weapons and piled their duffel bags on the enormous floor. While some decided to catch up on the sleep they had lost, Steve and the boys played video games and frisbee. Remembering his summers at the beach, Steve skipped the frisbee off the slick floor and played hard.

The metallic bang of an M-60 machine gun breach caught everyone's attention. It was a reality check given by Tony Rosini. Waving the lethal weapon in the air, he rounded up his Indians. It was time to go.

Steve picked up his gear and led Second Squad out onto the flight line. He was happy that his legs were moving without being coaxed. Approaching First Platoon's assigned aircraft, he looked up in awe. It looked like a building with wings. It was huge and, amazingly, the obese bird could fly. The boys climbed the wrought-iron staircase and ascended within the belly of the beast. It reminded Steve of the ancient soldiers who concealed themselves within the Trojan Horse. He took a seat in the rear, and then took a deep breath. There was no turning back now. Fear filled the cabin, but there was also a sense of adventure. Prepared or not, Sergeant Steve Manchester and his friends of many years were embarking on the adventure of a lifetime.

Chapter 6

Into the Eye of
the Storm

To the faint hum of the giant C-5A Galaxy's engines, Steve opened his eyes. He realized he had been daydreaming for hours. Shaking the cobwebs from his head, he sat up and lit a cigarette. Goose bumps covered his body. In order to remember the path that led to his predicament, his mind rewound the last ten years of his life. The haunting memories shook him inside. Taking a long drag on the smoke, he scanned the cabin. Besides Chuck Emond, he was the only man awake. Chuck offered an exhausted smile and threw a thumbs-up. The gesture brought Steve's thoughts back to his long lost friend, Wil Souza. Poking out the butt, he raised his eyes upward and whispered, "If I ever needed help, brother, it's gotta be now!"

Six cigarettes later, the crew chief popped his head into the cabin. "Rise and shine people. We're making our final descent into Torrejon, Spain."

They waited to hear the standard: Please extinguish all smoking materials and bring your seats to their upright positions, but it was a military flight. All seats were bolted into one position — uncomfortable. The stewardess sported a five o'clock shadow.

Steve lit another cigarette and prepared to venture into Europe for the first time.

On cue, the boys stood, stretched out and sluggishly filed out of the cabin. Carrying their weapons, all other equipment remained on board. The lay-over was only intended for re-fueling. In less than two hours, they'd be right back in the air. The war was patiently waiting.

Steve jumped off the last three steps into a world filled with unfamiliar lights and noises. It was night time on some flight line in Spain. It didn't matter. The Army was in control now. There were no windows on the giant green bird, so it felt like walking out of a time capsule. Completely disoriented, the blind sheep were led into an enormous hangar. After insuring that all his people had found their way off the plane, he walked in behind the group. One step in and he was ready to re-board.

The hangar was bigger than anything he had ever seen. From one end to the other, old army cots were lined in tightly spaced rows. Thousands of men could have layed shoulder to shoulder, and it still would have looked empty. It was nothing more than a large holdover for troops deployed into the Gulf, but there was an air of despair about it. Of all times to feel cheated, Steve considered never visiting Spain again and became strangely disappointed. There would be no bull fights, no beautiful senoritas and no tour whatsoever. There was just enough time for a quick siesta in the biggest homeless shelter in the world. Grabbing an empty cot in the sea of green, he kicked up his feet and practiced what the U.S. Army had taught him best — he waited.

Nearly two hours passed and everyone was still lying around waiting. Tony made his way down the long center aisle. His face showed signs of either good news or something deranged which he thought to be funny. Approaching his platoon, he said, "Boys, it must be your lucky night, or morning ... whatever." Shaking off the confusion, he continued. "That old beast we just flew here in, well, the oil pressure is down in one of her engines. The pilot says it'll be at least two hours before we're under way ...."

Interrupting, the C-5A's pilot entered the hangar and announced, "Looks like the damage can't be repaired for another week."

The expression on each young face surprised the man. The anticipation of war was brutally draining. They waited long enough.

The confused pilot went on, "Not to worry though, there are two alternate aircraft available to complete the trip. All vehicles and equipment will be transferred within the hour. This company will be split into two groups." He scanned the changing expressions. "Sorry about that folks," he finished and returned to the black night.

The last comment made the boys cringe. Everyone wanted to start this horror story on the same page. When the final tally was made, besides Steve and a handful of others, the 661st was taking the first aircraft.

Concealing his own worry, Steve called his small group. Trying to convey a careless demeanor, he informed them, "Okay, guys, it looks like we'll be flying in one hour after the majority of the company. It should be no big deal."

The worried expressions of the orphaned soldiers begged for more information.

He shrugged. "Yeah, so we'll be an hour behind everybody else. If worst comes to worst, we'll kill twice as many Iraqis when we get there!"

The humor lit up every solemn face. It wasn't the answer they were looking for, but it was timed perfectly. Returning to his cot, he sighed, "What a perfect way to start a war!"

Two hours later, the first aircraft took to the friendly skies over Europe and with it, almost the entire 661st M.P. Company. Steve sat on his cot, impatiently watching as one hour turned into three.

The first and only announcement was called to board the second aircraft. The crew chief jumped clear of the stampede. A small herd jogged past him and quickly disappeared into the plane. The delayed group was actually in a hurry to be dropped into a combat zone. Scratching his head in confusion, the older man followed the boys in. Within minutes, they were airborne.

Steve took his usual place in the rear, and opened a fresh pack of smokes. After inhaling two, he dozed off and didn't wake until reaching the dangerous southwest Asian skies. Wiping the sleep from his eyes, he realized that his final hour of peace had been appropriately spent in blissful slumber. At last, the moment of truth was at hand. Checking his weapon, he muttered a silent prayer. He pleaded, "Father, please bless my comrades and I with good health, both of mind and body. I ask that the fighting be swift. I pray for strength, that I may not cower, but lead with honor and dignity. I also pray forgiveness for anything I might be forced to do." Imagining the horrible scenarios, he felt unsure whether his prayer would be heard. It was then he remembered his mom's advice: "Keep the faith!" He smiled.

After unlatching the floor straps from his Humvee, Bug Light, Steve and his two-man crew locked and loaded their weapons. There was a comforting closeness felt by all. Each knew that, if necessary, one life would be forfeited for the next. The person, the situation, didn't matter. He acknowledged the bond and accepted it as a blessing. Whatever happened to one of them, would probably happen to them all. A large amount of body bags had been loaded onto the same aircraft, a visual reminder that death was a genuine possibility.

Breaking his morbid train of thought, the crew chief entered the bottom deck and warned, "Once the nose opens, you people have no more than five minutes to get these vehicles out onto the sand. This monster has to get back into the air A.S.A.P. Hussein's Air Force has been all but wiped out, but this son of a bitch makes for a pretty big target. Nobody knows if any of his defectors will fly back over the Iranian border to play. Personally, I don't want to find out!" Snapping a crisp salute, he finished, "Make us proud people and ... God Speed!"

The aircraft's hydraulic nose showed a hint of desert sunlight. It dropped open and the boys were moving. Yards away from the bird, Steve discovered a world unknown to most.

Though initially unaware of their location, he was informed, via radio, that they had landed at King Khalid Military City, or K.K.M.C. It was nicknamed Tent City, and that's all that could be seen to the south, east and west. There was row after row of drab green army tents. Bringing the Humvee to a complete stop, he quickly realized that the thousands of friendly forces were just camping. Each unit waited to be deployed elsewhere. Unlike their expectations, there was no immediate threat of danger.

Though anti-climatic, it was a fantastic start. He ordered, "Okay, guys, let's clear the weapons." Jumping out, he turned to the north, toward Iraq. While his pulse crept back to normal, all of his senses became peaked. He was ignorant to the fact, but his body was immediately overcome by a heightened awareness. As the hours of fearful anticipation drained out of him, those feelings were replaced by a curious excitement. Through the exploring eyes of a child, he observed a place unlike anything he had ever seen before.

The picture took his breath away. It was a world so different from his own that, for the briefest moment, he sensed he was dreaming. Standing in the midst of a barren wasteland, his speeding mind recorded every detail of the new environment. It was not what he had pictured in his mind's eye, a world of majesty and intrigue. Nor was it the living hell, as described by the military. It was a land long forgotten by mankind.

It was daybreak, and already 80 degrees. Walking away from Bug Light, he inhaled a warm breeze that carried the nauseating odor of diesel fuel. His lily-white skin tingled from a combination of adrenaline and that soothing breeze. Just yards ahead, a small herd of grazing camels caught his attention. Their front legs were tied together by short pieces of rope, insuring they could only travel a short distance before being retrieved by their owner. The rough terrain was sparsely vegetated, with nothing but sand in all directions. Reflecting on summers past, he thought it was like an endless beach without the relief of the cool ocean. Bending down, he scooped up a handful of sand and let it sift slowly through his fingers. The sand was as fine as powdered sugar, or worse, dust.

Gazing up, he stared into the most beautiful sky on earth. It was an enormous canvas where the artist had painted the bluest of blues, mixing in brighter colors toward the east. Turning his head in that direction, he watched as the relentless sun cleared Tent City. The colors, cast by the sun, turned from orange and red to an unbearable white. He quickly looked away and put on his sunglasses.

To his surprise, it was quiet. There was a solitude that embraced his entire being. It felt tranquil, but he knew it wasn't the time or place to become relaxed. Looking closer, the surroundings verified his instincts to be true.

On the horizon, a caravan of tanks and mechanized vehicles stretched out as far as the eye could see. They headed directly into harm's way. Though Steve had never witnessed such things, the line of lethal vehicles fit into the picture. He tried to estimate the distance between he and the convoy, when a pair of A-10 Warthogs, or tank killers, buzzed over. The fighting vultures instantly destroyed the simple beauty of the sky. They were also heading north, toward some strategic target. Opening the door to the vehicle, he took one more look out onto his new world and told Private Tripp, "It seems peaceful enough, and it sure is quiet. I hate first impressions!" Firing up Bug Light, he flicked his cigarette into the air. The Arabian Desert was now his personal ashtray. It was time to locate the 661st. In miles and miles of identical tents, it wasn't going to be easy.

It didn't take more than 15 minutes for them to spot The Dream Team parked outside the perimeter of Tent City. After an exchange of hugs, Tony welcomed his lost sheep with their marching orders, "As you can see, we won't be setting up camp here. We've been ordered north to Log Base Charlie. If we make good time, we can be there by sunset."

Steve glanced over at Chuck's sour face and whispered, "North? Any idea how far Log Base Charlie is to Iraq?"

Chuck shrugged and returned the whisper. "Nope. But at least there'll be no more guessing."

"So much for being stationed in the rear." Steve snickered.

When the small briefing came to a close, Tony informed Captain Wall, "We'll be ready in five, Ma'am."

Awaiting the order to move, Steve threw his heavy, protective flak vest onto the passenger's seat of Bug Light. Its only useful purpose was a cushion. There was no way the temperature would ever permit him to wear it. Private Tripp, the ingenious recruit, wired a Pioneer stereo directly to the battery. Throwing in a cassette, the music pulsated throughout the Humvee. Steve smiled. With a pair of fuzzy dice hanging from the windshield wiper knob, he tried to recreate the feeling of The Old Special. As the convoy started to roll out onto the road, it was clear that the attempt was futile. Bug Light felt like anything but the Special. He just hoped it handled better in the sand.

As the 661st drove up the eastern border of Saudi Arabia, reality set in deeper with each mile passed. Located in the middle of the pack, Steve monitored the army radio and absorbed everything with his eyes. It wasn't easy. The vehicle in front was kicking up a hurricane of sand. Visibility was terribly limited. Keeping their course on Main Supply Route, or M.S.R. Black, The Dream Team closed the gap between themselves and the enemy — a million-man army. Danger lurked up ahead, and the entire platoon sensed it. It was evident through the nervous and unnecessary chatter on the radio. Fed up with the bantering, Tony roared, "Okay, First, unless you're taking fire, I don't want to hear one more of your whining voices again!"

As practiced during training, each vehicle switched to an alternate frequency. This way, they could speak freely without being monitored. The silly game didn't last long, though. Everyone quickly simmered down to do some sightseeing.

Steve gawked out the passenger's side window. It was a desolate land with nothing to see but sand, rocks, an occasional palm tree and more sand. But it was peaceful. The only person shooting was Keith Robles, and he couldn't keep enough film in his camera. Every several miles, they passed a convoy of coalition forces. Whether American, British, French or Egyptian, the numbers of troops were a relief to see. Steve felt a fierce pride, however, as they exchanged waves or friendly smiles with other American soldiers. From the open turrets of tanks to the back of transporting trucks, each young face displayed the same look. There was determination peering from behind the goggles and bandannas that protected their faces from the blowing sand. Every American convoy flew the flag of freedom. These American flags were a chauvinistic display of strength, and Steve felt more reassured with each passing flag.

The troops' attitudes were typical of most Americans, only they were better prepared to defend their beliefs. It was obvious. America had arrived to defend Saudi Arabia, liberate Kuwait and embarrass the biggest bully of the post-Cold War era. This confidence, just shy of blatant arrogance, emanated from every single unit.

America's sons and daughters had come to exact justice. Their responsibilities were immense. There was so much at stake. Politically, there was America's leadership of the free world. Economically, there was one tenth of the world's oil resources. Morally, there was protection of human life. But silently, there was the rebirth of America's spirit. They came to heal the nation from a ghost that had haunted them for two decades — the poltergeist of Vietnam.

Hours passed and Steve didn't see one royal palace. There were no magic carpets and nobody was granted three wishes from a mythical genie. Instead, he observed a culture suffering from oppressive poverty. He witnessed the poorest of peasants living in a nation that had amassed great wealth. The run-down shanty towns, consisted of shacks and tents, barely suitable for protection against the harsh winds of the open desert. The people were thin and clothed in rags. Steve returned the waves. Most stood barefooted to greet their defenders. It was unbelievable. They possessed very little, but what they did have, they didn't want to lose to Iraq. To Steve's wonder, they looked happy, very happy.

From time to time, the convoy also passed tribes of Bedouin Indians. These natives lived as shepherds, tending to their flocks of sheep and goats. Like gypsies, they roamed the vast desert, setting up camp only when there was enough vegetation for grazing. Some stared with curiosity at the passing strangers, while others couldn't be bothered. These simple people were oblivious to what was about to transpire. Steve envied them.

It was sunset when the 661st got their first glimpse of urban life in Saudi Arabia. Traveling the outskirts, the lights of Hafar al Batin, a city less than 200 miles south of Iraq, glowed with mystery and intrigue. The unusual skyline was filled with dark rooftops that looked like upside-down ice cream cones. They were round at the bottom, forming pointed tips at the top. Some even had a twist to them. Straining his eyes, Steve watched as the city swiftly faded into the distance.

Turning to his left, his attention was diverted by a photographer's dream. The scene was absolutely hypnotizing. The sun was diving underground, creating the most perfect setting on the planet. With its southern hemisphere already sleeping for the night, the other half shimmered on the flat horizon. Its intense heat caused ripples in the royal blue sky. Throwing off waves of red and orange, the surrounding atmosphere turned to shades of purple, green and pink. Steve stared hard and watched the orange ball drop inch by inch, until it completely disappeared. Turning on the heater in Bug Light, he learned that the desert retained only a fraction of the day's searing heat. Within minutes, the temperature dropped 30 degrees. He thought about Monica. The setting of the sun was so beautiful, it was a shame that he couldn't share it with her. The chill of the night air caused him to desire the warmth of her body. He turned the heater up a notch and smiled. It was better for Monica to be where she was, no matter how many beautiful or cold nights separated them.

The head of the convoy finally turned left into the mouth of a walled perimeter. The perimeter was square, with embankments of sand piled 15 feet off the desert floor. Coming to a halt, First Sergeant Avery announced, via radio, "Welcome to Camp Lois, people!" Their little piece of the chapped desert was named after their fearless leader, the illustrious Captain Wall.

With a grin, Steve asked his team, "I wonder who suggested the name?"

No one answered.

Each platoon was assigned their own corner, and the entire company went to work. It was time to set up shop.

The Dream Team unloaded their vehicles and trailers under the faint light of a crescent moon. Starting with the first tent, a General Purpose Medium, the boys fumbled in the darkness. While holding up his end, Pat screamed, "This fuckin' sucks!"

Equally irritated, Chuck snapped, "Quit your crying!"

It was downhill from there. The tension was high, tempers were flaring and the platoon's two tough guys prepared to exchange blows.

"Knock it off, you two," Steve barked, "We're in this together. Everybody's aggravated, but let's save the fighting for the Iraqis."

The rest of the small camp was erected in silence. Three tents were put up, the chemical detectors were placed out on the perimeter and the generator was started. It powered up all communications and one bare light bulb per canvas shelter.

It took nearly two hours before the boys called it quits. The tents needed tightening and hundreds of improvements needed to be made, but for the first night, it was good enough. With a bite in the air, Steve threw on his cold weather parka. He made his final round of the armed guards posted out on the perimeter. All was well. Walking back toward the temporary camp, he looked up for a second and stopped dead in his tracks.

The black sky glistened with stars. There were more stars than he had ever seen. It was as if the heavens had opened. He felt that such raw beauty was wasted on anyone but lovers. Reaching into his pocket, he retrieved a harmonica. It had been a gift from his late grandfather. Though he couldn't play it, the instrument was a reminder of better days. Wiping off the mouthpiece, he fumbled through a broken tune. While mysterious silhouettes danced in the dim light of the tents, the hum of the generator played backup. He heard the muffled laughter of his friends. His mission was accomplished. It was time to go to bed.

Insuring his sleeping bag was free of snakes, scorpions, and any other critters in search of heat, he finally layed down. Closing his eyes, his thoughts drifted toward home. He closed them tighter and tried thinking of other things. It wasn't so difficult.

There was a rumble that shook the earth that first night. It was the continual flow of tanks speeding toward the front, toward the breach with Iraq. He felt the ground shake outside, but inside his sleeping bag, there was also a slight tremble. It was fear — fear of the unknown. Looking down the row of cots, he knew he wasn't alone.

The morning brought another miraculous sunrise, along with warmth. Finishing the day's first cigarette, Steve strolled with Chuck to the Operations Tent. The morning briefing was consumed by gossip. It was evident that there was no clear mission for the unit. Like magicians, he and Chuck disappeared out the back, while the upper echelon continued to talk in circles. Reporting to the mess tent, the two joined their squads for a nutritious breakfast. Two cups of coffee later, they went to work.

The first day was full of teamwork. The Dream Team rolled up their sleeves and turned their tiny corner of the world into home. The tents were fastened into place. Hundreds of sandbags were filled, while the remaining hole was converted into an air raid or fallout shelter. Before lunch, First Platoon's home base resembled the setting of *M.A.S.H.* There was a clothesline set up, along with a humorous road sign, indicating the amount of miles from Saudi Arabia to different towns in Massachusetts. The horseshoe and volleyball pits were easy to create, and the latrine was made of three, 55-gallon steel drums, which had been cut in half. A knotty pine plank was placed across the top for everyone's comfort. Steve marveled at the finishing touch — it was a flag to mark their territory.

Dennis, the platoon's artist, had drawn a shield. In the center, there was a gray cloud spitting a bolt of lightning. Behind the shield stood a horned demon. The monster's head and legs stuck out at the top and bottom, while its wretched fingers held the shield for protection. Above the picture, the words DREAM TEAM were written in red ink. A pitchfork divided the two words. Beneath, the platoon's motto read: EVERY ENEMY'S WORSE NIGHTMARE.

Before they knew it, the first full day was behind them, though most wondered how many more there would be before it was over. Steve finished the day's last cigarette, blew into the harmonica until he heard laughter and turned in. The screeching lullaby was now a nightly ritual.

The following morning, the majority of the company was rushed to a makeshift hospital. A handful of M.P.s were left behind to provide security for Camp Lois. They were considered some of the most fortunate soldiers.

The 911th EVAC hospital consisted of two small tents, an ambulance and five medical personnel. It was a traveling operation, for sure. Steve rallied his squad. Like sheep led to the slaughter, they filed into the first tent. With very little explanation and absolutely no paperwork involved, the boys were innoculated with America's solution to Iraq's nuclear, biological and chemical threats. The shots were labeled preventive medicines. From Botulism toxin and Anthrax to various chemical agents, each arm was tainted with a small dose of the viruses.

As they filed out, one of the nurses commented, "These should build your immune systems against anything Hussein might throw your way. Good Luck!" Handing out packages of tiny green pills, she added, "Take one every three hours, unless your body reacts abnormally, then cut down the dosage."

Chuck voiced his concerns. "And what are these for?"

Nonchalantly, she replied, "They're to build up your tolerance against an attack by nerve agent gas." With that said, the boys were released into the blinding sun.

Steve grabbed Chuck. "Ever feel like a guinea pig set loose after a demented experiment?"

Chuck shook his head and threw his share of pills into the wind. Furiously, he replied, "Let's get away from this damn laboratory and warn the platoon!"

Once they hit the road, Chuck pulled over and instructed everybody to get out. Formed in a horseshoe around his vehicle, the Overlord started, "Take those green pills and deep six'em. We all know that if we get hit by a chemical agent attack, the most we can hope for is that the missile carrying it lands right in our lap. Either way, we're dead, so get rid of that shit!"

A large pile of the green devils hit the sand. A few of the overzealous guys, however, had already popped one. As Steve kicked sand over the rising green mound, he found humor in their pale faces. Chuck had scared them to death.

Several hours passed before each soldier experienced unusually swollen and sore limbs. Steve's arms inflated like helium balloons. The tents were quickly over-run by flu-like symptoms. The Dream Team suffered from head and body aches, nausea, vomiting, diarrhea and the weakness that accompanies dehydration. Their bodies were attempting to combat the alien viruses, and it came as no surprise to Steve. Somehow he sensed that the odd doctor's visit would result in punishment. First Platoon rested and waited for their orders.

Steve fell asleep to the rhythm of his snoring friends, but soon awoke in sheer terror. For the first few seconds, he remained lying on his stomach. The intensity grew and he sprang to his feet. Grabbing at his chest, he struggled for air. It felt like someone was standing on him, and he couldn't take in enough oxygen. His heart raced out of control, while his limbs went numb. His nose began to tingle. Sensing danger, he looked around. There was no enemy. As his adrenaline pulsed, he realized that the enemy was within. "My God, I'm having a heart attack. It must be those experimental shots!"

He wanted to scream out for help, but didn't. Feeling overwhelmed and confused, he rushed out of the dark tent. As he gasped for air, he spotted Ryan's face. It was illuminated by the small orange glow of a cigarette. Judging from his broad smile, Ryan was probably dreaming about his unborn child. Without hesitation, the expectant father rushed over. The change in his expression scared Steve even more.

"Steve, what's wrong?"

He attempted a word, but it got caught behind the lump lodged in his dry throat. Finally, he managed, "I don't know. I think it's my heart!"

Before he realized it, he was in Ryan's Humvee, speeding toward the old 911th EVAC.

During the ride, his body rushed out of control, while his mind quickly followed. Every thought was negative and he funneled downward. As they pulled into the hospital's camp, he wondered if he was losing his mind. A loud irritating noise startled him. Ryan was sounding the horn. Placing his head in his hands, he said aloud, "My God, I feel so out of it!" The fogginess terrified him. Ryan was silent.

It didn't take long before a light came on in one of the tents. The same nurse who administered The Dream Team's violent illness, staggered out. She was half-dressed and barely coherent. She looked annoyed. She either hated to be bothered during a sound sleep, or Ryan had layed on the horn a few seconds longer than he needed to.

Steve explained the recent flu-like symptoms, along with the details of his current nightmare. The woman's attitude changed. There was a sense of urgency, as well as compassion, in her every action. She hurried him into the rear of the ambulance and began taking vitals. Calling for emergency assistance, she hooked him up to a portable E.K.G. machine. The doctor responded. He calmly read the results of the heart test and concluded, "You're not the first soldier to complain of a bad reaction to the inoculations, but let me reassure you, your heart is fine. As a matter of fact, besides being dehydrated, you appear to be in good health. I think that you may have experienced a severe bout with anxiety. I'm pretty sure that it was only a panic attack!" Offering some universal advice that was easier said than done, he winked. "Just try and relax, okay?"

Steve sat up on the gurney and looked at Ryan. It was impossible. He had experienced incredible amounts of stress before. The prison created tons of it. The doctor was wrong. He had to be. As his pulse slowed down significantly and his breathing returned to normal, he felt the blush of embarrassment. Left both physically and mentally exhausted, he stumbled out of the rear of the ambulance. Adrenaline overload had drained every ounce of energy out of him. Returning to the Humvee, the two friends drove away in silence.

A few miles down the road, he felt even better. The horrifying sense of being out of control was leaving him. The sense of despair was gone. Ashamed, he said aloud, "Ryan, let's . . . ," but Ryan finished the sentence for him.

"We'll keep it between us buddy, but if you feel this way again, let me know, okay?"

Steve nodded his head in appreciation. There were a lot of people counting on him. It was important they remain confident in him. He didn't want people walking around on eggshells around him, especially the Second Squad. Being awakened to the possibility of his own death scared him, but if it happened again, he'd presume it was anxiety. He'd deal with it alone.

Breaking the silence, Ryan added, "Steve, I know I've been in my own world lately, and you were the only one to care enough to talk to me. I also know that you're carrying a ton of weight from home. Monica being hurt, the mortgage .... All I'm saying is, let me be there for you, too."

Steve shook his hand. Ryan was a true friend. Unlike his fair-weather friends, who were only there to laugh with, Ryan was also there to cry with. He loved him for it. Shutting off the headlights, Ryan waited to turn off the ignition until just before reaching the tents. The Humvee coasted into its normal parking spot without anyone ever knowing it was missing. Slipping into their cots, the friends shook hands again. Not another word was spoken about the nightmare.

The following morning, Steve awoke exhausted, but there was no evidence of anxiety. He felt a great sense of relief and figured he'd chalk the night up to experience. There was no use giving the episode another thought, so he didn't. He went to work. The morning briefing was lengthy. The 661st was finally informed of their first mission. It came all the way down from the top, 7th Corps.

The 7th was the force stationed in Europe, with its sights on fighting World War Three. With the end of the Cold War, however, they were dispatched into the desert as one of the largest American elements. The majority of its force consisted of heavy armor brigades. Steve was confident that somewhere along the line, the 661st would be supporting one of them.

For the time being, they were tasked with a different job. The 661st M.P. Company was now responsible for providing security for Log Base Charlie, which was the ammunition supply point closest to the Iraqi Border, and it measured ten square miles in size. His company contained merely four platoons of 30 soldiers each, but was tasked to oversee all of it. And, as the orders read: EFFECTIVE IMMEDIATELY.

At the conclusion of the briefing, each squad leader was issued two maps, one of northern Saudi Arabia and one of southern Iraq. They were nothing more than tan paper, with fine black grid lines slicing them into sections. Studying them, Steve determined they would be of little use. The boys would have to rely on precise compass readings, accurate odometer readings from the Humvees and solid radio communication to find their way. Through prior training, he knew he was very poor at judging distances. His bearing on directions also fell short. He always depended on his map reading skills to navigate his way. The map provided, however, could have been put to better use in the latrine. He handed one of the maps to Pat, a man who possessed the instincts of a scout.

"Pat, we're gonna have to work together on this shit," Steve said.

Pat grinned, giving him an uncomfortable feeling. It was the sick feeling that his assistant was looking for the upper hand and had finally gotten it. In a joking manner, Pat responded, "I'll lead the way, Steve. If you get lost, I'll send somebody back for you!"

Unsure if Pat was kidding, Steve was taken back a bit.

Returning the same devious smile, he informed his assistant, "I'll tell you what. We'll drive in circles before you take the fuckin' lead. We'll either work together or apart!" With that said, the friends laughed, though it was a deadly serious situation. Waving goodbye to Pat, he mounted up the squad and took to the rugged terrain. Six miles from Camp Lois, Bug Light approached a fork in the road.

Without being asked, Pat volunteered his expertise over the radio. In a professional tone, he confirmed, "Swamp Yankee, up ahead, bear right."

That was it. The radio was silent again. Steve smiled to himself. Pat was working with him, though his enthusiasm for the war disappeared shortly thereafter. He became unusually quiet. When he did speak, it was brief. Everybody noticed it. Pat O'Malley was a born leader. If he couldn't lead, he became a victim of boredom.

Log Base Charlie was huge and Steve doubted his squad had covered every inch within their first twelve-hour shift. It was a bustling place, with a constant flow of tractor trailers dropping off every round and missile imaginable. They watched with astonishment, as the logistical nightmare was handled relatively gracefully. Mother Liberty brought more hardware than she'd ever need. Even more amazingly, whether by land, sea or air, it was all going to be delivered to Iraq. Steve doubted they'd appreciate the lethal gifts, but nonetheless, they were carefully chosen as the recipients.

Finishing their first full shift, they realized their mission was a farce. The ammo supply point was so vast, it would have taken a battalion of M.P.s to effectively provide security. Instead, there were three lightly armed Humvees per shift. Evidently, the word security looked good on paper. With the daily chaos inside Charlie's borders, nobody ever took notice anyway. Returning to base camp, Steve decided that whether they were playing toy soldiers, or not, was irrelevant. They'd put in their twelve hours per day, complete their assigned duties and accomplish their own major objective — to return to camp, every day, unscathed.

For the first two weeks, they settled into their routine; twelve hours on and the other twelve to adapt to their new environment. Adjusting to the desert was the key. To fight it was a losing battle. The sand was a prime example. There was no getting away from it. They slept with it in their sleeping bags. They ate it during their meals. Millions of grains of sand also invaded every hygiene session. Whether it was brushing teeth, taking a sponge bath, cleaning up with baby wipes, or washing the laundry by hand, the white powder penetrated everything. The sand was a part of life. Acceptance was the answer. Any other attitude could have easily led to insanity.

Unavoidably, there were times when each of them let out a scream. This venting brought laughter. Everybody felt the same. When one shrieked in frustration, he did it for them all. It was therapeutic. For Steve, it was a combination of the sand and the merciless sun. It caused him to sweat profusely. Consuming a liter of water per hour only caused his pores to gush open like faucets. As if he were a refrigerator and the sand, magnets, he was constantly covered from head to toe. On more than one occasion, he howled at the sun.

At first, their little adventure felt like a sort of vacation. There were twelve hours of security, patrolling within a mountain of munitions that grew by the day. The only true benefit of the mission was that the boys helped themselves to all the ammo they could carry. Accountability for machine gun, rifle and pistol bullets didn't exist. Crates upon crates were taken, but never missed. Eventually, the grande theft larceny ceased, but only because there was no more room to store the loot.

After their shifts, the boys played hard. With three squads in the platoon, the shifts rotated. Catching twelve hours off during the day was a real treat. While engaged in competitive tournaments of horseshoes and volleyball, each man watched the months of stored fat melt away. In the meantime, every toned body turned a bronze tan. It was weird. Though the wondrous sky hosted every war bird in America's arsenal and the northern horizon produced an uninterrupted flow of Allied tanks, for the time being, the war was doing just fine without the 661st M.P. Company. Steve became more relaxed with each passing day. Life was almost good.

Returning to Camp Lois after another long and boring day of armed patrols, the Second Squad stumbled upon the opportunity of any desert experience. Steve's eyes widened and he halted his patrol. Parked on the side of M.S.R. Blue was an enormous convoy of tractor trailers. From a mile away, it was obvious why the convoy had stopped. They were overloaded and were losing a good part of their inventory. There were cases of bottled water, which was difficult to locate and even harder to keep in stock. Each bottle was cherished as a luxury. They had stumbled upon thousands of bottles, just lying in the middle of the road.

He jumped out of Bug Light and placed the heavy Kevlar helmet onto his head. Though he was smiling on the inside, outside he attempted a look of rigid professionalism. He posted two men on the road to direct traffic around the soldiers who were attempting to re-load their trucks. He approached the lead tractor. With a look of disgust plastered across his face, he barked, "Where is your convoy commander?"

The driver appeared nervous. He immediately called for the commander. Within minutes, a U.S. Army major made his way up to Steve. In spite of the man's rank, Steve threw caution to the wind.

He introduced himself, while maintaining the look of disgust. Then, he lied to the high ranking officer with a nearly convincing sincerity. "Sir, I've been tasked with the responsibility of keeping M.S.R. Blue clear of all debris, so that the ammunition and fuel trucks, both priorities, can quickly make their way to the front. I'm sorry to inform you that your convoy is blocking their way. I must also inform you that you're carrying more than you can handle. I'm sure that even if your people can quickly clean up this mess, we'll be faced with the same dilemma a few miles up the road."

The man looked sick with rage. He snapped, "So tell me sergeant, what am I supposed to do with all this water for a Division up front?"

Steve shook his head. As if the answer were so simple, so obvious, he advised, "Carry what you can and dispatch another vehicle to retrieve the cases left behind. In the meantime, I'll have my people watch over the goods."

The major chuckled. He saw straight through the bullshit story, but there wasn't one thing he could do about it. He didn't have the time or patience to try. Sarcastically thanking Steve, he informed him, "Another truck will be along in two hours." Climbing into the cab of his truck, the officer looked back and laughed again.

Steve sensed that the older man appreciated the cunning game, so this time, he laughed with him. They both knew. The major wasn't outfoxed. He was just a victim of the pirateering that accompanies war.

Steve summoned the entire company from Camp Lois to pick up the Mother Load. The story of the big score spread like wildfire. First Sergeant Avery commended him for taking the initiative, though he was more pleased that Steve took the fresh water. He stole some valuable items intended for another unit. Instead of catching hell, he was praised. The rules had certainly changed. It took hours before the hundreds of cases were transported back to Camp Lois, with a good majority being stockpiled within The Dream Team's borders. Nobody complained about how it was divvied up. On the contrary, they were all grateful. Since their arrival, they had been forced to swallow the sludge being reprocessed at the desalinization plants. Before the episode was over, Steve had nearly earned himself a medal for his lies. The Army, however, wasn't authorized to reward a man for such acts of trickery and deceit.

Camp Lois eventually became their home away from home. Each platoon tucked themselves into the corners of the perimeter, while the remainder of the company claimed the safer center.

The Mess Section found their duties relaxing. Their most challenging task was boiling water to heat the Beefaroni lunch buckets. Headquarters, or the Operations Section, also sat on their hands most of the time. They, however, tried harder to conceal it. Appearing busy became their goal. The charade was easily detectable though. Captain Wall could never be found without her trusty companion, a Nintendo Gameboy. The Motor Pool did their fair share by improvising with faulty or damaged equipment. Whether it was covering the Humvees air filters with panty hose or repairing a stolen trailer for bathing purposes, they kept reasonably busy. The Supply Section spent most of their time trading or stealing things the company needed, while Staff Sergeant Volmer, the company clerk, lived alone in a tent that looked quite handsome on her. She was responsible for only one thing — the mail. For the first few weeks, she was the busiest of them all.

Mail call brought on an onslaught of letters and packages. The majority were addressed to *Any Soldier*. The overwhelming support from back home was both humbling and inspirational. Besides the expensive 15 minute phone call allowed once a week, and the daily propaganda of Armed Forces Radio, it was the only link to the real world. Steve received nothing at first. Then, the over-worked postal service caught up with him.

It was a late mail call. He was lying on his dusty cot, writing a letter to his worried wife. He began,

Dear Monica, It is so difficult to explain how much I miss you ....

The camp's delivery boy, a flustered young soldier, blew right through the tent. As he approached the exit flap, he threw a handful of envelopes onto Sergeant Manchester's chest. Sitting up, Steve chuckled, as the boy's shadow quickly vanished into the early dusk. He opened the first letter before even looking at the sender. From the stationary, he knew right away. It was from his mom.

The stationery heading contained the poem, *Footprints*. Though the author was unknown, for Steve it was a great source of strength. In many respects, the poem symbolized a special gift of hope to him from his faithful mother. The heading never changed, and the poem spoke directly to his soul.

One night a man had a dream. He dreamed he was walking along the beach with the Lord. Across the sky flashed scenes from his life. In each scene, he noticed two sets of footprints ... one belonging to him and the other to the Lord. When the last scene had flashed before him, he looked back at the footprints and noticed that many times along the path, there was only one set of footprints in the sand. He also noticed that this happened during the lowest and saddest times in his life. This really bothered him ... and he questioned the Lord. "Lord, you said that once I decided to follow you, you would walk with me all the way. But I noticed that during the most troublesome times of my life, there was only one set of footprints. I don't understand why ... when I needed you most, you deserted me." The Lord replied, "My precious child, I love you and I would never leave you. During your times of trial and suffering, when you see only one set of footprints ... it was then that I carried you."

Each time, in Nancy Manchester's flowing penmanship, the letters were signed, *So long for now and Keep The Faith!*

No different from Monica or Billy's many letters, Steve's mom kept him updated on recent events at home. There were always requests for more details of his daily life, as well as pleas for him to write more. His mom's letters, however, were special. They included the priceless artwork of his baby sisters. The girls either traced their tiny hands or drew pictures of things he couldn't make out. It didn't matter. It was always fun to guess. Even the other guys in the platoon attempted in laughter. Through sentimental eyes, he treasured the beautiful pictures. They were Crayola masterpieces, sent halfway around the globe, from two little girls who he adored and missed sorely.

He did his best to write, but after the first few letters, there was very little to share. The days were either spent in boredom, or with events he had no intentions of sharing through correspondence. The first Scud attack he witnessed was one of those experiences.

It was on a late shift, similar to all the others. The Second Squad was sitting on a giant hill overlooking Log Base Charlie. It was a small mountain shadowing the ammo point. After weeks of driving in circles, the boys decided to conduct non-stop surveillance from a stationary, more comfortable position. Initially, the spot was named Solsbury Hill, after the famed Peter Gabriel tune. Days later, their British allies found a more suitable title. Dubbed Barter Hill, the site became an active trading post for all Allied Forces.

As every single convoy heading toward the front needed to pass Barter Hill, most pulled over to swap anything and everything. From full uniforms and berets to food and drink, The Dream Team eventually set up their own pawnshop. Their policy was quite clear: All trades were final and if any soldier approached the high ground, he was obligated to offer one war memento for another. The word spread quickly. Before long, business was booming. Within a week, however, Private Tripp's cache of Vietnam-issue bayonets were completely depleted, while the boys had gained all the British and French souvenirs they could handle. The policy was then amended to include the exchange of stories. Steve enjoyed this bartering the most. It was on one such night, while he was engaged in a discussion with a British counterpart, that the attack took place.

Sipping English tea, while one of the Limeys heated American coffee, he initiated an interesting conversation. "So tell me, where are you guys normally stationed?"

The older man grinned. He looked over at Donnelly and Ahern. In his thick British accent, he proudly responded, "Northern Ireland, mate, where we kill'em when they're not killing each other!"

Hearing the crude answer, some of the boys left. Steve was glad that Pat was out of earshot. There would have been a blood bath. It was obvious that the British despised the Irish, even Irish-Americans.

Feeling the need to defend his friends, Steve defiantly informed the allied soldier, "See, that's one thing you Englishmen don't understand about American soldiers. We're a mixed breed, whose bloodlines can't be identified through a simple name."

Sensing the tone in his voice, the Brit also became defensive. He replied, "Is that right Englishman?"

Breaking the thick tension, Steve laughed. "Wrong again, my friend. I'm half French, half English, but all American!"

Looking down at Steve's arm, the soldier quipped, "I can see that from the flag on your bloody arm." The man extended his hand and introduced himself, "The name's Cornish, Sergeant Major John Cornish."

Steve's first international friendship was born. He accepted the handshake, along with another cup of tea. At that very moment, the attack took place.

One split-second before it was announced over the radio, Steve saw it in the sky. It was a Scud missile, the Iraqis inaccurate and indiscriminate weapon of terror. Strategically, it had no bearing on the war, but from a terrorist's standpoint, it did its job. It produced the second largest fear in the Gulf. The first was Hussein's possible nuclear capabilities. The second was a chemical attack. For all Steve knew, he was sitting directly in the middle of one of them. Quickly donning his protective mask, he insured that his people did the same. Everyone was covered. While his blood pumped hard, the boys sat in place, unable to do anything but watch and wait for the outcome. The apprehensive moment was over in seconds.

Staring at the burning ball, he thought it looked as if someone had lit a tennis ball on fire, then lobbed it into the black sky. Then, what appeared to be a fire fly, dotted across the sky and hit the ball, causing it to spin out of control. A second Patriot missile was fired. This time, there was a direct hit. The dual was over. The Scud was successfully intercepted. Muffled cheers exploded from beneath their masks. While shrapnel rained out of the sky, The Dream Team celebrated their lives and the success of America's Scud-busters. Coming from New England, they were Patriot fans. This night, however, gave that term a whole new meaning.

A mere five minutes later, Central Command announced, via radio, "All clear." This meant the masks could be removed. Steve reluctantly pulled off the suffocating rubber shell and listened to the empty promise of Tony Rosini. On an alternate frequency, Tony relayed some information from Central Command.

"Don't worry guys, the boys at the top don't believe that the Scud's head was filled with anything, chemical or not. They say that even if it was, the poisonous gases have already dissipated into the atmosphere, leaving all ground troops unharmed. According to them, the danger factor is low, very low."

The radio squelched once, then went dead. Steve looked at Pat, Doug and Dennis. They were all thinking the same. Tony didn't sound the least bit convincing. It was because he didn't believe it himself.

"How in the hell do they already know whether or not the Scud was loaded with chemical agents?" Steve asked. Before anyone could answer, he inquired further, "Would those potential chemicals be dissipating into the same atmosphere that we're currently breathing?"

There was no response to either question, but each face searched for answers. Though brief, it was their first brush with danger. There were two more Scud attacks. Each time, they were left to wonder whether or not they were contaminated. Central Command's response was always the same. They answered nothing and left the boys to fear for their future health.

For the remainder of the night, Steve listened attentively to the descriptive tales of his new friend. Right from the start, he knew that his prison stories would seem like children's tales to a soldier with such experience, so he kept quiet. The man liked to talk. Steve secretly enjoyed his accent the most.

Her Majesty's army arrived from Northern Ireland and the southern United Kingdom. Nicknamed, Desert Rats, the two divisions were considered some of the best desert fighters in the world. They were well-trained, possessed combat experience and traveled light, using white phosphorous as their ammunition of choice. As white phosphorous will burn through four inches of plated steel, the Geneva Convention had outlawed its use on personnel. Equipment was singled out as its only potential target. The British, however, later defined equipment as being helmets, boots, etc. They were a mean lot.

Cornish shared his candid motto of war. According to him, it was the philosophy of most British soldiers. He said, "Kill everything and take no prisoners. Believe me lad, prisoners will slow you down. You have to feed them, water them and they're a pain in the ass. Even children. If you don't kill them right off, who knows, maybe 20 years down the road, your own kid will have to hunt down the dirty little bastards!"

Steve was shocked, but chose to react with indifference.

Cornish coldly added, "And believe me, my American friend, war is not for the weak at heart!"

The man's deepest beliefs were transparent and his outlook, drastically inhumane. Yet, he knew war. He had experienced combat. Steve understood that confidence was a must, but catching the sparkle in Cornish's cold eyes, he doubted that killing was to be enjoyed. Instead, he believed that weakness had relatively nothing to do with it. Cornish was sadly mistaken. War was not for the *good* at heart.

Rallying up the squad after the exciting night, he bid farewell to his cruel comrade. Trading cases of Chef Boyardee for English sausages, a delicacy much like hot dogs, it was time to go. Then, in a gesture unheard of, the man extended an open invitation to his camp. Steve promised he'd take him up on the generous offer and turned to leave. As he reached Bug Light, Cornish yelled out, "At least you have bloody women in your ranks, mate, for the chilly nights. Too bad most of them look like a bulldog chewing on a wasp!"

As the Second Squad descended Barter Hill, Steve still heard their laughter. Gazing over his shoulder, he was glad that both females in his squad were monitoring the radio back at base camp. Still, he silently chuckled at the dark humor of the sadistic man. It was a strange experience in international affairs, but he intended on following it up with a future visit.

The next night, Second Squad took their respected place on Barter Hill. Looking into the threshold of heaven, Steve jumped off of the vehicle's hood to watch another parade heading north. They were British and had pulled up roots to get a closer look at Iraq.

Lighting a cigarette, he heard it before knowing what it was. There was a distinct crackle, then he saw the dirt fly up not ten feet in front of Pat. One of the British soldiers in the rear of a truck screamed, "Sorry about that, Chap!" The truth hit him. The crackle, the flying dirt; it was all due to an expended bullet. The soldier was clearing his rifle and accidentally discharged a round. Pat was the first to be shot at, even if it was friendly fire. Steve thought about the contradiction in terms and wondered if any bullet was ever friendly.

Walking toward Pat, he stopped. The reality of his friend's reaction smacked him even harder. Pat never flinched. He simply went straight to his back pocket, retrieved a can of dip and placed a pinch between his cheek and gum. If the shooting had affected Pat any more, it would have bothered him. Sensing the eyes burning into his back, Pat finally offered the British soldier the global sign of love. He flipped the man a bird.

The night crawled into morning. The squad returned to base, only to find Tony in the rarest of moods. Tony never left Camp Lois, as any contact with danger could have easily triggered a flashback from his first war. Nobody questioned it. Steve figured it had happened anyway, the night before. The Scud attack must have jarred his tortured memory and brought him back in time. Watching Tony from the perimeter, Steve's body shuddered with a sick sense about his friend's mental health. It was as if he was watching the making of a B-rated movie. Tony cut off the sleeves of his T-shirt and tied a bandanna across his wrinkled forehead. With the Humvees stereo blaring the rebellious tune, *Fortunate Son* from Credence Clearwater Revival, Tony inhaled his cigarette as though he was smoking a joint. The scene became complete when a chopper cleared the perimeter and flew directly overhead. The gunship's blades cut violently through the air, creating a raucous mix with the music.

Tony's gears were slipping, and the upper echelon found it entertaining. For The Dream Team, however, the ramifications were life threatening. For the next week, the madman kept his own agenda. Every diabolic decision he made was unauthorized. Each one involved his 30 pawns, the First Platoon, and Steve found that, before long, he and his friends were exposed to some very unnecessary dangers. On the other hand, there were also lessons in courage.

Labeled Recon Missions, they were actually just a couple of deranged ideas thrust into action. Tony Rosini, the mastermind, became a man searching for adventure through the eyes of his men. He got away with it twice, but during the second trip, Steve realized it had already happened once too often. It served no purpose but to quench Tony's thirst for excitement.

A carbon-copy of the night before, Steve and his squad watched the fireworks from the top of Barter Hill. It reminded him of sitting in the dunes on the fourth of July, even if there was no reflection cast off of the ocean of sand. The nightly shows were extraordinary, though in time, they became routine. While the Allied forces poured certain death upon Iraq, the virtually defenseless enemy retaliated by firing wildly and sending a barrage of anti-aircraft fire into the smoky sky. The subtle winds then carried the smells of gunpowder and sulfur all the way to Barter Hill. For some time, it was the only reminder that there was a war going on. In an attempt to hit something, anything, the Iraqis kept shooting. It was no use. Hussein even admitted that the Americans were the technologically superior, yet he still refused to lose face to the Arab world. As a result of his self-serving pride, the Iraqi people paid the price. They paid dearly.

Steve was summoned over the radio, then informed to switch to an alternate, safer frequency. Turning the knob four clicks, he heard the annoying rumble of Tony. "Swamp Yankee, be advised, you are ordered to abort your present mission and proceed due north. There are recent intelligence reports indicating that friendly troops are being hit with small arms fire. You should approach the skirmish at mile marker 72. Good Luck!"

With no further direction from Camp Lois, Second Squad responded to the alleged scene. This was the second call for assistance in as many nights. The first was a false alarm. The boys had their suspicions that Tony was fabricating the stories, but there was no logical reason for lies. They didn't remember that it was Tony Rosini they were dealing with. Either way, they had to check it out. In the meantime, they also checked the strength of each other's backbones.

Several miles into the voyage, the squad began to leapfrog, as two Humvees constantly covered the lead. Radio communication was held to a minimum. Steadily, the three vehicles were right on schedule for their first fire fight. Watching the mile markers count up to 72, Steve's body began curling itself into the fetal position. His senses were keen, his mind alert, but his body was paralyzed with fear. He knew it and the reality of it was crushing his spirit. Though it initially made his heart sink even deeper, he suddenly saw two moon-lit silhouettes. They were unknown men, just yards from marker 72. It was time to react.

As if a switch was thrown, his body straightened out. With little thought or effort, he pressed the radio's microphone and ordered, "Pat, cover the left flank. Dennis, you take the right. We'll cover the targets head-on!" He could hear his commanding voice, see his body quickly reacting, but he felt as though he were on the outside looking in. It was as if he were observing the dangerous scenario from the safety of a window.

The boys halted the shadows and learned that they had nearly hunted down two American scouts. Yet, Tony's intelligence report was somewhat accurate. There was a fire fight in the area. Steve cringed, however, when one of the soldiers informed him, "We appreciate the backup, but we cleared from that clash over six hours ago. Whoever sent you, must be getting their information by Pony Express!"

The two men chuckled. Steve could only picture Tony's lying face. With a cordial, but insincere apology, the squad left.

The ride home was conducted at a leisurely pace, allowing Steve the time to consider the recent events. He was tired from the adrenaline, yet his body continued to rush. He thought about the paralyzing fear, but gradually the frown was replaced by a weary smile. He was partly elated and partly relieved at his instinctive reaction. The Army's famous advertising was right. Courage was merely setting fear aside to get the job done. They neglected, however, to describe the intensity of such fears.

Everybody got pumped up, but while they all came down, his body still peaked. Trying to analyze his feelings, he became confused. He wasn't disappointed with the outcome, but in a strange way, he felt that things were unresolved. He sensed that if they fought, it would be over. It was the apprehension that tore at his soul. His mind knew it was done, but somehow, it couldn't relay the important message to his body. He closed his eyes and rode out the rest of the adrenaline wave. Unaware of the change, the false mission triggered his most primitive instincts. During times of peril, he reacted calmly, but during times of peace, his body refused to rest. He made the transformation. He wasn't just a man anymore, he was now a warrior, who anticipated the worst even when things were good.

Returning to home base, he woke Tony. In a calm and collected tone, he informed his boss, "This will be the last time anyone in this platoon chases a ghost for you!"

Like an embarrassed child, Tony shrugged and smirked with a hint of mischief.

Steve snapped, "And for the last time, no more fuckin' games!"

With that off of his chest, he went to bed. His sleep was anything but restful.

In order to get some extended time off, the Second Squad worked two double shifts in a row. The hard work took a week, but the time off couldn't have been any better. As usual, a vote was taken. The consensus was to venture into Hafar al Batin for the first day. The second, they decided, would be spent taking Cornish up on his invitation. They were the best two decisions they had made since their arrival almost five weeks earlier. They had chosen to spend 48 hours living in two very different cultures only 60 miles apart.

Only one mile into the city limits, Hafar al Batin lost its enchantment, but the mystery remained. As if he were leading a field trip, Steve decided to cruise the crowded streets before making any stops. He attempted to keep an open mind about the different culture, but found it difficult. In training, they were taught about the Arab ways, but to see it all first-hand was a rude awakening.

The filthy streets were flooded with people dressed in disguise. The women, clothed in black abayas, scurried from shop to shop. Most traffic was military, with the majority of civilian vehicles being Datsun pickup trucks. While stopped at a traffic light, Steve looked toward his left. One of the many Datsuns pulled up alongside. The simple picture of ordinary life said it all. The driver was a dark-complected man, smiling from behind a full face of hair. Propped up in the passenger's seat, sat his companion, a goat. In the back of the truck, sat the man's wife, along with other goats. The crew laughed, then watched as the insulted native sped off. It was so bizarre, but at the same time, explained so much. The Saudi men had great difficulty accepting the American women serving in the military. Their feelings were conveyed several times through some very bad looks. Steve chuckled. It was no wonder they had a problem with women in authority. They were a medieval society, where barnyard animals held a higher status than wives and daughters.

As a similar truck passed, Steve caught the seductive stare of another submissive woman. From behind a sheer scarf, her penetrating eyes were blacker than coal. There was no feeling behind them, just an intriguing sex appeal that caused him to become aroused. Smiling, he realized that he hadn't gotten an erection since landing in the huge litter box. Sex was the last thing on anyone's mind. The sensation passed quickly, but stayed long enough to assure him that his equipment was still in good working order.

Several times during the morning, the bells of the city rang out, calling all of its citizens to prayer. The storekeepers locked up their shops and the shepherds came in from their sandy fields. Even the Saudi military ceased all operations. The entire city walked to their Temple, took an extended moment of silence, while meditating and worshipping God. Watching this, Steve was unsure whether the people were so devoutly religious, or if the six-to-eight daily periods of reflection just provided a lazy outlet from the unbearable heat. He decided it was a combination of the two.

After seeing the entire city, the boys stopped for lunch. It was a small grimy shop, with whole chickens slowly roasting in the window. The sight of poultry stopped them, but it was the drifting aromas that lured in the big sale. They each purchased the house special — one-half of a chicken, a heap of rice, some pita bread and a couple of cold Pepsis. The price was only two American dollars. As if devouring their last meal, most of them ordered the other half of their chicken. Steve sat back, lit a cigarette and enjoyed his third Pepsi. The view from the open cafe was fabulous. He was in no hurry to leave. Without having to look back at the table, the grunts and groans of his friends told him that they weren't ready to go either. Content with the drinks, they did some people-watching. There was no better place.

From training, he understood that everything he witnessed was common for the region. It still didn't seem right. Men walked hand in hand down the streets in conversation. It was the native sign of friendship. As he gazed down the street, a heated argument caught his attention. It was an American soldier who appeared gigantic next to his Saudi Arabian adversary. From the gist of the traveling vulgarities, he figured out that the American was waiting for the telephone when the Saudi civilian cut in front of him. For the culture, however, the cutting of a line was not uncommon, nor even considered impolite. He turned to Pat.

"Back home, someone could get killed for something that disrespectful."

Before Pat could comment, it happened. The G.I. threw a haymaker, knocking the tiny man to the ground. With mixed emotions, Steve watched as the fragile Saudi jumped up and ran for his life. There was a severe lack of communication between cultures. These heated differences of opinion had been commonplace since America's arrival. Steve thought the violence was typical of his people. Force was usually the chosen solution.

Taking a long draw on his Pepsi, he turned to Pat. "Did you just see that beef?"

Pat grinned. "No wonder we got sent here to protect these cowards. If they do have hearts, they must be pumping Kool-Aid!"

Chuckling at his friend's cynical wit, Steve tore the labels from the three empty Pepsi bottles. The Manchester's would love the souvenirs. There was PEPSI written on one side and the Arabic version printed on the other. Besides the soft drink, there was no other hint of the Western world. The Saudis did quite well keeping American influence out of their country. With money to burn, however, G.I.s had flooded their market with American currency, causing an economic imbalance. For the first time in their history, the average peasant was making a killing peddling his goods. Without regard for concentrated wealth or oppressive poverty, the ancient Kingdom of Saudi Arabia was being introduced to the fundamental principals of free trade and the power of the almighty dollar. Steve doubted the royal family appreciated the business.

Finishing the delicious lunch, the crew paid their bill, leaving a generous American tip. The waiter was pleased. The city bells chimed once again. This time, the tone and interval was different, more somber. Using his vivid imagination, along with the creative hand signals of the grateful waiter, Steve put the puzzle together. The people of Hafar al Batin were being summoned into the city's square. It was Friday, the customary day for public punishments. It was rumored that if a prisoner's neck withstood a single, striking blow from the executioner's ax, he would walk home a free man. Consumed with a morbid curiosity, the boys attempted to witness the rare event. They were quickly ejected from the area. Outsiders were not permitted to observe the people's justice. Most left disappointed, but as they rallied back at their vehicles, the issue gave way to a strong discussion of the advantages of Marshall Law.

In total disagreement, Steve told Dennis, "No doubt, corrections are handled differently over here, but are they wrong? It's one of the last places in the world where the hands of thieves are removed, the castration of rapists are carried out. You consider it barbaric and inhumane, yet compared to our country, Saudi Arabia has relatively no crime. It makes you wonder which society is truly the uncivilized?" Steve wasn't sure the Arabs were doing it right, but employed for Corrections within the United States, he was convinced America wasn't handling the problem effectively. The sensitive issue gave way to more debate.

They arrived at no agreement and finally headed off to the black market. En route, they nearly ran over a man who was urinating in the middle of the street. With a smile spread across his soiled face, the nasty native squatted and actually relieved himself in open public. Again, it was common. Most Saudi men did it. With no catch drains, or gutters, the pool of urine simply trickled down the littered street and waited to be evaporated.

No further evidence was needed. Hafar al Batin was a dirty place. The exposed man, however, gave Steve an idea.

Taking a sharp left, he halted his squad in the front of The King Fahd Hotel. There was no valet parking, so the boys found three open spots and jumped out.

Pat asked, "Getting a room, Steve?"

He grinned, but kept walking toward the virtual palace.

Pat was less trusting of the Saudi people and was getting restless. "Steve, what are we doing here?"

Steve stopped, turned around and announced, "I just want to enjoy a healthy shit like a normal human being!"

With that said, each face lit up with excitement. They'd already spent over a month in the field. The thought of a toilet overjoyed them. From the look on their faces, Steve realized that he had taken so much for granted. Such simple pleasures were considered luxuries in other parts of the world. Filing it away, he led his rambunctious friends on a passionate quest for an ordinary ceramic commode.

After receiving some vague directions in broken English, they finally located the hotel's powder room. Steve was the second man and thought they had taken a wrong turn. There were no toilets and not one roll of bathroom tissue. Instead, there were small holes in the concrete. Behind them, bolted to the wall, were water spigots. As they tried to figure it out, everyone got a first-hand lesson in Arabian potti-training.

The door opened and a Saudi man walked in. Lifting his heavy robe, he squatted over one of the holes. With eight pairs of eyes watching him, the gentleman defecated, unbothered and unashamed. Steve caught himself staring and grabbed the boys to leave. There was no need to watch the man rinse his ass off with the sprayer. Half disgusted, half disappointed, they had seen enough. Mother Nature would have to wait.

The open marketplace bustled with more vendors than customers. It was like a large flea market, with a sweet citrus smell freshening the stagnant air. The incense made Steve's head pound. The area was infested with beggars and conmen, but the American intimidation factor worked well. Like a pack of frustrated women, the boys embarked on a wild shopping spree. Steve enjoyed watching his happy friends. As one potential sale after another was negotiated, the Saudi's rattled on in their own tongue, while The Dream Team haggled in English. Through all the chaos, there was communication. The exchange of currency tore down language barriers and brought about instant understanding.

The entire afternoon was comical. They purchased handmade works in copper and brass, detailed Persian rugs and snack foods, such as pita bread and pistachios. The Humvees were loaded. Hours passed and Steve watched, as most of the squad shopped like they were at Macy's during Christmas. Remembering his financial dilemma at home, he kept his spending to a minimum. By the time it was over, he had conservatively purchased two prayer rugs and a brass lantern for Monica. The rest of the money had to go home. The bank was still pressuring for funds that weren't there. His army pay was less than half of his regular salary and Monica was still out of work due to her injury. It was no time to be frivolous. He was happy to go without.

As the final team mounted up, the Saudi Arabian police skidded to a stop and blocked their exit. Steve approached the police jeep. He was determined to get some answers.

The closer he got, the more he realized that the Arabian people were so much smaller in size. The scared look in the police officers' eyes made him wonder whether their hearts were equally tiny. He wasn't ten feet from the patrol jeep when they hit the gas and sped off. Steve threw up his hands.

"You gotta be kiddin' me?" he yelled. "Pat, I think you're right about these people."

He heard laughter. Shielding his eyes from the glare of the sun's powerful rays, he saw the real reason for the cops' rapid departure. Private Tripp, seated in the turret, was pointing his M-60 machine gun directly at their heads.

They headed back to camp, never knowing why they were swarmed upon. Personally, Steve didn't care. He was just proud of Tripp. Right or wrong, they were prepared to fight.

After some much needed rest, the sun signaled the start of another scalding day. Breakfast consisted of a cup of coffee and some corn bread, then the Second Squad was on the road again.

Welcomed with opened arms, the British went out of their way to show their American friends a good time. Their best homemade alcohol was taken out of storage. The boys wasted the lazy afternoon away by exchanging stories of home. With a little buzz on, Cornish challenged the squad to a friendly game of football. Pat never hesitated. He reached into his truck for his pigskin. The whole British contingency erupted into healthy laughter, while Cornish returned from the darkness of his octagonal tent. In his large hands, he held their own version, a soccer ball. The joke was understood and the boys accepted the challenge. Two sweat-drenched hours later, Second Squad found that they hadn't represented the U.S.A. with any dignity. Beneath a scorching sun, they got their asses kicked. In an attempt to redeem their honor, the pigskin was kicked off. Another exhausting hour later, the British also learned the agony of defeat. They had to quit. The sky was getting unusually dark. For an hour, each man attempted to rehydrate his body, while staring at a bleak sky. Alternating between booze and water, it was a losing battle.

It was late into the afternoon when it finally happened. Everyone froze in place. The overcast skies opened up and the dark clouds dumped buckets of cool, refreshing rain. Like children, some of the men danced beneath the showers. The cracked desert let out a sigh of relief. It was magical. Steve tilted his face upward and drank from the generous sky. It felt like forever since rain had touched his skin. It was long overdue. Then, as quickly as it started, it stopped. The black clouds blew north, while Steve sat to enjoy the latest spectacle.

It was a rainbow, and the first he had seen since childhood. It was perfectly shaped. Every color in the spectrum was stacked, one on top of the next. It looked like it started in Hafar al Batin and ended up somewhere in Massachusetts. Steve was sure there was a pot of gold at the end. As one color bled into the next, the rainbow softly faded away, leaving a breath of fresh air. The shifting desert wasn't accustomed to the cool clean breezes and quickly rejected them. Within seconds, the blazing sun reared its ugly head, while the soldiers sat together, each feeling alone.

Casual comments eventually arose about the spiritual experience. Nobody could articulate what they felt, it was so powerful.

The evening rolled in with a kind of serenity that only close friends could acknowledge without feeling ashamed. That night, they did just that. From the cover of a cozy camouflaged patio, two nation's soldiers sipped bitter cocktails and spoke about the wasted beauty of the desert. Steve felt a warmth generate throughout his body. It was happiness, a sweet taste of pure contentment. They had spent a full day playing games with men of a distant land. Though now, the British weren't just men, they were genuine friends. Steve recognized their refined behavior, their gentle mannerisms and the etiquette of blue-blooded royalty, but beneath, there was more. There was death. He could see the ice water flowing through their veins. He had witnessed the same look on the faces of murderers in the prison. It was in their eyes. Each pair were shallow pools of hatred, rage and a hunger to exterminate life. Ironically, they were men who also appreciated the simplest beauties. In such a time and place, however, it didn't matter. He accepted their friendship, without conditions, thanked his new friends and said goodbye.

Two days passed and the Second was perched on Barter Hill. The traffic was picking up when Dennis yelled out, "Hey, it's our friends. They're heading north!"

Steve stood at the crest of the hill and snapped an American salute. Most returned their inverted version, but the vehicles were moving in a hurry. With the fluttering flag of the United Kingdom leading their way, Steve silently wished for their success and their health. Then, he did a double take.

One of his good-natured soccer buddies was urinating out of the rear of a truck when the rapid convoy stopped abruptly. It then sped up equally fast. The accordion effect caused the man to be thrown from the truck. In the limited visibility caused by billows of flying dust, the following truck ran him over. It tossed his body beneath its axles like a rag doll. Steve instinctively screamed out. They all did. It was too late. As the boys helplessly watched, the old chap's body was twisted and mangled under four sets of tires. The chaotic convoy was finally halted. Steve sprinted toward the base of the hill. The man's comrades threw his corpse into the back of another truck and quickly moved on. There were no tears. There was very little emotion of any kind displayed over the tragedy. If he hadn't seen it with his own eyes, Steve would have never believed these men had just lost a brother.

He was right. There was death beneath those British eyes. They saw it, they caused it, and without question, they suffered it. Climbing the hill, he lit a cigarette. Though he had just witnessed his first useless death, he realized that he didn't feel any grief over the incident either. Instead, he had finally observed something that he had expected to see plenty of. Statistically, his dead friend was only one of many expendable casualties. Tragically, it was an accident that made no sense. The only thing that actually bothered him, was that the death seemed so completely normal. He turned to watch the rear of the convoy vanish into a cloud of dust. His British friends were making their final leg of the journey. They were going into battle. Finishing his cigarette, he wondered when the 661st would make their big move. Tossing the butt into the wind, he looked at Dennis and said, "I bet we don't go for another four weeks."

Dennis merely shrugged. It was clear that they controlled very little of what went on around them.

The Dream Team proudly displays the flag that will mark their territory in Saudi Arabia and Iraq.

Chapter 7

Hell – through a Soldier's Eyes

A few more boring, uneventful nights passed before the Second Squad was back on duty. With the three Humvees parked on the ridge of Barter Hill, Steve looked down at the ammo dump. Most of the munitions had already been transported to the front. With the exception of a token number of soldiers, the entire area was deserted. Everyone had pulled up stakes and headed north. Searching the interior of Bug Light for another pack of smokes, he located his lost watch. It was still working. The time was 8:35 P.M., the date, February 23. Finding a brand new pack, he tossed the watch back onto the floor. Except for the frustrating feeling that they were serving time, time was irrelevant. The date was also insignificant. As the evening progressed, however, Steve learned that February 23, 1991 was forcefully ushering in another milestone in his life. It was a turning point from which there was no return. Danger stowed away in the shadows, while death was less patient. The Grim Reaper was waiting to claim the hardened and tormented souls of fighting men. It was the eve of the ground war.

Lying on the warm hood, he stared into the black sky. As his cigarette smoke drifted upward, it was carried away by a slight northern wind. Concealed in darkness, in much the same way, elite ground troops moved silently over the border of Iraq. Dual-propped Chinooks and the fierce Apache gunships were hidden in the cover of a starless sky, and flew all through the night.

Bouncing sonar waves off of the desert floor, they flew blindly, using the terrain as their highway. They hovered dangerously low and were virtually undetectable by Iraqi radar. Even the boys couldn't see them. Their whining motors, however, announced that they were going to work.

Steve gazed back up at the murky sky. He saw what appeared to be distant stars rotating in circles. They were A.W.A.C.S. aircraft flying high above the light cloud cover. Their job was to jam radio signals, radar waves, all enemy communications. Normally used in support of ground operations, they were the last clue he needed. The time was drawing near. The U.S. Army and Marine Corps were getting ready to flex their muscles. It was time to finish off Iraq. Steve turned up the volume of the army radio and waited. The call didn't take long.

Tony Rosini, the bearer of all news, finally called out to his people.

"Pack it up, First Platoon. You are ordered to abort all present missions and immediately report back to base camp! The apple is red. I say again, the apple is red!"

At last, the time was at hand. Tony's idiotic code meant they were entering the ground war. There was no more waiting and worrying about the future. There was no more wondering.

Rounding up the squad, Steve placed his hand into the center of the huddle. In silence, one hand after another was placed upon it. From nerves, most were covered in sweat, but each was held firmly in place. He gazed into the eyes of each of his friends. There was fear, but there was also a silent promise offered by each. Do or die, they were in it together. Though no words could have ever expressed the group's feelings, Pat screamed out, "Let's get some!"

With confidence, Steve led his friends back to camp. During the short trip, Armed Forces radio played the same motivational words, over and over. It was the voice of General Norman Schwartzkopf, successfully inspiring his troops. "You are the thunder and lightning of Desert Storm!" he roared. The message boosted everyone's morale. Even Steve got caught up in the camaraderie, though he also pondered the recent eviction notice from the Kingdom of Saudi Arabia. Smiling over the recent change in events, he decided he was ready, or at least as ready as he'd ever be.

Second Squad pulled into Camp Lois and found a good part of the mobile unit already dismantling itself. Private Tripp positioned Bug Light's headlamps to face The Dream Team's tents. Steve and the boys tore down their old houses. The work went quickly, but it was still a pain. Loading the last tent into the rear of Chuck's trailer, Steve joked, "This sucks!"

The Overlord grinned. "Become attached to the place, have you?"

"No, it's not that," said Steve, "I've always hated moving."

The friends shared a laugh and headed for Operations. It was time to get their marching orders.

The mission was clear, concise and easy enough. Captain Wall advised, "We've been ordered to travel in a wedge formation, approximately five miles behind the Third Armored Brigade. Any Iraqis found alive and moving, capture them, then Operations will transport them back to the rear for interrogation purposes. That's it people. We've been tasked with the collection of enemy prisoners of war, or E.P.W.s. Let's grab our share, set up camp when we get further instructions and cover each other out there!"

She finished and looked up to field questions. There were none. She was reading the instructions directly off of a piece of paper. She knew less about what was happening than any of them. Leaving the tent, Steve and Chuck shook hands.

"Well, this is it, brother," said Chuck.

Steve nodded. "For once and for all, let's get this shit over with!"

Within minutes, they were moving. Steve placed the headphones onto his head to hear the radio traffic. There was no reason to alarm everyone else in the vehicle. If they needed to know something, he would tell them. Ignorance usually meant bliss. Looking over his shoulder, he watched as Camp Lois disappeared into the distance. There were only three tents left standing. The rest were being moved to the unknown. Looking toward the north, he locked and loaded a full magazine, then turned the rifle's selector knob to semi-automatic. It was dawn.

Saddam Hussein had sworn it would take the Americans months to cross the breach, a tall berm of sand. It had taken hours, and it only took that long only because the 1st Infantry had utilized armored bulldozers to lead the attack. The Iraqis carefully arranged rows of lethal obstacles. These proved no match for good old-fashioned American ingenuity. The large, bulky machines buried every barrier within their path. The fields of barbed and razor wire were easily trampled. The land mines, which littered the desert, exploded within the steel buckets of the dozers. The Allied Forces moved fast, crushing the first of three Iraqi lines of defense. The enemy had been dug in for weeks. Now, they sat totally entrenched within their fighting positions. As if they weren't even there, the American war machine rolled right over them. Relatively unopposed, the U.S. Army stormed in, discovering that they had overestimated the enemy. Even the dreaded oil trenches were quickly plowed over with tons of sand. This created a hellish grave of man-made quicksand for those caught beneath. Many Iraqi soldiers drowned at the bottom of those greasy pits. Soon after, the 661st M.P. Company was called forward.

Behind the safety of countless tanks that valiantly traveled abreast across the great desert, the visibility was extremely limited. It didn't last. In a whirlwind of flying dust, Bug Light finally crossed the breach. They entered Iraq. There they witnessed the after-effects of 41 days of uninterrupted bombing. It was as if someone had raised the curtain to hell.

The land was strewn with unexploded bombs. The ones that did hit their targets left hundreds of destroyed tanks and artillery pieces lying about. As far as the eye could see, tons of scrap metal had been torn from the war machines and catapulted into the open desert. It was obvious. The Arabian Desert had been used as a testing ground for every new weapon in the American arsenal. It looked like an old military junkyard, but there was something more. Death. Steve saw the carnage. Driving at no more than five miles per hour, he observed his first Iraqi corpse.

The man's upper body was lying half out of a destroyed T-72 Russian tank. As they got closer, Steve realized that the soldier had met an agonizing ending. He had burned to death. His hair was completely singed off. His entire body was charred from head-to-toe, and his black skin was raised and cracked. What little uniform did remain, was melted flush to his body. The man had actually cooked in his own fat and the smell of burnt flesh caused Steve to gag. Cautiously passing the wreckage, he saw that the corpse no longer had a lower body. It was blown away with most of the tank. "What the fuck?" Steve asked. Tripp never answered. His eyes were glazed over from shock. The scene was savagely grotesque, but proved common for the first few hours of the ground war. Over the radio, someone blurted, "Did you see that one on the left, he looks done. Cajun style!" Tripp looked like he was ready to vomit.

It immediately became clear that while Hussein chose to sit out the air campaign, his people were being annihilated in masses. The Iraqi people bore the brunt for their ruthless dictator and, like all victims of war, they paid with gallons upon gallons of their own blood. There was a massacre.

Through outrageous aggression, Hussein had provoked an unforgiving world. The plundering, torture and terror could not be tolerated. No matter the price, Iraq had to be ejected from Kuwait. The deadly chess game was unfolding as planned. Remembering the Vietnam experience, America insured a decisive victory. With a revolting astonishment, Steve observed the magnitude of the stupendous defeat.

Throughout the first day, The Dream Team kept their distance behind the iron killing machines. Their jobs proved easy. There were no Enemy Prisoners of War to be found. There were no survivors anywhere. Every Iraqi soldier was toasted and left partially disintegrated within their steel caskets. As the day progressed, Steve felt relieved. Most of the fighting was already done. After seeing one dead soldier after another, however, he started to wonder how the heavy losses were inflicted. From smart bombs to hell-fire missiles, America had unleashed all of her fury upon Iraq. This not only maimed its Army, but nearly decimated it. But there was more. Every corpse was burnt to a crisp, while the crippled equipment was covered with a white powder. Each similar scene sent more discomfort up his spine. The burns were obviously caused by chemicals. The powder was some type of residue. He didn't like the looks of it. He detested all the death, but he also started to question whether Allied troops were being placed in danger.

As they drove, the Allies received relatively no resistance. Hussein forced the unwilling to defend his crimes. Unlike the American force, which was completely volunteer, the majority of the enemy force consisted of civilians. These farmers, shepherds and laymen made up the first two lines of defense. They were penetrated with ease. The amount of casualties left behind was catastrophic. In such a time and place, it didn't matter. They were wearing uniforms. It was war. There was no choice but to destroy, or be destroyed. The American force was determined that the latter wasn't even a remote possibility. They forged on. Throughout the fighting, Hussein's only true soldiers, five divisions of the elite Republican Guard, elected to retreat like scared rabbits. Their chain of command was collapsing from within. They were already beaten. It was only a matter of time before the surrender.

With little rest and less instruction, the 661st played follow the leader. Like Bedouin Indians, they found themselves homeless, wandering the trackless desert in search of prisoners. There were none. There was only death. With Kuwait to their east, they continued north toward the Euphrates River Valley. At one point, the map indicated a place called As Samawah on their west flank. Steve figured that they must have missed the landmark. There was nothing there but sand.

Night melted into day, while they turned east toward An Nasiriya. They saw nothing but desolate land. It was the fourth morning since the start of the ground war. Steve looked toward Kuwait and saw billows of thick black smoke envelope the sky. Before retreating, Hussein had ignited over 500 oil wells. The inferno created a hell on earth, while the smoke formed a man-made eclipse of the sun. He stepped out of the vehicle, lit a cigarette and looked out onto the dark morning. The vulgar scene was an appropriate symbol of the days of senseless destruction. In the end, even the beautiful sky was destroyed.

It took four days, or a mere 100 hours, before the ground war was ceased. History was made. In triumph, Kuwait was liberated, while Hussein was humiliated before the whole world. An unconditional withdrawal was ordered. This time, he wasn't in the position to ignore the instructions. Politically, the sadistic demon was slain. In reality, unlike thousands of his own people, he still lived.

America's moral crusade was complete. On February 28, 1991, Iraq surrendered. The rest was damage control. The only thing left was to pick up the pieces. It was then that the boys were truly called upon. While the world celebrated euphorically, The Dream Team's work was just beginning.

Operation Desert Storm proved different from any other war. Technology had claimed victory in one battle after the other. Unlike other wars, machines had exterminated most of the enemy. There was no hand to hand combat. Most soldiers didn't even need to fire their sand-plugged rifles. The art of killing was more advanced. To some degree, the boys were spared pain. The Dream Team didn't travel the Highway of Death in Kuwait, nor did they take part in the battles of Khafji or Medina Ridge. Yet, in four long days, they had still experienced it all. They had seen war and witnessed enough death for ten lifetimes. Then, only when the war was won, did they begin to face their own battles.

It was the fifth day since they entered Iraq. Although 18,000 Iraqis surrendered within the first hours of the war, Steve didn't see one. The 661st continued driving around the killing fields, discovering that all of their potential prisoners were fried. Not one Iraqi corpse could be forced to offer any intelligence information. Then, Steve spotted his first white flag. Four walking skeletons were waving it nervously.

Flanking Chuck's Humvee, Steve and his team jumped out. Each aimed his rifle at the heads of their enemy. For a good ten seconds, they held their aim, while the Iraqis screamed, cried and pleaded for mercy in their foreign tongue. Horror darted from their dark eyes. Looking over the front sight of his rifle, Steve realized that their first prisoners looked like anything but an enemy. They were no more than racks of bone covered by leather-like skin. Dropping to their knees, the Iraqis began to whine and pray. Doug and Pat quickly searched them. Confident that they were unarmed, the boys dropped their aim. The Iraqis continued to cry, only their tears turned to joy. They were saved — saved from starvation, dehydration and Hussein's reign of terror. It was pitiful. One of the men handed Tripp a pamphlet that was dropped by an American bomber. It was a list of Arabic instructions on how to properly surrender. Each man had precisely followed the directions.

Calling Operations for the transport of four, Steve broke out some water and four M.R.E.s. The prisoners ate like it was their first meal in weeks. It probably was. Watching them devour the meal, he peered deeply into their eyes. They were people, not animals. They were no different from the Americans. They were just on the losing end of a bad situation. They didn't want to fight. It was clear by their meek behavior. Even if they were aware of the reasons for the great conflict, not one of them felt it personal. Steve couldn't hate them, as he had been taught. Watching his friends offer more food and water, he saw that they felt the same. Cornish was wrong about killing them all. The real enemy was Saddam Hussein. All hatred was reserved for him. If Hussein had been one of the four, Steve would have assassinated the tyrant himself. He would have shot him in cold blood.

As the four prisoners were loaded into the rear of a truck, they thanked the Americans in their own language. Steve returned to Bug Light and looked over at Dennis. He shrugged. "They were a little different from the inmates back home. I don't think I would have given them any water if they weren't."

Dennis smirked. Rolling his eyes, he replied, "It makes you wonder. We probably should have dropped food and water rather than bombs. Who knows, maybe we'd be home by now?"

Left with that thought, Steve took off into the untamed desert. The search for more prisoners was on.

For the following two days, herds of Iraqis came out of hiding. There was no more bombing and no more shooting. It was safe to surrender. They all looked alike. Some were missing limbs, eyes, even their spirits. They were all starving. Due to the increasing numbers, they were quickly considered refugees. They found food, water, medical treatment, but most importantly, a sanctuary behind American lines. Most were civilians, caught in the clash of combatants. With no homes to return to, they were happy to be sent to the overcrowded enemy prisoner of war camps. The longer the stay, the better. Upon surrendering, their own war-torn country didn't want them any longer. The numbers piled up.

Before long, the heavy flow of deserters diminished, and the 661st was given coordinates for their new base camp. It was time to find their home. It was time to get some much-needed rest and settle into some sort of routine. The news was invigorating.

Within hours, the camp was erected south of An Nasiriya, only miles from where the 1st Infantry Division had made camp. It was rumored that the 1st, or Big Red One had sent scouts as far as Karbala. What was known, however, was that the 1st was considered the front line in Iraq.

Although it strongly resembled Camp Lois, it felt like anything but. Steve quickly decided that it wasn't home at all. While he unloaded some gear, Tony stuck his head into the tent. "Stevie-boy, the captain called for a meeting. It's time for our new mission." Leaving the mess, he followed Tony out.

Arriving a few minutes late, they sat in on a briefing that was already in progress. The captain stopped, shot a bad look toward The Dream Team's tardy representatives and continued.

"Okay, people, for the past week, we've been riding on the current of the Third Armored Brigade. That's over. No more surfing. We're on our own now, sink or swim." Clearing her throat, she sat down on a footlocker, removed her cap and broke the news. "In support of the 14th M.P. Brigade, we've been tasked with a complex mission and a lot of ground to cover. Each platoon will patrol 120 miles of Main Supply Routes, with land mines littering both sides. The collection of E.P.W.s will continue, but from now on, we must concentrate on keeping all friendly forces out of the miles of mine fields! There are also bunkers out there, most of them booby trapped. It's our job to keep everybody out of them." Standing up, she finished, "This means that tomorrow each platoon will be split in half. One half to cover the first 60 miles, the other half, to patrol the second. For tonight, however, everybody gets a full eight hours of sleep. You've all earned it and deserve the rest. I'll see you back here tomorrow morning, 0600 hours." Without saying goodnight, the commander exited the tent.

Returning to The Dream Team's cluster of shelters, Tony, Steve and Chuck conducted their own informal meeting. The decisions proved to be the greatest misfortune Steve could have ever encountered. Chuck was taking his own squad and half of the third. Steve, his own, and the other half of the third. This meant that for the remainder of their stay in Iraq, Steve would no longer see Chuck or Ryan, his most trusting and supportive friends. Fortunately, he retained Dennis, Pat, Doug and Keith.

After advising the platoon, he retired to his tent for a few hours of hibernation. Clearing off his cluttered cot, he picked up his harmonica, considered a tune, then decided against it. Throwing the instrument back into his duffel bag, the chrome mouthpiece fell to the bottom. It was never to be seen or played again. Things had changed. The rest of the group waited for their bedtime lullaby. It never came. They eventually dozed off, knowing that things were different now. Their vacation had ended a week before. Iraq was anything but home.

Just before nodding off, Steve picked up a letter sent from his mom and opened it. His sister's hand prints, which had brought such happiness in Saudi Arabia, now brought sorrow and pain. He couldn't think about home. It felt like he hadn't been there, nor seen his family in years. That was a whole different lifetime. At that moment, he decided he wouldn't read any more from home. Grabbing a stack of white lined paper, he began to write. He wrote three months worth of letters and assigned them all fictitious dates. There was nothing good to report and he needed the distance. Every few days, he'd mail one out. His family didn't have to know. It was best that only he knew the truth.

Closing his heavy eyelids, he was asleep only minutes when he awakened in a struggle for air. Feeling suffocated, he realized it was another anxiety attack. It was a severe one and the first since his introduction to them in Saudi Arabia. Leaping off his cot, he tried to get his breathing under control. It was no use. His throat, his chest, everything felt constricted. Again, it felt as if he were suffering a heart attack, only much more intense than he remembered. He walked rapidly away from the tent and concealed his terror within the shadows. His mind sent a horrifying monsoon of fear and panic pulsating through his body. It was agonizing, traumatizing, then completely over in 15 minutes. Composing himself enough to return to the tent, he jumped back in bed. He was determined to keep the scary little secret to himself. No matter how bad, how intense, he wasn't going to tell anyone. He vowed to be strong.

It took two solid hours before his fearful mind gave in to his exhausted body. His life had dramatically changed one week before. Since arriving in Iraq, the boys had been at full throttle. He felt normal, almost good, but only because there were valid reasons for all of the hype. With the many dangers, the destruction and death, everyone's adrenaline was peaking. After seven days, though, it was time to relax. He couldn't. His body was still stuck in the alert mode. His most primitive instincts for basic survival had been triggered. During times of trouble, he felt normal. During times of peace, however, he hardly functioned normally. His little secret was tearing him up inside, one brutal piece at a time.

Before the sun rose, Chuck and his 14-man crew, began their attack on the unfamiliar terrain. They set out on a quest for a satellite camp positioned at least 60 miles north. Watching their vehicles vanish into the early dawn, Steve's shaky hands sipped British tea. He tried to forget the nightmare he had recently lived through. He tried to convince himself that it was a new day, filled with promise. Analyzing his dilemma, he promised himself to keep busy. That was the key. In three days, he would be relieving Chuck's crew. In the meantime, he and his people would scout out the land surrounding base camp.

The next three days reflected their daily lives for the next three months. The Dream Team discovered that their frequent engagements with the Iraqi people were never truly anticipated, usually proved painful and were always impossible to forget.

Receiving last minute instructions from an unreliable Tony Rosini, Steve hardly listened. The information would soon be forgotten — any orders, totally ignored. Still, Tony rambled on.

As Tony repeated something unimportant, Steve saw a small white pickup race into the base camp. Skidding to a stop, the Iraqi driver found over 20 rifles aimed at his head. One of those belonged to Steve. He cautiously approached the unwelcome visitor.

Before he reached the truck, the man jumped out and threw his hands into the air. He was terrified, but not from the weapons being pointed at him. There was something more. Steve carefully approached the stranger, while Dennis thoroughly searched him. He was clean. Steve dropped his aim, while his attention was diverted to the rear of the truck. In a heart-stopping instant, he understood the reason for the man's impatient pleas for help. There was a small child, lying in the bed of the truck. The girl's right arm was missing and her right leg was severed in half. She was lying in a pool of her own blood. Steve threw Tripp his rifle and screamed "medic." He lifted the broken doll out of the bed liner. His desire to save a life became so much greater than his wish to take one.

Softly placing her fragile frame on the ground, he could tell she was still alive, though barely. Her big brown eyes stared in horror. He removed his shirt and called for more bandages. Pressure dressings were applied in an attempt to stop the profuse bleeding. Within seconds, they became saturated with the thick crimson blood. Her tiny lungs filled with fluid. The gurgling sounds made her eyes widen more, then mercifully, she went into shock. It was an eternity before the medic jumped in. While Steve, Dennis and Pat worked on her, they waited for a medevac. Besides losing two limbs, the girl also suffered a broken sternum. This caused her rib cage to float outside of her chest, so C.P.R. proved impossible. They were losing her and they knew it. They worked faster, but to no avail. Steve stared into her innocent eyes and saw the reflection of his own baby sisters. Remembering Darlene and Jenny, he knew she was no different from they. She was a beautiful little girl, standing on the threshold of death. With great pain, he could feel the exact moment when her unblemished spirit drifted out of her wretched body. She was gone and, though Steve knew it was a blessing, he stood and apologized to the girl's father. Steve felt the loss as well. The man humbly nodded.

The tiny child was wrapped in a green, woolen blanket and handed back to her father. To everyone's wonder, the farmer appeared elated. He lifted the corpse toward the sky, released a high-pitched, joyous scream, then threw her lifeless body into the back of the truck. Smiling and waving, he finally drove away. In shock, Steve lit a cigarette and tried to understand the happiness. He couldn't. The culture was so different. Perhaps the man was only expressing his relief over the end of his child's brutal suffering. It was still too bizarre. Sulking near the tent, he was approached by Tony Rosini. Smirking, the giant asked, "Don't tell me that the death of that little sand nigger's gonna bother you? It's war and kids die!"

Flicking his cigarette over Tony's head, he returned the smirk. "I'll tell you what, fruitcup, when shit like that stops bothering me, then I'll know that I've become as deranged as you. Until then, I hope it rips my frigin' heart out!"

Steve stepped into the musty tent and silently mourned the violent death of a pure and innocent life. She was so defenseless, so undeserving. It was more senseless death. Iraqi or American, a kid was a kid. The grief was evidence he hadn't lost his own soul. There was great comfort in that alone.

Only minutes after the cruel interruption, he headed out of base camp, with five Humvees in tow. Though he had avoided another panic attack, a whole new emotion arrived. It was depression.

As war made no time for emotions, the boys reconned their area of responsibility. Just yards from the camp, Steve was awed by the amount of land mines, just lying in the sand, waiting to be tripped. There were thousands marked by engineering tape. He was sure there were thousands more concealed within the fine powder. The soldiers spent most of the day playing run-down. They drove up and back a 60-mile stretch of road until

Steve determined the best locations for the platoon's communication relay stations and traffic control points. Once he was satisfied with the breaks in the long stretch of road, they returned to base camp at early dusk. Their 14-hour workday was complete.

Another anxious night was finally brought to a close, while the morning started with a bang. It was the distinct bang of a sniper's rifle.

The radio yelled for assistance. "Base . . . this is Oscar 19. We've takin' fire at mile marker 133. I say again . . . we've taken small arms fire at 133." Members of the third platoon needed help.

In no more than five minutes, Second Squad responded to the scene. Upon arrival, Steve observed an Iraqi sprawled out on the sand. The man was smoking a pipe. Jumping out of Bug Light, rifle in hand, he asked for details.

In quick, nervous chatter, a young soldier disclosed, "We were driving by when we took fire." Pointing to his team leader, he continued, "Joe stopped, took cover, then returned fire on the sniper. I saw the muzzle flash, then the son of a bitch just collapsed to the ground, wounded. The next thing I know, he puts his hand into the pocket of his cloak and comes out with some hash. He's been smoking the shit ever since!"

Steve listened to the end of the story, while Pat approached the gunman. The soldier wasn't handled with any care. He was placed face down, searched, then forced onto his knees. Looking back at Steve, Pat insisted, "We'd better clear out of here. I didn't find any weapon. I think he's unarmed!" Steve knew exactly what his friend was saying. Pat was a good cop in civilian life and made an equally competent soldier. There was going to be an investigation into this one. The boys wanted no part of it. The war was over and everyone was liable for their actions. This shooting was going to be a tough one to explain.

The remainder of the day was spent patrolling the dangerous roads. Weeks before, the Allied engineers had cut the roads into the shape of a snake. It made perfect sense at the time, but since the threat of an enemy air attack was removed, the winding trails created a dangerous ride. Yet, it was important to be able to drive them blindly. The sense of sight couldn't always be depended on. With the blowing winds and dark nights, there were many trips driven by memory. One mistake, one wrong turn could easily spell out an explosive death. Everyone paid attention.

On the third afternoon, Steve was looking forward to seeing his old friends again when his team happened upon a large, beat-up truck. The rear was loaded with passengers. Some were in uniform. In a calm, professional tone, he ordered, "Okay, people. L-frame ambush!" As if practiced a thousand times, each Humvee dove in and swarmed the confused Iraqis. The unidentified vehicle was halted and covered toward the front and side.

Through tunnel vision, Steve watched the vehicle stop. Something was different though. He could sense the danger. By the way his friends reacted, they all sensed it too. Three machine guns were pointed directly at the Iraqis. Concentrating on the passengers in the rear, Steve noticed that every one of them threw their hands up, all of them but two. He pulled his .45 caliber pistol out of its shoulder holster and rushed the tailgate. With the help of Pat, Dennis and Doug, he began throwing the potential killers out of the truck. As he tossed the first, he was surprised at how light they were. Like small rag-dolls, one after the other flopped onto the sand. Making his way to the front, he came face-to-face with one of the tough guys. The stubborn bastard still refused to raise his hands, so he helped him. With an open hand, he cracked the soldier across the face, causing him to fall backward. As the furious Iraqi gained his balance, he found himself staring down the barrel of Steve's pistol. The lifeless piece of cold steel was now an extension of his spirit and the Iraqi knew it. He saw fear in his enemy's black eyes.

Steve also felt fear, but a different fear. He was only seconds from taking a human life. With the hammer cocked, his enemy's actions dictated whether or not he lived. Steve didn't care either way. The soldier was still thinking about his options when he struck him again. The second blow to the face assisted him in making up his mind. Very slowly, he placed his trembling hands into the air. He was ready to go peacefully. Steve's adrenaline was pumping hard and he was seeing red. At that very moment, he learned he could kill. The act itself would be rather easy. He was going home. No matter what, he was going home. Being slow to the trigger would never be the reason for his death. The Iraqi soldier saw every thought in his eyes and became completely cooperative. It was too late. Steve had different plans for the fierce Iraqi fighter. It was time for a lesson in humility.

While half the crew searched the truck, the other half attempted to gain some order among their chaotic prisoners. Jumping off the tailgate with his new friend, Steve decided to speed up the process. It always amazed him. Although the Iraqis never understood the English language, everyone felt they could relay their information by screaming. The louder they yelled, the more their instructions should have been understood. It never worked. This time was no different. The only way to solve the problem was through visual aids. People understood demonstrations, especially when they were violent and painful. Steve was grateful for his enthusiastic volunteer. It was an easy philosophy: If the big bully followed the directions, while losing a little self-esteem in the process, then they'd all get the life or death message.

For the third time, he left the imprint of his open hand on the man's cheek. The heavy blow brought tears to his enemy's eyes. Everyone froze. He then stiff-armed the soldier's head into the sand. It took a few times before the ignorant fool realized it was time to play Ostrich. The entire episode wasn't pretty, nor was it fun, but it was the safest way to establish law and order. Nobody would be shooting Iraqis if their heads were buried in the sand. More importantly, there was a slimmer chance any of the boys would get hurt. That was the goal. They bound each set of trembling hands with plastic flex cuffs and conducted a thorough search. They quickly discovered that they were right to have taken precautions.

The truck was loaded with weapons. From rifles to hand grenades, the 14 prisoners of war, now crying for their lives, could have easily started a small war of their own. With the amount of hardware on hand, they could have shed a great deal of American blood. Steve understood why his foe had such a difficult time deciding his next move. He was sitting right on top of a loaded AK-47. Steve threw the enemy rifle into a pile of many and lit a cigarette. The adrenaline was making him high.

Chuck's crew was summoned to assist in the transport of the prisoners. They were treated just as kindly in the hands of the Overlord. Loading them all into the back of an American truck, Steve shot his Iraqi friend a wink. The man didn't smile.

Pat joked, "My God, if looks could kill!"

Everyone laughed.

"It looks like Sparky, here, is still pissed off. He should be kissing your white ass. He almost left here in a bag!"

Pat was right. He knew how Steve felt, because he handled the other tough guy the same way.

Before they left, the boys rolled them for all of the cash they were carrying. It was actually funny. The armed robbery meant nothing, as the war had dropped the value of the Iraqi Dinar through the floor. Besides, where they were going, there was no need for currency. The weird bills were shipped back to the states as souvenirs, with hopes that nobody would ever have the chance to spend them. Laughing at the thievery, Doug asked, "I don't see Iraq becoming a hot tourist spot any time soon, do you?"

Steve shook his head. The soldiers all laughed and headed home. It was time to switch posts.

During the lengthy trip, Steve contemplated just how close he had come to taking a human life. He was faced with a decision that few men ever encounter. In the real world, the irretrievable act of murder was considered immoral and punishable by a life sentence in prison, or even death. In this bizarre world, the same act could earn a man a medal, while easily elevating his military status to hero. In an attempt to put the frightening experience behind him, he turned up the radio. The questions of morality were leaving a queasy feeling in the pit of his stomach. He knew he had been just inches from crossing the line. He turned up the volume again. It took some time before the churning within his guts subsided.

Chuck took over at base camp, while Steve and his crew ventured out to the satellite compound. Pulling in, Steve chuckled at the large sign that greeted them. It read: THE PONDEROSA. They still had their sense of humor.

There was only one tent set up, with a picnic bench in the rear. The cozy patio was covered with some old, shredded camouflage netting and the entire camp was surrounded by razor wire. Though it was in the middle of nowhere, Chuck chose to set up a perimeter. It was hilarious. Taking a walk around, Steve saw it all within three minutes. It felt even less like home.

The Ponderosa was a place of excruciating boredom and 101 panic attacks. It was the most desolate, sorrowful place on earth, and it epitomized Steve's every thought and feeling. Yet, for three days at a time, it was home. Steve despised every minute spent there.

And so the routine went, three days here, and three days there. There was either nothing to do, absolutely nothing, or there was everything all at once. One minute, they were at a standstill and the next, their bodies were speeding at 100 miles per hour. Nothing changed. There was an excessive amount of senseless death. The majority of those casualties were innocent Bedouin children who played where they shouldn't have. Land mines didn't discriminate. There were also encounters with more Iraqi prisoners, and there were calls for assistance at random skirmishes. Then, there were monotonous days that seemed to turn into weeks. It was a time of torment, where the searing days took their toll and the lonely nights were filled with the nightmares of 1,000 faceless victims.

Steve was mulling around the compound one afternoon when Tony approached. "Hey kid, got any plans today?"

Placing a stick of gum in his mouth, he gritted his teeth and hissed, "Yeah, I think I'll head to the mall."

Tony chuckled. Walking away, he waved Steve toward him. "In that case, you can give me a ride into Saudi Arabia. My knee's been acting up, so maybe they'll give me some pain killers. Either way, I could use the time away and, from the look of it, so could you."

"Whose vehicle?" Tony never answered. He just slid into the passenger seat of his own, A Horse With No Name.

They were making good time, and traveled down the dusty road at a fast clip. Moving along, Steve was surprised to find Tony in a giddy mood. Even stranger, he shared the older man's feelings. They joked and laughed, with only 40 miles between them and the Saudi Arabian border. Before long, the radio traffic ceased. They were out of range. Steve noticed they had been the only vehicle on the road since they left. He continued to scan the vast terrain to insure they were alone. The Republican Guard was still out on the loose in the form of soldiers who came out of hiding during the dark hours. The farther they drove, however, the less it mattered. They were only an hour from safety.

While laughing at Tony's sick humor, Steve slowed down. They hit a dust storm, a bad one. He could hardly see three feet past the windshield. In the blink of an eye, the blue sky turned a blinding orange, as the harsh winds of the open desert rearranged the landscape. With the help of hurricane winds, tons of sand leapt into the atmosphere and flew around. Maneuvering the Humvee right and left, he slowed down even more. The snake-shaped trail was one hairpin turn after another. Squinting his eyes, he concentrated and drove on.

Approximately 30 miles from the border, he heard the bang. It was a loud crash that came from the right side of the vehicle.

In super slow motion, the vehicle tipped left, toward the driver's side. The windshield cracked at the top, then spidered throughout the center. The desert spun in circles, end over end. He felt something heavy smash into the back of his bare skull. It was an army field phone, flying around aimlessly, until it found a target. The piercing pain was quickly followed by numbness. His tense body went limp. He felt as if he were being submerged in a pool of warm water. Unlike any peace he had experienced before, the sensation was heavenly. With no choice but to accept the comfort, his eyes slammed shut. In one brief moment, he watched his life play out before him like a slide show, in one vivid picture after another.

He watched himself and his brothers playing war under the protection of their trusty fortress. In their imaginary battlefields, their happy faces were proof that nobody ever got hurt. He saw other clips from his childhood. Then photos of his parents flashed. Scene after scene was displayed, reminding him of all he was, of all he'd done, of all he loved. He saw himself and Monica exchanging vows. He saw his sisters taking their first steps and speaking their first words. He watched his entire life unfold before him. He was euphoric. He was at peace.

But he didn't want to die in a Humvee accident. He fought it off with everything inside of him. He didn't want death. It wasn't his time. He fought, but the struggle was brief. There was no more pain, no more peace and no more pictures. There was only darkness.

He opened his eyes and felt a rhythmic pain surge throughout his body. His entire body throbbed, but it was his left arm and neck that caused him to groan. Attempting to lift his heavy head, his mind whirled, fogged from the pain and disoriented from the shock. Turning his head slowly, he looked down at his fingers. The only thing missing was his wedding band. Turning right, he saw the Humvee. It was almost 40 feet away, lying on its roof. It looked funny, like a helpless turtle resting on its shell. Reality struck. With all his might, he pushed himself to his knees. The Humvees motor screamed for help. It was running at full idle. Trying to clear his blurred vision, he choked on the smell of gas and oil that leaked from the wreck. He took two small, painful steps toward the Humvee, then he saw him. It was Tony.

Like a bat, his platoon sergeant hung upside down inside the wreckage. He was suspended in mid-air by a seat belt. Steve's heart jumped into his throat and started to beat wildly. Tony was in trouble. He needed help. Picking up the pace, Steve ignored his own pain. He screamed, "Get out! Tony, get out!"

Tony never moved, the motor raced faster. Without hesitation, he dove into the Humvee.

Tony was out cold. Instinctively, he unbuckled the safety belt and awkwardly pulled his friend out. He was dead weight, but he continued to drag him, hoping that he wasn't causing more damage. There was no way to tell if Tony had broken his back or neck. He wasn't even sure whether Tony was alive. He dragged faster.

A safe distance from the Humvee, he laid Tony onto the warm sand and took his pulse. The old horse was still kicking. Feeling the greatest sense of relief, he was promptly reacquainted with his own pain. The intensity made him nauseous. He felt as if he were going to pass out, but fought it off. Though he wanted nothing more, there was no time for a nap. Tony was coming out of it.

For awhile, he just sat in the sand, with Tony's head in his lap. The motor finally seized up. Tony talked in riddles. His gibberish told Steve that he was in shock. So, as the Army had trained him, he treated the symptoms accordingly.

He loosened the man's restrictive clothing and elevated his feet. He moistened Tony's lips with water. Bending over, he shaded his platoon sergeant's face from the sun. Unsure whether he could understand or not, he also began reassuring his friend. It was the biggest act of his life, but he promised, "Don't you worry, Tony. I'll get us out of this one. We'll be okay." The empty words drifted off into the lonely desert. He was overcome with guilt. He whispered, "My God. Tony, what have I done?"

Tony never answered. He just mumbled and shivered from the cold. The shiver scared Steve. It was more than 90 degrees and his friend was freezing. Removing his shirt, he covered his platoon sergeant's upper body, then headed back to the smashed Humvee. He needed a plan.

The closer he got, the more he understood. In the midst of the heavy dust storm, they had hit a boulder with the right front tire. The Humvee flipped three or four times, completely crushing the driver's side. It finally landed on its roof. The driver's side door was lying 20 feet from the scene. His spine tingled when he saw it.

It was too bizarre to be coincidental. He wasn't wearing a helmet, which allowed the telephone to knock him out. In turn, his body was thrown around at will. His seat belt would have trapped him under the weight of the wreckage, but that was never a problem. He had forgotten to put it on. The door flew off, throwing him out of the truck and away from the final landing. That was the clincher. If each factor hadn't happened, in sequence, he would have been smashed like a grape. For reasons unknown to him, he was still alive. It was no less than a miracle.

Searching the ruined interior of the wreck, his suffering mind was consumed with worry. They were in the middle of no where, with nothing but sand in all directions. There was no food and maybe enough water for six hours under the relentless sun. Worse of all, there was no communication. The antenna was buried under the wreck and though he tried again and again, it was no use. Nobody heard his pleas for help. Nobody knew they existed. The boys at base camp didn't expect them back for a whole day. There would be no search for at least that long. Helplessness welled up inside of him. Like a stranded child searching for his parents, he called for a medevac one last time. He waited. There was a terrible silence. Fighting off despair, he grabbed his rifle, a box of ammo and a ragged blanket, and returned to Tony.

In his absence, Tony had become more coherent.

"What the hell happened?"

He explained the accident, adding an apology at the end.

Tony raised his hands toward the sky. He muttered, "You worry too much, Stevie-boy. Just get us the hell out of here!"

Steve smiled, then lied straight into his friend's frightened eyes. "No sweat, boss. I made the call. Help should be here in no time."

Tony said nothing. He just grinned weakly, then returned to unconsciousness.

Rocking him back and forth, Steve looked over at the wreck. The hopelessness tore at him. Looking down at his older friend, he knew it was better that Tony didn't know the truth — a truth which meant probable death. There was nothing he could do. They were both in rough shape. Traveling on foot was impossible. The radio was no longer operable. The only thing to do was wait. He hated that lack of control. As the steady breezes covered he and Tony with sand, Steve felt as if they were sitting in an hourglass, with their time running out. With all Allied forces heading farther north, the chances of someone driving past were very slim. Sitting somewhere on the southern tip of Iraq, under a drift of powdered sugar, they were in big trouble.

The two longest hours of Steve's life passed without change. With each passing minute, the outcome looked more bleak. Tony was in and out of consciousness, unaware of time. Steve sat alone, wincing from his physical pain and struggling with the mental torment. It was too much. His platoon sergeant was getting worse, and there was nothing more he could do. He feared Tony's death more than his own and was carrying the guilt for both. Then, as if seeing a mirage appear on the horizon, he struggled to his quivering feet. Waving his good arm in the air, he realized it was no delusion. There was a vehicle heading straight for them. It was another miracle. Help was on its way. For the first time during the entire episode he cried.

The Humvee was identical to their own. The driver pulled up slowly, hesitantly. He was an older man, with a bloated white face and green eyes that showed panic. Steve stepped in front, causing the rolling vehicle to finally stop. He approached the driver's side window and pleaded.

"Sergeant, I need your help. A few hours ago, I flipped our Humvee and my platoon sergeant is in pretty bad shape. I have the call signs and frequency needed to bring in a medevac. I just need to use your radio for one minute?"

The man's eyes widened. He began to stutter, "I can't. I have to find my convoy . . . I lost them . . . I can't!" He completed his shocking response, hit the accelerator and sped off.

Consumed with a murderous rage, Steve drew his .45 caliber pistol and aimed. With two pounds of pressure deciding whether the man lived or died, he slowly dropped his sights. He couldn't kill the coward. The American stranger was lost, and from the direction he was traveling, he was probably heading straight toward death's door.

Steve dropped to his knees and wept. Why would the man refuse to help. Filled with fury, abandonment, and regret, he thought about the situation. Throughout his life, he had always tried to do the right thing, and be there for anyone when they needed him. The first time he ever extended his hand for help he desperately needed, that hand was batted away, and he was left for dead. In two short minutes, one jellyfish of a man had erased his faith in mankind. With everything inside of him, he hated the son of a bitch, and regretted not pulling the trigger. Ironically, since arriving in the Middle East, that coward was the only person he had truly wanted to exterminate. He had his chance and blew it. As a result, he and Tony were as good as dead. He began to wonder whether it was he who was the coward.

Time crawled by, though it was irrelevant. Tony was dying from his wounds and Steve was all but dead inside. He continued to console his trusting friend, while compassionately stroking what little hair was left. Tony spoke in riddles, crying every once in a while. Vietnam was creeping up behind him. Steve watched as he tried to fight off the horrifying dreams.

Steve sat deserted, stranded in the wild. He had never felt so broken and alone. Tony was there, but only in the physical sense. Steve sobbed in guilt, despair, even self-pity. He didn't want to die alone.

The hand of an angel rested upon Steve's shoulder. Looking up, he stared into the face of the blackest man he had ever seen. The soldier bent down and gently whispered, "Lay down, Sarge. I'm gonna take care of you now. It's all over. We're gonna get you out of here."

He collapsed onto the hot sand. He could finally rest. His tortured mind had been put at ease. Catching the twinkle in the medic's saintly eyes, he believed every word the stranger said. With all his heart, he trusted him. Years of ignorant bigotry and prejudice, which had been learned in the prison, were erased in an instant.

Sergeant Jason Matthews, the medic, called for a chopper, then worked feverishly. Steve was strapped to a long-board, while his pants and shoulder holster were cut off of him. His arm was splinted and his neck, placed into a bulky brace. An I.V. was administered and through it all, he slipped in and out of the real world. Awakening again, he felt cold. Gazing up, he saw the shadow of a man standing over him, blocking the sun's heat. It was the Chaplain, praying. Steve's dog tags indicated he was a Christian, and he was receiving his Last Rights. It was a strange feeling, though he knew that the kind man was wasting his time. He hadn't lived through something so bizarre, only to die.

As the medevac chopper flew in for the pick-up, Steve heard Tony cursing the Army priest. "Get away from me," he screamed, "I was shot up twice in the Nam and you think that a fuckin' auto accident is gonna end it for me?"

Steve smiled again. Tony was going to be okay.

Tony screamed once more, only this time in pain. A second medic, trying to remove his pants, had cut too far and snipped into his scrotum.

With an apology, he informed his irate patient, "That's gonna require a stitch or two."

Tony went ballistic. The laughter made Steve's body ache.

Sergeant Matthews covered him from head to toe with a warm foil wrap. The incoming chopper kicked up a mountain of the powder with its giant blades. The medic placed his entire upper body over Steve's face, shielding him from the blowing sand. Touching down, the airborne ambulance's motor was cut down to a high-pitched whine. It was the most welcome screech Steve had ever heard. Four men lifted up the canvas litter and at a sprint, he was rushed into the helicopter. Looking back at Matthews, he yelled, "Thank You," though there was no way the angel could have ever heard him. The chopper was too damn loud.

With a look of urgency, Matthews ran over. He grabbed Steve's hand and placed something into the palm. With a wonderful smile, he threw a thumbs-up. The gesture gave Steve chills. When he looked up again, the man was gone.

Steve opened his hand. It was his gold wedding band, slightly deformed, but shining brightly. Goose bumps raced over his body. It was too much to believe. He had lived through it. He slid the ring back onto his finger and the chopper took to the air.

Sergeant Matthews was half right. He took care of him and got them out of there, but it wasn't over.

It was the ride of a lifetime, though neither man could enjoy it. Landing at Log Base Echo, in southwest Saudi Arabia, Steve and Tony were rushed into the nearest Evac Hospital. The doctor asked, "What is it that hurts most?"

Steve winced. "My bladder. I've gotta take a leak."

The man laughed at the honest answer before summoning a nurse for a metal pitcher. As she held the container, Steve held his penis. For the next minute or so, he relieved hours of stored urine. Finishing, he noticed four female nurses looking on. He didn't care. Embarrassment and shame were the least of his worries. Life had been rudely placed into perspective. Then, the doctor went to work.

His body was treated for bumps and bruises, sprains and small lacerations. As a result of the strange accident, he had suffered a mild concussion and a severely sprained arm.

But it was his mind that truly needed mending. As hard as he tried, though, he couldn't get the haunting picture out of his head. It was the coward who left him for dead. His heart and soul were consumed with hatred and rage; his mind, with depression. He still couldn't believe it. They wore the same uniform, came from the same military family, yet his brother-in-arms had all but served him to the vultures. Jumping down from the hospital gurney, he attempted to wipe the horrid thoughts from his mind. The vivid memories made his stomach twist and turn. Maybe I expect too much from people, was his last thought before starting his search for Tony. In a hospital so small, the quest didn't take long.

Physically, Tony was less fortunate. His weathered body had been beaten senseless and needed time to heal. Steve approached his bed and asked, "So, what's the prognosis, Doc?"

Tony grinned. In a tired, raspy tone, he answered, "Seems you took care of the knee that's been bothering me. They say it's all done. They also say I have whiplash, a concussion and an ingrown toenail."

Smiling, he waited for Steve to return the grin.

He couldn't.

Tony continued, "Steve-boy, accidents happen. It wasn't your fault. Who knows, maybe it was a blessing. Maybe they'll finally patch me up right from Vietnam?"

Steve shook his friend's hand. He hoped Tony would be taken care of. He hoped all of Tony's war wounds would finally be healed. He wished for nothing more.

Per doctor's orders, Steve was rudely asked to leave. There were still more tests to be conducted. The physician, with the crusty bedside manner, informed him, "Sergeant Rosini may have to be shipped off to Germany for surgery. We still don't know."

Thanking the doctor with a sarcastic tone, he headed for the door. Over his shoulder, he asked Tony, "Oh ... did they stitch up your pouch?"

Tony smiled and flipped him the bird. Steve walked out of the room and into the bright day. Looking around, he realized that he didn't have to search far to find others who were worse off. There were servicemen, basking in the afternoon sun, who had lost legs or arms. Most were missing a limb or two. Others displayed facial scars from artillery or mortar shrapnel. They were a group of fighting men in pretty bad shape, but Steve could only see their physical scars. Like him, most had also sustained deeper wounds. Walking out onto the compound, he decided it was time to mingle and get acquainted. Everybody was a potential friend. It was just a matter of breaking the ice. These were people he wanted to know. They had each paid a price for the liberation of Kuwait. Some, however, had paid more than others.

As he strolled over toward the mess tent, the sight of a young soldier stopped him. He could see a hint of short orange hair under the red beret, but it was the man's face that caught everyone's attention. Both of his eyes were covered with white patches. Hearing the sand crunch under heavy footsteps, he called out, "Hey, buddy, you got the time?"

Steve stopped and looked down at his wrist. He started to shake his head until he realized that a blind man had asked the question.

The soldier sensed the confusion by the short delay, and laughed.

Steve apologized, adding, "I lost my watch somewhere along the way."

"I suppose we've all lost a few things along the way," the stranger kidded. Patting the seat next to him, he gestured for Steve to join him.

He happily obliged.

After a few seconds of awkward silence, the soldier continued, "Actually, I could care less about time. I'm just content with knowing whether it's night or day. I hope you don't mind. I heard you passing by and thought it would be nice to have some company." Extending an open hand into space, he introduced himself, "I'm Sergeant Daniel Calis. My friends call me Red."

Grabbing his new friend's hand, Steve shook it firmly. "Nice to meet you, Red. I'm Steve Manchester."

Some cordial, small talk, revealed that Red had been in the Gulf for months. He was a paratrooper assigned to the 101st Airborne Unit. Working in the capacity of a scout, he was behind enemy lines long before the start of the ground war.

"My job was to bring the laser guided missiles directly onto their targets. It was incredible, precision bombing on a magnificent scale!" Pointing to his eye patches, he shrugged, "Then, sitting in the turret of a Humvee, my driver wandered into a mine field and hit a small anti-personnel mine. It was big enough to splinter the hood into my face, though. I haven't seen a damn thing since."

Steve listened attentively and felt sorry for the young warrior. Red had traveled a rough path.

He apologized for controlling the conversation, and asked Steve the reason for his hospital visit.

Almost ashamed, he started to explain the accident. Halfway through the story, another soldier took a seat and listened in. He never introduced himself, but as Steve finished, the man shook his head. "So much pain and suffering, only because America chooses to be the police of the world!"

Just as soon as the words spilled out of his mouth, Red was standing. He screamed, "You ignorant bastard. No matter how much sacrifice it takes, this is a noble cause. I took a purple heart in Panama and this is my second. It was worth it! Even if I never see again, it was all worth it!" Calming down, he added, "If America is the only country powerful enough to free the world of tyranny, then it's our job to do so. Remember, Hitler nearly exterminated an entire race before we stepped in. Six million innocent people were slaughtered before the police of the world decided to do the right thing!"

Steve swore he could see tears falling from beneath the eye patches.

Red concluded, "Besides, the Iraqis are the people who have paid for this dictator's sins, not us. We may have lost a few, but we've been very fortunate. For combat, it's been very few!" Finishing his passionate speech, he took his seat. The other soldier just walked away. His face was the color of Red's beret.

Patting his friend on the back, Steve gently whispered, "I agree with you. This is a just cause. Unfortunately, the views of some become fogged from their own pain."

Red just nodded. Someone who had paid dearly reinforced Steve's ideals. Red was blind, yet he saw better than most people.

For the longest time, the two men sat together in silence. It didn't matter if anything was said. They were just happy to be together.

Five days elapsed. While Tony was healing better than expected, Steve was winning big money at poker. During one of the games, Tony hobbled in. "Let's go, Lucky. They said I can wait for my knee surgery, so I hooked us up with a hop back to Camp Lois. Nobody knows where we've been. For all they know, we were killed."

Steve said his goodbyes, took his money and jumped into a waiting chopper. Within 20 minutes, she was touching down at Camp Lois.

Hopping out, he spotted Chuck and Ryan running to greet him. With a bear hug, Chuck yelled, "You asshole, we all thought you guys were either killed, or picked up by some unfriendlies! Thank God, you're all right!"

Turning to Ryan, Steve and his old friend said nothing. They just hugged.

Walking toward the parked Humvees, Tony called out, "Hey Steve, if you want to chill out here for awhile, you can. The war's over. There's nothing happening up north any more." Raising his big paws, he finished, "What do you want to do?"

Steve waved goodbye. "My friends are up there, and the war never mattered. We've done all our work after the cease fire. I need to go back."

Shaking his head, Tony slid into the seat beside Ryan. In a somber tone, he said, "Okay, let's go see the boys." And off they drove, all four men, due north.

During the long ride, Steve filled his friends in on he and Tony's accident.

"Some fuckin' coward actually left you guys for dead?" Chuck asked.

Steve nodded, but because of the look on his face, the subject was quickly changed.

Ryan filled Steve and Tony in on all of the latest news. They hadn't missed much, considering that most of the platoon aborted their mission to search for them. Laughing, Chuck added, "You're gonna love this one, Steve. The Humvee you totaled was stripped clean. When we found it, there were no tires, no radio, even the doors were gone. The scavengers got to it before we did. But that's not the best of it . . . ." Smiling harder, he added, "You, Sergeant Manchester, are under investigation by Battalion for reckless driving and driving to endanger. The damage — $44,000!"

Steve was stunned. "You're kidding, right?"

Chuck shook his head. "If you're found guilty, that's a lot of weekend drills to pay for the wreck!"

It was so sick that even Steve laughed. The laughter lasted straight into base camp.

It was night when they arrived, but everyone was waiting. Steve and Tony were welcomed with hugs and even a few kisses. The soldiers were convinced that they had lost two of their own. The celebration was glorious, but Steve longed for his cot. He needed the rest. His interrogation was scheduled for the morning.

Following an inedible breakfast, he reported to the Battalion's compound. He sat before a full-bird Colonel and was quickly slammed with questions. After answering the first two, he thought his blood pressure was going to make his head explode. He was forced to recall the horrid and unavoidable accident, and was enraged about having to answer for his actions. He remained calm, however, and explained the whole experience to the older man. At the end, he added, "There was nothing more I could do."

The Colonel attempted a compassionate grin. It was empty.

Steve had heard enough. He informed the Colonel, "I know what happened out there, and I also know that one of our own left my sergeant and I for dead. I'll have to live with that. As far as the Humvee, well, I also know that I can't be blamed for its damage."

Raising his eyebrows, the Colonel asked, "And why is that, sergeant?"

Staring straight into his eyes, Steve gave the only answer he could, "Because I never signed for the vehicle. It wasn't mine."

The last sentence said it all. He was quickly dismissed. It was bizarre. In the military, a person could ruin anything and not be held accountable, as long as he didn't sign for it. Whoever signed on the dotted line owned the equipment. In this case, the signature was Captain Wall's. There was no way they would be forcing a company commander to pay the outrageous amount. The officers took care of their own. Right or wrong, Steve got off on a technicality. To the Army, the details of the accident were insignificant. But, those cruel details changed his life.

Jumping right back in the saddle, he returned to his team. It was no different from any other evening. He mounted up the big squad and set out on their dangerous mission. With 60 miles of Main Supply Route to patrol, it was imperative that the boys stay alert, keeping all Allied forces out of the mine fields. It was no easy task. The night became uncooperative. The high winds changed the terrain and the dark sky blinded them from the engineer's land mine markers. Nonetheless, they performed their duty.

Cruising along, Steve was pleasantly surprised to pick up some interference over the army radio. It was two men conversing in Arabic. They had chosen the wrong frequency. He waited to switch to an alternate net. Their gibberish was the most entertainment he had enjoyed in days. Finally joining the conversation, he created chaos, and heard the laughs of his friends in the background. The Arab men were hardly amused, but it still made for 15 minutes of fun. No sooner had they stopped talking, when Steve heard the crash. It was a small explosion that sounded as if it came from within the interior of Bug Light. Without instruction, Tripp stomped on the gas, while Steve hopped on the radio for assistance. Everybody was thinking the same thing. They had just taken sniper fire.

One mile from the loud bang, Tripp pulled over and Steve jumped out to look for the bullet hole. Through the red lens of a dim flashlight, the search resulted in negative findings. There was no evidence of small arms fire. It didn't make sense.

The entire squad was rallied. For the next two hours, they set out to find the alleged gunman. Leapfrogging over each other, the methodical sweep also produced nothing, leaving them scratching their heads. It was too odd. Something hit them, something unfriendly. Without further discussion, Steve ordered they return to camp. The sun was coming up. Their frightening shift was over.

Pulling into base camp, he advised Tony that they had found nothing, but that it wasn't for the lack of trying.

Tony laughed. "This desert is loaded with ghosts, isn't it? I think that you and your people need some sleep."

The doubting words infuriated him. "The only ghosts I've ever noticed around here are still dancing in your head!" he snapped.

Tony's grin was wiped clean from his face, but there was no response. Instead, he folded his hands behind his back and started his morning stroll through the compound.

For good measure, Steve flipped him off. Tony never saw it, or at least pretended not to. Watching the old war horse, he felt bad about the outburst. Tony couldn't be held accountable for the things he said. He had earned that.

Steve returned to the vehicle. He opened the back door and saw it right away. It nearly knocked him over. It was an enormous hole, which had almost taken out the entire floorboard. Like a can of sardines that was ripped open, the floor was gone. It was located not one foot behind his seat. A cold sweat quickly formed on his brow, and ice water rushed through his veins. The damage was the result of a land mine. They had hit a land mine, and if Private Tripp hadn't been speeding, as usual, the explosion would have blown Steve's torso in half. Collecting small chunks from Bug Light, his stomach churned. His tortured mind reeled. It was too bizarre. Maybe he really was on borrowed time. The war was over and he was still dodging the Grim Reaper. That black cloud that hovered over him was starting to get darker, thicker. He had barely escaped death again, and wondered how long his luck could run.

Several full moons came and went, while things had changed, but only for the worse. There was more death of sinless children and innocent shepherds. Each was a Bedouin Indian, dressed in rags, with a runny nose and dirty face. The war had been over for weeks, but as Steve had learned, land mines refused to surrender. The soldiers tried desperately to save each child, but it was always the same story. The choppers either arrived two minutes too late, or the wounds were just so extensive that the flying medics were never called. Most of the kids smiled before they left the desert forever. It didn't take a genius to figure out why.

Personally, his body was consumed with pain. His head constantly pounded and his digestive system was completely out of whack. Yet, it was his mind that carried the greatest burdens. Never realizing that the chronic problems could have been caused by inoculations, Iraq's Scud attacks or the white chemical residue that covered everything, he was always down. The depression engulfed him, and though he fought it, his body was just too tired. Every waking moment was spent in a vice of anxiety, or all-out panic. Like clockwork, each night, his restless sleep was interrupted by severe panic attacks or demented, life-like nightmares. He could hear the shrills of grown men, smell smoldering human flesh and count each cruel and excruciating death he had witnessed. Each time, he awoke and tried to separate himself from the hellish dreams. But his life was the nightmare. He merely replayed the torment during his sleep. After weeks of the intense suffering, he decided to write a letter.

Though he addressed it to no one, he wrote: Though it's only been months, it seems like forever since I've been home, or have seen the people I love. I guess it has been forever. Forgive the lies I sent in my previous letters, but to tell the truth, it hasn't been a real good time over here. Something is horribly wrong with me, and I can't figure out what it is. Of course, I've seen things that nobody should see. I've watched children die, men leave their brothers for dead, land mines claim victims — the list is endless. Most of these things have been random and infrequent. They are no worse than the cruelty I experienced over the last four years working in the prison. And that's my problem. I can't figure it out. I feel sick. Every day, I feel sick and I wish it were only physical. Something has happened inside of me over here, and the more I search for the answer to make things right again, the more I feel lost. I'm not sure if the other guys feel the same. I suppose fearing that some of them might lose faith in me, I haven't dared to ask. I need you to know that, although I've felt an inexplicable fear since I've been here, I never once dishonored my family's name. I've done my best. I wish I knew what it is that's turning me inside out. I wish it were easier. I'm sorry.

The camp was quiet, with everyone tucked in for the night. Steve looked out into the black desert. Picking up his rifle, he removed the banana clip, but left one round in the chamber. Alone, he walked slowly into the darkness. Overwhelmed and confused, the months of anguish had brought despair. His body and mind were both tired. Looking back at the camp, he decided that he had walked far enough. He collapsed onto the cool sand and gazed up at a majestic sky. He searched hard, but couldn't find the beauty. He released a river of tears. The salty droplets streamed down his tanned cheeks, moistening his dry lips. He wept hard. He cried for his life, wondering whether or not he was minutes from ending it. Closing his eyes, he searched within, but couldn't find any goodness there either. He was on empty. There was nothing left. With no relief in sight, the present was unbearable and the future held no hope. He cried harder. It was the third time he had faced death. But this time was different. The first time he fought it off with every ounce of his strength. The second, he was completely unaware of it until it was over. This time, he only wished to embrace it. As the last tear turned to dust, he opened his eyes and looked back into the starry sky. To his surprise, he remembered his old Army partner, Wil Souza.

"Where were you, you son of a bitch?" he screamed in rage, "I needed you. I really needed you . . . ."

Steve remembered Wil's suicide. The memory had been stored away for years.

Sitting up on the sand, he remembered the vow he had taken at the beach and felt ashamed. Not only had he contemplated suicide, he had actually taken several quivering steps toward it. He recalled the grief over his best friend's death. Suicide wasn't an option. Wil had inflicted tremendous pain and suffering upon his family and friends. It was unfair of him. Yet, Steve could finally understand the last seconds of his friend's life. Wil was no coward, nor was he crazy. Like Steve, he simply feared living another day more than facing death. Staring hard into the brighter sky, Steve's tears turned sentimental, perhaps grateful. Wil was with him. He could feel his friend's presence. The thought of Wil's premature death, however, was only half of the reason for Steve's second chance at life. The other half was his mom.

For the first time in too long, he pictured Monica, his parents, his brothers and young sisters. He hadn't thought about them. He hadn't considered the devastating consequences of his selfish contemplation. He could hear the faint echo of his mother's gentle voice. "Steve, Keep The Faith!" He cried uncontrollably, knowing that he had lost his faith. Ashamed, he knelt on the desert floor, a shell of a man. His spirit was all but crushed when, for some unexplained reason, hope arrived. He couldn't kill himself. He couldn't do that to his family. The love they shared wouldn't allow it. Unloading his rifle, he tossed the brass bullet into the black void. Regaining his composure, he started back toward camp.

As he walked, he realized that his life was saved by two people. Neither one would ever know, nor were they there in person. It was the strength of their spirits that had awakened his lost soul. He could feel their comfort. Looking up, he thanked Wil for sticking by him. Thinking of his mom, he thanked God. She gave him life and without realizing it, she had saved it. Her faith was strong enough for them both.

Reaching camp, he looked back and felt his hair stand on end. The moon cast the softest, most angelic light, illuminating a perfect set of footprints in the sand. Thinking of his mom and her poem, he knew that he wasn't traveling alone. His mom was right.

Crossing himself, he thanked the Lord. He also asked forgiveness for having forgotten Him. The experience changed his life. He had been given another chance. He silently vowed to make the most of it. He didn't know what the future held, but he was confident in the strength of his personal promises.

He burned the letter of sorrow he'd written and, for the rest of that fateful night, read two months of unopened letters. He longed to be with his family. He desperately needed them in his life. Their words were encouraging, comforting and overflowing with love. No matter how much it hurt, he was never going to cast their words aside again. As the sun played peek-a-boo with the sleeping desert, he finished the last letter. Folding it back up, he smiled. It was a last reminder from his mom, a letter he should have read weeks earlier. From then on, her advice wouldn't be taken lightly. "I understand now," he whispered, "I'll Keep The Faith!"

The boys set up a satellite camp in Iraq and name it "The Ponderosa."

Even in the midst of an M1-Abrams tank, Papa White's sense of humor cannot be shaken.

Four Iraqi soldiers are taken prisoner just after the cease-fire. The dog doesn't make it out alive.

A lone soldier stands in the dunes of the Arabian Desert — overlooking the Persian Gulf.

Chapter 8

A Hero's Homecoming

In less than an hour, the camp stirred from an uneasy night's sleep. Steve rallied his people. It was time to relieve the Overlord's crew at the Ponderosa.

Making the trip in record time, he met his long lost friends at the barbed-wired entrance. In transit, they exchanged pleasantries, but it was very rushed. Chuck's gang was anxious to return to anything that resembled society. Steve shook Ryan's hand and felt a familiar tap on his shoulder. It was Chuck. "Anything new, Steve?"

With a phony laugh, he replied, "What in the hell could be new around here? We're either trying to save kids or watching the wind blow mountains into valleys!"

Chuck nodded with understanding, then mounted up his people. Within seconds, the hooting and hollering vanished into a tornado of dust. They would be back in three days. In the meantime, Steve assigned his soldiers to their traffic control points, then sat under the minimal shade of camouflaged netting. It was going to be another long day. He tried to get comfortable. It wasn't even a possibility.

With a fresh start on life, he attempted to adjust his negative attitude. As always, he expressed himself through his twisted humor and the boys loved the amusement. On the outside, the happy clown had returned. On the inside, however, he still fought desperately to find anything positive. The internal battle raged on, and his humor eventually turned to cynical sarcasm that fed off of a deep-seeded anger. Too much had happened.

Every once in a while, a Bedouin Indian wandered into camp, begging for food, cigarettes and a drop of precious diesel fuel. As they rattled on in their foreign gibberish, Steve responded, "No, thank you. We have plenty!" His audience held their sides in laughter.

The visitors were normally sent on their way with some food, a few cigarettes and a Polaroid picture of themselves. The photo dumbfounded most and brought others to joyful tears. The ordinary snap shot was something they couldn't imagine in their wildest dreams. They left without any fuel, a hot commodity that needed to be conserved, but they always walked away happy. All were unaware that they served as the butt of Steve's harsh jokes.

There were other times when Arab truck drivers, transporting crushed gravel and similar road-building materials, stopped. Steve simply forged the invoices with every name from George Bush to Chuck E. Cheese and instructed them to dump their cargo into the open desert. Within days, piles upon piles of stone were just sitting in the middle of nowhere. Whenever the boys passed one, they enjoyed the same hysterics all over again.

To top it off, Steve and his crew responded to the aid of some Saudi civilians who got their vehicle stuck in one of the many deep tank trenches. Before lending a hand, Steve had the foreign men dancing and singing silly songs. As Dennis winched the truck out, the Saudis chanted, "Triple A. Triple A." Everybody screamed in delight, everybody but Steve. As usual, he wore his false smile. Nothing made him laugh anymore.

Time waited for no man, but it never ran away from anyone either. At a snail's pace, life dragged along, while the boys settled into their daily routines. Most of The Dream Team found the boredom to be less welcome than the emergencies. At least during times of crises, they knew they were still alive. Most of the time, however, each day was a mirror of the one before it. The hours slowly turned into days.

Desert life was like serving time in miles and miles of solitary confinement. There was no escape from the sand trap. Still, they made the most of it.

A shower was constructed, with four pieces of plywood used as the walls, two wooden pallets as the floor and an old diesel tank used to hold the water. Locating the shower head was the key, but once accomplished, the boys were in paradise. The tank was painted flat black and was always filled to the brim in the morning. The scorching sun beat off of it the entire day, allowing five to seven people a warm, gravity-fed shower at night. The rotation permitted everyone at least one shower per week, providing that they lathered up and rinsed off quick. Everyone was pretty fair about it. And the black biting flies, attracted by the moisture, helped to insure integrity. Any more than three minutes in the shower and the black swarms chewed a shin to hamburger. Most of the boys were grateful it was only once a week. Besides, their sand packed ears and muddy bodies were never really clean anyway. The combination of the white powder and untamed winds didn't allow it.

The raunchy latrine also attracted insects of all shapes and sizes. This caused most of the soldiers to use the kitty cat method. At first, they'd walk a mile before digging a hole and squatting over it. In no time, that ended. It didn't matter if it was a mile or 100 feet. They lived in an open desert where privacy was non-existent. Shame and embarrassment was quickly stricken from their minds. Even the women did what they had to do when nature called, not to mention that special time of the month. It wasn't pleasant. It wasn't clean. It was reality.

When they weren't working long hours on the dusty trail, they played cards or tried to sleep in the sweltering heat. The sun got hotter by the day and outside sports were no longer an option. The games could prove fatal. Most of the guys consumed at least a liter of water per hour. Steve, the sweat hog, took in more. The smarter soldiers would dig a hole at night, line it with a trash bag and fill it with bathing water. By submerging six to eight bottles and covering them, the night air created an underground refrigerator. Those taking the extra initiative produced some refreshing water for the brutally hot mornings. As the day progressed, however, and the thermometers shot up, they were all forced to drink water at the temperature of the desert. That meant 100 degrees plus. There was always a question of parasites or bacteria in the drinking water, and diarrhea became an accepted part of daily life. Inevitably, it was either live with the runs or dehydrate and die.

The menu never changed. Meal times remained erratic and everyone was placed on a diet whether they chose it or not. In a sudden barrage, the packages started arriving from home. Most were filled with candy or sweets of some type, giving the boys the empty calories needed to make it through each day. Darlene's elementary school was one of the biggest contributors. Before long, Steve wrote Monica, requesting some liquid refreshments. In a wasteland where alcohol was forbidden, the group decided to throw a party. It was nearly Easter when the mother lode arrived.

Picking up his prize, he noticed the large box was nearly crushed. Its brown paper wrapping was carefully addressed in black marker and the many stamps told him that it traveled around the globe. As if opening his first Christmas present, he tore through the wrapping and searched its contents. The whole clan back home had pitched in. They were more than generous. For entertainment, Randy had even included a paddleball. Chuckling at his brother's light-hearted wit, he looked closer. There were nips concealed in every nook and cranny. Monica had followed his instructions to the letter. Opening the large green bottle of mouthwash, he immediately detected the faint odor of vodka. The green food coloring, an old trick he picked up at the prison, was just an insurance policy in case the customs officers got their greasy fingers on it. He popped a few nips, stashed the rest for the party and returned to duty. With a warm and wonderful feeling lighting up his belly, he responded to a call for assistance. It was Dennis Ahern's calm voice. There was an accident. It was a fatal.

As he pulled up, the mangled Humvee was being dragged from the bloody scene. Lighting a cigarette, he got out and asked for a rundown. An M.P., assigned to a different unit, filled him in.

"What a crazy night, Sarge! I was right behind them when I saw the fuckin' tank just run them down. It was like they weren't even there. They never had a chance. They were crushed to death!" Shrugging his shoulders, the young soldier walked away. He grieved terribly, as his friends were taken away.

Steve felt the man's pain. It was obvious what happened. A full tank brigade was pulling back to the rear, when one of their steel beasts became blinded by the flying sand. Without ever seeing them, the tankers drove right over the unsuspecting M.P.s. Two men died in the chaotic accident. Steve had never seen them before, had never known them, but he still felt the loss. They were Americans, so they were friends. Now, they were dead. Grabbing his people, he drove off, wishing he had consumed a few more nips than he had.

The days turned into weeks.

The boys were allowed to make one telephone call per week. They drove three hours into northern Saudi Arabia, waited two hours in line, then talked for a timed 15 minutes, knowing that it was another three-hour trip back. Each call was outrageously expensive. Steve alternated his calls home between Monica and his family, and asked that they share the information. Monica didn't care for it, but he hardly had the strength to deal with his own dilemmas. When he spoke to her, she spent most of the 15 minutes complaining about the house. The mortgage was falling way behind. For many reasons, he just didn't care any more. Somewhere along the way, his perspective had changed.

During the telephone trips, they always passed the scene of he and Tony's accident. Every week, at the same location, there was a witty comment blurted over the radio. Prepared for the jokes, he usually returned an even wittier response. Everyone laughed, even him, though only on the outside. Inside, he could hardly stand being in the vehicle. He felt smothered in the enclosure. In fact, as soon he returned to duty, he took himself off of passenger status. He could no longer stand being out of control of any situation. From then on, Private Tripp sat back in comfort, while his boss did all of the driving. They had their different reasons, but it suited both of them fine.

The nights were normally quiet, though the local wild life became more active. Critters of all types either crawled or slithered under the Humvees in search of heat. The snakes and scorpions were most unwelcome. Sometimes they received the death penalty just for being there. On separate occasions, however, the group adopted two beasts with different attitudes.

The first was a reptile of some sort that measured over two feet in length. Nicknamed Spot, the cold-blooded grump refused to eat or even blink his eyes. After three days of his protesting stubbornness, Doug untied the leash and set him free. The scaly creature just sauntered off and never looked back. With his rebellious attitude, he would have never fit into the program anyway.

The second animal was a wild dog that decided to abandon his roving pack and camp out with the boys. He was as white as snow, so they appropriately named him Snowflake. Steve felt uncomfortable with a wild dog hanging around, but the mutt soon proved his worth. He became a good watchdog, scaring off other creepy critters and barking at any strangers who happened by. The Dream Team's pet found himself living the life he could only have dreamed of. While everyone else was losing weight, the dog got fatter by the day. He gratefully ate the scraps from the hands of 30 masters. Then, on one spring evening, he met his violent demise.

Steve was sitting on the hood of his Humvee when he spotted Snowflake wandering through one of the many minefields. He called out to the dumb mutt, while the other guys sat back to watch the show. Snowflake was doing quite well until he took a wrong turn. There was a loud explosion and then the old dog vanished into thin air. He was there one second, and completely gone the next. The spectacle made most of the boys laugh hysterically. Even Steve realized that it was funny in a sick way. After seeing so many children meet the same death, the boys would have traded 1,000 mangy mutts for one child. Besides, Snowflake had lived like a king right up until his last minutes on earth. The familiar child-and-land-mine scenario took place the following night.

The radio called out for a medevac. The voice belonged to Keith Robles. Steve could tell by his tone that this one wasn't pretty. At breakneck speed, he responded to the scene.

Upon arrival, he saw Keith bent over a young Bedouin child. It was a boy, no more than ten, and he was wearing the clothing of a shepherd. Several goats stood off in the distance, watching, as Steve stepped in closer. The child was missing half of his face, as well as his right arm. Keith worked frantically on him. While administering C.P.R., every breath he blew into the child was another second the boy lived. Keith was his lifeline and everyone knew he was keeping the boy alive. The medevac chopper informed the crew that they would be late, as they couldn't fly in the current windstorm. The deadly news made Keith work harder.

Several minutes passed and Steve saw the boy's eyes wander off into space. The blank stare was all too familiar. He had died. At that very moment, a piece of Keith died with him. As the child's blood poured out and strained through the sand beneath him, Keith's grieving tears were mixed in. Then the chopper touched down. They were two minutes too late. Heartbroken, Keith walked away.

Watching him, Steve realized that his friend had become one of the bonafide heroes of Desert Storm. He hadn't shot or killed any enemy. He had never even taken fire himself. Instead, he offered his own soul to a dying child. It made Steve wonder about the worth of one life — any life. It also made him think about his friends, and their diverse experiences since arriving in the Gulf. The differences dumbfounded him.

Every day was a roll of the dice. Some guys witnessed very little and always found themselves in the right place at the right time. They saw nothing. Others were not so lucky. They were the men who were magnets to trouble or heartache. Keith had just joined the ranks of the not-so-privileged. In his heart, he was sure that his friend would see that boy's face for the remainder of his days. The cruel experience was a part of him now. There was no getting rid of it. He knew the feeling only too well.

Steve thought about his other comrades and their varying job performances. He learned that some of the guys were blessed with blinders, and were relatively unaffected by anything. Doug Donnelly and Pat O'Malley were two prime examples.

Doug remained quiet in Iraq, and never got his chance to prove his theories on the art of guiltless killing. Steve never doubted, however, that he would have been one of the first to pull a trigger. Instead, both his words and rifle were silent.

Pat, on the other hand, truly possessed the spirit of a warrior. Steve was certain of it. With no fighting to be done, he spent most of his time in quiet slumber. He became a power sleeper. Initially, some of the boys were unsure if it was merely an escape mechanism from reality. Steve knew better. Pat was just bored, and that boredom caused him to log in countless hours on his cot. Although swept away by his own oblivion, when something did occur, he rose to the occasion. Pat always possessed a keen sense for trouble.

Though he was separated from Ryan and Chuck, Steve knew they were both as solid as rocks. Chuck was the tough guy, while Ryan possessed more compassion. Together, they complimented each other perfectly. They were the ideal team, and Steve missed working with them. He missed them dearly. As far as the others: Keith had proved himself many times over, as had Tripp. Dennis eventually went one step further. In Steve's eyes, he leapt from zero status to hero status.

Out of them all, Dennis was the most consistent with his caring assistance. He quickly smashed his label as a coward and taught the entire platoon a lesson. The group had been a little too quick to judge. Dennis was the complete soldier who was ready to fight, or help, depending on which situation arose. When it came down to it, Dennis was the only one there for Steve. He became a true friend. Over the long weeks in the wild, the two bonded. Dennis sensed his great pain and eventually told him, "Steve, you don't always have to make people laugh, you know." Those simple, yet kind words brought relief. Dennis' care and concern also brought the first genuine smile from Steve in weeks. Like a handful of others, they had sealed their friendship for life.

At the same time, other friendships within the platoon were severely maimed, and would never heal. It all had to do with personal perceptions. It was amazing. Two people could witness the same event, experience an identical situation, yet perceive it totally differently. Depending on where their hearts and minds were, those differences either separated them forever, or brought them closer than brothers. Steve had experienced and accepted both. Difficult times had a strange way of removing all falsehoods.

With all of the aggression building and no release valve in sight, he was surprised that everybody got along as well as they did. Reflecting back on the days of carefree fun, The Dream Team had become an entirely different group of men.

The weeks crept into months.

Working the long shifts, Steve and the boys witnessed more senseless death, and accidents that should have never occurred. One night, a couple of soldiers went on a quest for souvenirs. As they hunted through one of the many booby-trapped bunkers, one of them got more than he bargained for. He picked up two pineapple grenades and threw them onto the floor of his Humvee. Satisfied with the loot, the bandits raced away from the scene. They didn't make it 200 yards before one of the grenades exploded. The passenger lost one of his legs, right up to the knee, and the foot of the other. His blood curdling shrill echoed through the infinite of the desert. Though he lived, he would never walk again. Such accidents claimed more lives and limbs than the Iraqi Army could ever take credit for.

The very next evening, the army radio called out to Swamp Yankee. Steve acknowledged the radio traffic, only to find the caller's voice too distant to understand. Through all the static, the message was gobbled up. He pressed the microphone button again, saying, "Be advised, I did not copy." He waited.

As if his friend were standing right beside him, Ryan said, "Swamp Yankee, this is Papa White. Prepare to copy a message from home. Over."

Surprised by the curious request, he responded, "Papa White, this is Swamp Yankee. Send message."

Without further delay, Ryan sent it.

It was a tape recording sent from home. Leaning closer to the radio, he strained to listen. A small group formed around him. A few focused seconds passed and still, he heard nothing. Then, in the faintest of sounds, the message came through. There was some static and the quality of the recording was poor, but he heard something. It was a rhythmic beat and it sounded as if it were under water. Listening hard and thinking harder, the recording continued, "Boom, boom … boom, boom …." It was a heartbeat. It was Baby White's heartbeat. Finally unscrambling the puzzle, the boys ran off into different directions. The message was so powerful, so overwhelming, that each set of tired eyes erupted into tears. Tears of pain and joy rolled down Steve's face. The recording was a glimmer of hope in a world full of despair. After all of the death, at last, there was life. His tears dried quickly. He had spent so many on Iraqi children who had died. He could read the sign. It was only a recording of the heartbeat of an unborn child living halfway around the globe, but it was hope. It was life.

Steve walked back to the radio, while the rest of the group stood at a distance, weeping. They had all carried the same burden of helplessly, watching one child after another die. The message was received loud and clear by each of them. Baby White was a sign of innocent and protected life. The fetus was also a reminder of a better life back home. Reaching the radio, Steve heard Ryan's emotional voice searching for him. "Did you copy that Yankee . . . that was my kid!" His voice drifted off in tears of pride and elation.

He tried to answer, but couldn't. He shared his friend's joy and, at the same time, envied him for his careless courage. Ryan was crying over the radio for all to hear. He couldn't have cared less. Steve wished he could do the same. Instead, the lump grew larger in his throat, so he waited. Like an abandoned child, Ryan called out to his friend. Steve finally managed two words.

"Congratulations, Brother!"

Ryan received the response and obviously sensed his friend's emotions. In a serious tone, he broke radio procedures. "Thank you, Steve. Thank you for everything!"

The radio went dead, and Steve walked away. There were a few tears left.

Morning finally arrived and with it, some news that came as no surprise. The Pentagon had released a classified document revealing that heavy doses of depleted uranium were used in certain areas of the Gulf. The message explained the charred corpses and white powder that covered everything. The Pentagon strongly warned that any ground troops stationed in these areas should protect themselves with the full chemical ensemble, from the mask to the rubber boots. Steve shook his head in disgust. They had been working in those very areas for over three months. Nobody once wore a chemical suit. The notice had arrived a little late.

Lighting a cigarette, he looked down at the salt rings that tie-dyed his T-shirt. There was no more sweat. His perspiration was evaporating as soon as it left his pores. Squinting into the white sun, he decided that with the temperature reaching triple digits each day, he'd rather take his chances at surviving the radioactive waste. Summer was coming and the heat was getting more unbearable. In the heavy chemical suit, he wouldn't make it three hours before cooking in his own juices. With a sadistic snicker, he told

Dennis, "You just have to appreciate the options. Die quickly in the monkey suit, or prolong the agony over a span of years! Damn, you gotta love the United States government!"

Dennis never answered. He just crumpled up the report and threw it into the wind.

Remaining unprotected, a few more long weeks passed, while The Dream Team watched the Army pack it up and go home. Everyone was heading south. The boys continued their tedious mission, even though the novelty of it had worn off months before. They were aggravated and frustrated with their present situation.

The radio called out for immediate help. Ironically, it was their last mission and the only one Steve ever missed. Of all times, an angry rainstorm had picked up the Ponderosa and torn it to shreds. While the satellite camp began floating away in one massive gully, Steve and Tripp stayed back to chase it down. Pat grabbed the rest of the squad and went on the hunt. Steve didn't mind. With a pounding headache and burning diarrhea, he was glad to see Pat get a chance at the helm.

There was a small team of Americans who were surrounded by a group of armed Iraqi Rebels. Enthusiastically, Pat and the boys swooped in on the hostage situation. Like veterans, they cleared up the problem within five vicious minutes. The Iraqis were treated with the usual care, while their weapons were confiscated. The prisoners were transported to the rear, while Pat returned with enough AK-47s for everyone in the squad. Throwing one to Steve, he said, "We had to take seven Iraqis into custody, but what a shame. They were Rebels, out hunting the Republican Guard to overthrow Hussein. Instead, when we leave, these people are going to be exterminated, like the Kurds!"

Since the beginning, President Bush had pleaded for the Iraqi people to stand up and overthrow their dictator. As soon as they had found the courage to do just that, the Allied forces were ordered to pull out. In turn, Hussein requested permission to fly his choppers. The request was granted and the rebels were hunted down. Pat was right. Steve responded, "It's never going to be over for these people. But like most other things, it's completely out of our hands!"

For days afterwards, the boys took target practice on any abandoned vehicles they could find. One was a bus, containing an old dirty sign of segregation. It read: All Women Must Ride In Back. They fired it up. A row of 15 men laid on their bellies and fired everything from pistols to machine guns. The bus was completely obliterated. Standing, Doug asked, "Don't you think we should have checked to see if anyone was aboard first?"

Everyone laughed. Doug was the only one who didn't check it out beforehand. They burned the remains. It was the most fun they'd had in weeks. Then, Chuck had a brainstorm.

It was time for a party. Steve broke out the vodka, Pat, his tequila, Chuck, some spiced rum. Whatever they could find was thrown into the pot. Sitting in the faint light of a small musty tent, they all started drinking. Each bottle was passed from one greedy hand to the next. Keith took out his camera and took group photos. He offered one to Steve, who thankfully placed the memento into his pocket. They sang their favorite songs and told their reminiscent stories, but things were different, and everybody knew it. Within the hour, some were puking, while others watched the tent spin in circles. The remainder passed out. Their tolerance was down, but they had given it their best shot.

Along with the worst hangovers, the long anticipated call arrived. With no prior warning, the 661st M.P. Company was ordered to pack it up and get out of Iraq. Their job was done — mission complete. It was time to go home. As abruptly as it had started, it was ending. Nobody had to tell them twice.

The Ponderosa was left to rot, while base camp was dismantled within the hour. The latrine and shower were soaked with diesel, and anything not worth carrying was thrown into the heap. Everything from AK-47s to extra uniforms were thrown in. The pile grew high. In a strange ceremony of jubilation, Tony lit the bon fire, while the boys sang and danced. It was a time of celebration. Chuck filled two trash bags with diesel and tossed them into the blaze. The diesel bombs caused an explosion that lifted the fire another 20 feet into the stifling air. The soldiers screamed with excitement. Steve, however, stood at a distance, feeling detached. He, more than anyone, wanted out of Iraq. Yet, he couldn't even bring himself to smile at the thought. Instead, he ducked into the shadows to ride out another frightening anxiety attack. They were getting stronger and more frequent. He hated every second of them, and feared the ones to come even more. He just couldn't fake another smile.

It took some time before the fire burned itself out. Steve grabbed Ryan and loaded crates of food into two Humvees. No different from soldiers of other wars, the First Platoon shared their food with the children of Iraq. Now, for the last time, they brought them all they could carry. At 60 miles

Once The Dream Team is ordered to pack it up and get out of Iraq, The Ponderosa is burned to the ground.

per hour, they threw the cases from the vehicles, while the Bedouin children ran for the big score. Steve looked back and watched a small girl, waving goodbye. He turned his head and silently wished she would live to remember this day. With the number of land mines awaiting her throughout the treacherous desert, the odds were against her. In a solemn mood, he and Ryan drove back to camp.

The convoy of the 661st wasted no time before heading south. As they traveled Main Supply Route Blue for the last time, Steve remembered every twist and turn in the road. He could have driven it blindfolded. They all could have. To his surprise, the radio remained silent. There were no jokes or comments piercing the airwaves. There was total quiet, and it was nice. Everybody was thinking about the long months that had passed. Some remembered it as nothing but one boring day after the next. Others recalled it as a living hell. Strangely, they had all started on the same page. They all came with the same fears, but each was leaving with a different experience. Everyone was elated to finally see the Iraqi breach pass behind them. Steve doubted anyone would look back. Nobody did.

The company arrived back at King Khalid Military City, the Saudi Arabian starting point, and were ordered to clean their equipment. When they finished, they were ordered to clean it all again. It was scheduled to take four days, but the orders were clear. The military didn't want to carry any diseases or viruses back to the states. The crew went to work and cleaned like they had never cleaned before. The outdoor G.I. party lasted a full six days. Then, the rumors of their departure started to fly. These rumors brought more torment than any empty promise Steve had ever believed. The departure date changed four times and, each time, the hopes of The Dream Team were crushed. The waiting game was agonizing.

Though they were at the end of their stay in the Gulf, the platoon's tents were overrun by a mysterious illness once again. The flu-like symptoms were no different from the beginning, with simultaneous bouts of diarrhea and vomiting. Left weak and concerned, they attempted to help each other through the disabling illness. Steve wondered if the unexplained and recurring illness wasn't a souvenir they'd all be taking home. For the time being, however, the major goal was to board any aircraft heading home.

Fed up with their depressing ailments and the sick game of waiting, the boys decided to play a game of their own. No different from their summers on Cape Cod, the crew set out to make a mockery of their chain of command. It was time to wreak havoc.

A pair of Staff Sergeant Volmer's underwear was strung up the flagpole for all to see. The least impressed was the Battalion Commander. Shooting flares and other booby traps were set up around the camp, making their unsuspecting victims scream out in fear. The group laughed in pain. Steve was finally summoned to Captain Wall's tent. She said, "I think Sergeant Volmer's underwear must be dry by now. Let's knock off the games, okay Sergeant Manchester?"

Steve replied, "I understand Ma'am. I guess the boys have been getting a little antsy. I'll make sure it stops."

The company was finally bused to one of the many flight lines and funneled through customs. Both of Steve's duffel bags were packed with souvenirs. He had knives, hats, berets, foreign uniforms and the flags of two nations. He destroyed the AK-47, which would have cost him some big time at Fort Levenworth Federal Penitentiary. The customs officer conducted his thorough check.

"Not too much equipment left, huh?"

Steve giggled. "No. Those would be considered combat losses."

The man laughed, never knowing that it had all burned in the finest bon fire ever.

As the man finished his search, Steve asked, "Hey, buddy, what's the strangest thing anyone's tried to smuggle through here?"

The man's smile was wiped away. In a whisper, he responded, "Some sick son of a bitch actually wrapped an Iraqi arm in a trash bag. He almost got it through before we caught it. It was burnt and smelled horrible. The M.P.s ended up taking him away. I still can't figure out what he was going to do with it."

Steve shook his head. With an equally serious look, he replied, "Maybe it would have made a nice ashtray stand."

As he walked away, the officer looked at him with disgust. Steve just laughed. It was obvious that the man hadn't seen any of the death or destruction. The dark humor, an effective defensive trait, completely eluded him. The stranger couldn't understand, and Steve had already learned that many never would. Grabbing his bags, he led his squad onto the dark flight line. The gorgeous plane was waiting.

At last, they boarded a NorthWest Airlines flight, destination; Anywhere, U.S.A. Steve entered the plush cabin of the Boeing 747. Before taking his seat in the rear, he conducted one final head count. There were seven men and two women. The Second Squad was all accounted for. They all made it. In fact, The entire Dream Team had survived Operation Desert Storm. The realization made him smile from ear to ear. An incredible burden was lifted from him. He was no longer responsible for anyone but himself, a task that was already proving to be more than enough. With an ignorant, but comforting sense of relief, he took his seat.

Buckling up, he felt the energy within the interior of the aircraft. Each face glowed with excitement. They were going home. After all of the setbacks, and all of the tormenting rumors, they were finally going home. The plane's motors screamed a final farewell at the dawn. The desert remained hauntingly silent. Like the answer to a prayer, the jet took off down the runway.

Steve peered out of the tiny window and captured his last memories of a difficult time in a harsh land. The dark desert sped past the window. The endless beach had changed his life forever and he knew it. On the horizon, he caught the very peak of the rising sun — the ball of fire that once sent rays of fear ripping through his soul. The plane lifted off the runway and took to the air. Everyone had held their breath for that very moment. It wasn't going to be over until they were in the air. Cheers, clapping and tears broke the thick silence. The entire group cried with joy and celebrated the completion of a successful mission. After giving Chuck a high-five, Steve looked out the window one last time. It was just another morning in the Arabian Desert, but it was the last one he'd ever see. As the plane banked sideways, the whirling winds and shifting sands of the desert floor disappeared forever. He wouldn't miss it, not any of it. It was time to go home.

Over the happy yells, the plane's intercom called for everyone's attention. It was the pilot, welcoming his military passengers.

"I'd like to be the first to thank you people for a job well done! America is anxiously awaiting your safe return and I feel privileged to be the one to give that to them. Enjoy the long flight and, again, on behalf of the whole crew, thank you!"

The cabin exploded with the proud and grateful cheers of 300 soldiers. The faceless stranger responded with a gift that touched the hearts of every person on the flight. The captain played the anthem of Desert Storm, *God Bless the U.S.A.,* by Lee Greenwood. From the very first words of the song, the heavy sighs of men trying to fight off their churning emotions replaced the cheering. Steve hung onto every word and contemplated the true meaning of being an American. There was no better feeling. Tears rolled down his face. He thought about the sacrifices made for freedom. It wasn't easy, but it was worth it. It was all worth it. He had only paid a small price, but still, he had helped pay. The song reminded everyone of the reasons for the suffering. It was a generous gift and the last note rang out in total silence.

Before long, Steve was approached by a beautiful flight attendant. With a perfect smile, she offered him a cold drink. As she started to pour out the cola, he politely asked for the whole can. The smile brightened and she handed it over. The sweaty can was ice cold. He fondled it for a few seconds before placing it to his dry lips. It had been months since he had felt anything cold. The refreshing liquid extinguished an old fire in his throat. He savored every sip. It was an ordinary can of soda, but it quenched a long-standing thirst. It was the best he ever tasted. After having so little, having a little something meant so much. He vowed to never take even the smallest things for granted again.

A few hours into the flight, the pilot announced. "We are currently flying over the great pyramids of Egypt. If you look out the left side of the aircraft, you can see them." Steve stood, stretched out his cramped body and walked to the left side of the plane. The sight was breathtaking. They were 30,000 feet above the earth and he could see three small triangles as plain as day. As he started back toward his seat, he changed his mind and headed for the bathroom. It had been months since he had seen a toilet.

He relieved himself in luxury, but as he washed his hands, he looked up and saw a strange image in the mirror. The undeniable changes startled him. The baby face was gone. The chiseled features of a man replaced it.

The months of sweat, malnutrition and hard living had taken their toll. He leaned in closer. The reflection of his tanned face looked unfamiliar. He gazed hard into his own eyes. They were tired and somewhat sunken, but there was more. There was something missing. As hard as he tried, he couldn't define it. After a few long seconds, he gave up. It was time to get some rest.

He was nearly asleep when the pilot announced. "We're making the final descent into Germany." He sat up, fastened his seat belt and thought about cold beer. The boys had missed Oktoberfest, but he hoped the Germans would still have a few cold brews on hand.

They marched off of the plane in formation. Not 40 yards from a large Quonset Hut, a soldier up front, broke ranks and made a beeline to a tall oak tree. He wrapped his arms around the trunk, collapsed to his knees and kissed the rough bark. The entire company laughed. It was so appropriate. It had been an eternity since any of them had seen a tree. Half of them had been thinking the same thing. Steve whispered to Chuck, "That boy either has enormous balls, or he's as stupid as a stump!"

Chuck giggled. "Does it matter? Nobody's gonna do anything to him that hasn't already been done!"

In less than an hour, they were shuffled back onto the plane. They saw less of Germany than Spain. There was no cold beer on hand. Some large German woman, though, was quite generous with cookies and lemonade. Nobody complained. The lemonade was cold and the cookies were still warm. With a full belly, Steve reclaimed his seat in the rear.

Minutes later, the landing gear was up and The Dream Team was making their final leg of the journey home. Steve lounged back in his comfortable seat. No sooner had he closed his eyes, than the stewardess tugged softly on his uniform. "Are you hungry?" she asked.

Before he could answer, she placed a filet mignon on the tray in front of him. She affectionately patted his shoulder and said, "Enjoy." He was sure she meant it.

The steak was absolutely delicious, but four bites into it, his stomach began doing back flips. His body was having trouble accepting the foreign food. It had been so long since he had indulged in meat so rich. He pushed the food away and closed his eyes again.

His body was tense with anticipation. Sleep wasn't an option, but it was a perfect opportunity to daydream. For several hours, he imagined his emotional reunion with his wife and family. The mental pictures sent chills throughout his body. Yet, he continued to play out the future scenario. He could finally think about them without sorrow. It was time to let go of the desert and adjust back into his old life. It was already proving to be the most difficult mission of all.

It was a long flight and the landing seemed to take forever. Under dark clouds, the plane touched down on the slippery runway. The squeal of the tires caused the cabin to erupt in the loudest chorus of cheers Steve had ever heard. The hair on the back of his neck stood at attention. He searched out the window for his family. There was nothing but pouring rain. Then, the plane turned right and taxied down the last stretch of road. He saw it. It was the same hangar they had departed from months earlier. He choked on his own tears. There were thousands of people swaying back and forth, attempting to get a better look. The colors red, white, blue and yellow covered everything. It looked like the entire nation had showed up to welcome the boys home. Steve looked back. All of his friends were wiping their eyes and straightening their desert uniforms, preparing themselves for the most overwhelming experience of their lives. His heart beat faster. In spite of months of agonizing panic attacks, he welcomed the similar sensations. It was raw excitement and he savored every second. The plane finally stopped in the middle of the runway.

It took another eternity before the door flew open. There was a distant hum. Steve sucked in a deep breath. The muffled sound was that of a thousand screaming families. Putting one boot in front of the other, he reached

The Dream Team touches down on a wet runway at Westover Air Force Base in Chicopee, Massachusetts. There's no place like home!

the doorway and took his first step out onto the metal staircase. The hard, driving rain felt exhilarating. He stopped for a moment and looked toward the cheering crowd. His body tingled from the top of his head right down to his toes. It was as if The Dream Team just won the World Series, or showed up to play for a sold out concert. But there was more. There was the Manchester family waiting somewhere among the masses. The emotions welled up inside of him. As hard as he tried, he couldn't hold back. He picked up the pace. The rain pelted his face and mixed in perfectly with his salty tears.

Reaching the bottom stair, he stepped onto the flight line. He was home. He was back in the states. He screamed out in joy. Making his way toward the hangar, he pushed through the extended hands of one politician after the other. They were lined up on both sides. He couldn't have cared less.

Reaching the end of the row, he stopped to receive a salute from an older soldier. From the patches on the warrior's soaked uniform, he saw that the man was a Vietnam veteran. Without hesitation, he returned the salute. Above the piercing shrills of the restless mob, the soldier yelled, "Thank You!"

Steve's tears rolled faster. He smiled, with a hint of understanding. "No ... Thank You!" he replied.

The man didn't expect the simple, yet sincere response. He knew that Steve wasn't being cordial or polite. He was finally being thanked for his own service 20 years earlier. His own tear ducts were forced open. With pride, he stiffened his salute.

Steve turned back toward the hangar. It was time to find his family.

A few yards before reaching the hangar, he stepped onto a red carpet. He felt buzzed. He scanned the crowd and looked into the faces of a hundred people. Not one looked familiar. Yet, they were all clapping and screaming their affections at him. Some were even trying to touch him over the barricades. He was overcome with deep emotions. The electricity of the crowd carried him, and a powerful charge surged right through his body. Looking right, he finally caught the eyes of someone he had loved since his earliest memories. It was his brother. Like the hundreds of strangers, Billy was stretching over the barricade, struggling to touch him. The sight of it rocked him down to his bones. Billy was weeping openly and his eyes showed the love and relief that he felt. He screamed, "Stevie ... Stevie ...."

Sprinting, Steve rushed over and wrapped his arms around his big brother. Billy nearly crushed him with love.

Amidst a mob of supporters, Steve Manchester reacquaints himself with his baby sister, Jenny.

"I love you, Steve."

Steve couldn't say anything. He just tightened his grip.

Billy finally let him go and pointed down at the carpet. Without another word, Steve knew what he meant. There was still more road to travel. There were still more people to hug.

His head was spinning, while he shook the hands of hundreds of supportive Americans. The nation's arms were opened wide. Slowly, he followed the red path. Then someone jumped out of the crowd and blind-sided him. Before he could see who it was, he smelled her perfume. It was Monica. They hugged until they became one. It all came out. He couldn't hold anything back. He cried into her shoulder, "I love you, Monica. My God, did I miss you . . . ."

She kissed his dry mouth and hugged him again.

"Thank God it's over!"

She was right. For her, it was over. Hand-in-hand, they tackled the rest of the crimson maze together.

They had just cleared a bend in the path when Steve saw them. His dad was holding both of his sisters. They were looking straight through him.

Bill Sr.'s face became flushed, while his Adam's apple started to bounce up and down. The man finally spotted his long lost son. He placed both girls on the floor, pointed at Steve and let them go. Steve dropped to his knees and caught both of them running. Darlene jumped into his arms. Jenny was a little more reluctant. He grabbed her. From the look in her big brown eyes, the months were just as long for her. As if he were a stranger, she gawked at him. The baby hardly recognized him and it sent his mind back in time.

While they hugged and kissed, he pictured the eyes of the Arab children who had died. He tried to push the haunting memories from his mind, but he couldn't. At the same time, he enjoyed being caught up in a hero's welcome. It was so confusing. He had learned there was no glory in war. There was no honor in helplessly watching children die. Valor was in the eye of the beholder. He stood and took a deep breath. He needed to sort out his mixed emotions. Pushing them aside, he focused on the fact that it was a time to celebrate. Not because Iraq lost so decisively, but because he was being reunited with his family. He approached his dad.

Bill Sr. had a difficult time letting him go. He held him tight, sobbing, "Good job, Steve. I'm so proud of you!"

Steve could hear the respect in his father's voice. That, alone, almost made the trip worthwhile. Looking over his dad's shoulder, he noticed Randy making his way through the crowd. Steve broke one embrace and locked onto another.

As if they were children again, Steve and Randy cried together. He had missed his little brother, but was so glad that Randy's unit never made it to the Gulf. He was incredibly grateful that his baby brother had been spared the pain.

Nancy Manchester appeared out of nowhere. She was frantically searching the crowd when Billy found her and led her to the emotional reunion. Everything froze in place when their eyes locked. The family stood back. She ran to Steve and pulled him to her. Without saying anything, they hugged for some time. Then, she pushed away and grabbed his face. She peered into his eyes. He could see her tears turn from joyous relief to sorrow. She was looking into the eyes of an old man. The innocence that was once there, had been stripped away. She could see what he had missed in the mirror. She could see the pain and torment. Yet, she couldn't see why. He was holding on to that alone.

The family also searched his eyes for anything different. Everybody was curious to see if he had changed. Sensing it, he felt uncomfortable, but he wasn't going to make it easy for them. He answered the questions that were never asked and made his family laugh. He talked about the Middle East as though it was a joke. He was less than convincing, though the humor sliced the tension into shreds. His mother never bought a word of it.

The first few notes of America's song ceased the laughter. Over some giant speakers, the National Anthem called out to its desert warriors. He snapped to attention and threw up a crisp salute. As he listened to the song, he understood every word. The words meant so much more now. The tears welling up in his swollen eyes told his family the truth. He had paid a hefty price.

Immediately following the Anthem, Lee Greenwood's voice belted out the song of an era. An echo of sobs and sniffles consumed the hangar. He cried again until the final tear turned to dust. He had finally used them all. The memorable tune ended and the party began. The boys had two hours to get reacquainted with their loved ones, then it was back to Fort Devens. They were still the property of the U.S. Army.

Billy produced a large cooler and slid it over to Steve. He opened it and found a quart of beer lying in a bed of crushed ice. His eyes lit up. He chugged his first taste of hops and barley and thought he was going to vomit. It had been a long time, and his body's reaction was less than accepting. He passed the bottle and the remainder was consumed as part of a toast.

While talking in a tight circle, a little boy broke through the Manchester perimeter and handed Steve a T-shirt. "Can you sign this, please?" the boy asked.

He smiled and gave his first autograph. The hero routine was making him uneasy. Looking around the hangar, he saw that he wasn't alone.

Ryan was too busy kissing his wife's belly to notice anything else. All the other guys were either huddled with their own families, or making out with their lovers. Steve spotted Tony. He was the only soldier still crying. Tony was quietly weeping in a dark corner, and seeing it made Steve's chest heat up inside. He could see what was happening. Tony's wounds from Vietnam — open wounds that were two decades old — were being healed by love. The incredible amount of love that engulfed the huge hangar was just enough to make the platoon sergeant forget a different homecoming. Steve shed one last tear for his long-suffering friend.

It felt like only minutes before the 661st was called to a formation. It was already time to go. Steve said his goodbyes and walked toward the buses. He would see his family in a few days. In a few hours, he would be alone with Monica. There was a lot to look forward to. With a happy smile, he jumped on the bus and waved at the dwindling crowd.

Taking his usual seat in the rear, he closed his eyes. He was exhausted. His body was drained from the overwhelming experience, and all he wanted to do was sleep.

Gasping for a breath, he sat erect. It was the beginning of a full-blown panic attack, and he couldn't stop it. His body trembled, then his arms and legs became numb. As his heart raced wildly, his mind spiraled downward. It lasted no more than ten minutes, but the attack was proof that his struggles were far from over. Operation Desert Storm was complete, but Steve was embarking on a more painful mission. He was being carried away in the eye of an unexpected storm. It was a storm that raged out of control deep inside of him, tearing at his spirit, his whole being. There were two enemies to fight this time. The first ferocious battle raged within his heart and mind. He had helped to win the war, now he needed to win the peace. The second battle was with the U.S. Government.

Chapter 9

Fighting on Two Battlefronts

As the bus carried The Dream Team back to their old barracks, Steve was caught in the clutches of another anxiety attack. It was a premonition of things to come. For the second time in his life, the Army had broken him down, only this time, the damage reached him on all four deepest levels of his being. He was affected physically, mentally, emotionally and even spiritually. Left shattered, the burden of putting the pieces back together was buried in his desire to reclaim his life. It was like starting over from inside a deep, dark hole.

The squeal of the bus' tires signaled that The Dream Team reached their final destination. Seated in the rear, Steve knew better. He knew only too well. He was embarking on a great quest for inner peace and, if he was fortunate, a small taste of happiness. The passionate search was going to take everything inside of him. With no choice, he jumped on the emotional roller coaster and held on for the wildest ride of his life.

They were at Fort Devens for no more than ten minutes before Captain Wall announced, "Next formation will be at 0700, tomorrow morning. Company, Dismissed!" The thunderous applause was deafening. Steve waited for Monica. Within the hour, she pulled up and threw open the passenger door. He closed it and walked around to the driver's side. She just shuffled over, never questioning it. He stomped on the accelerator and they were on their way to a hotel. They had waited months for this very moment. The look on their faces said it all.

The door had barely closed behind them before clothes began flying around the room. It felt like the first time all over again. He ravaged his wife, only to find that his stamina was at an all time low. It was seconds before he was smoking the night's first cigarette. It didn't matter. The lovers had until morning. It was a time to rediscover each other.

Finally dozing off from total exhaustion, he awoke in a struggle for oxygen. Slipping into another horrifying attack, he turned to find Monica staring at him in terror. He looked into her wide eyes and attempted to speak, but was saved by her nervous question, "My God, what is it, Steve?"

He could only shake his head. He eventually told her, "I haven't slept in three months. I close my eyes, but I still hear things. I can still sense everything that's going on around me!"

With no reply, she wrapped her trembling arms around him. Through a pool of Monica's tears, the look of horror remained. The vision sent more fear ripping through his body. Her hug felt different. Peering into her eyes, he wondered if the tears were for him or for herself. They had traveled different paths for awhile, and it seemed like those paths led in opposite directions. The brief war had created an enormous distance. He hoped that time would bridge the gap. He longed to feel the embrace he had missed.

Morning arrived and he returned to his squad. He hadn't missed any one of them. From the look on their faces, they hadn't missed him either. The boys had spent an eternity together and now each man needed his space. Another bus carted them off to the fort's gymnasium. Appropriately enough, it was where it all started.

Steve prepared to outprocess from the big, green machine. He and the other soldiers stripped naked, expecting to be bounced from one station to the next. It was a misguided assumption. Instead, a lone doctor arrived and quickly informed his patients, "Get dressed people. If need be, we will examine you on an individual basis. Please, take one of the questionnaires and pass the rest to your right." Without another word, he left.

Steve's body quivered. It wasn't from fear or panic. It was from a rush of pure anger. The cruel game was sinful. After the meticulous pre-war exam, the veterans of Operation Desert Storm weren't even going to receive a token physical examination. The Army wasn't even pretending to care. Like their Vietnam War predecessors, Uncle Sam just wanted them off his menial payroll. Steve looked down the ranks. His fury became magnified.

Almost every one of his comrades had been violently ill with flu-like symptoms. They had all experienced long bouts with diarrhea, fatigue, head and body aches. Most were still feeling sick, but now they suffered from shock. Not one of them could believe what was happening. After their months of selfless service to their country, they were being dismissed without so much as a proper medical screening. With all of their physical and mental maladies, they were being booted out. It was criminal. Steve was outraged and decided to test the system — a decision that only caused more bitter pain. The government's giant machine knew exactly what it was doing. It had practiced and perfected the blatant lies 20 years earlier.

He truthfully completed the questionnaire and was quickly called for a medical evaluation. Besides taking the basic vitals, the annoyed doctor spent very little time examining him. There was no blood or urine extracted for testing and his physical complaints were virtually ignored. At the completion of the three minute exam, the man barked, "You will not be released from the United States Army until you are psychiatrically cleared!" The strict order was not meant to detect any legitimate problems. It was a threat and that threat was carried out immediately.

Leery of the dark forces he faced, Steve stepped into the Army's psychiatric ward. He sat before a middle-aged captain and explained the many physical ailments he had suffered while on active duty, along with the feelings of stress that accompanied them. The man grinned coldly throughout the explanation.

"Sergeant Manchester, we can document your complaints and attempt to detect the real problems. In the meantime, you will remain on active duty and be confined to this ward for months of observation. It's your choice."

The captain was only doing his job.

Steve imagined more time away from his family. He pictured the prison and the screaming men locked inside of padded rooms. The mental photos of the Army taking full ownership of him were petrifying. The doctor could read his face. Awaiting the answer, the government's representative accepted his shaking head as a no.

With a simple wave of his pen, the military shrink released him into civilian life. As far as the Army was concerned, Steve Manchester sustained no injury in the Gulf, physical or psychological. The interview reached beyond neglect. Through intimidation, coercion and the threat of lost freedom, they won the first round. Enraged, Steve knew it was far from over. It was going to be a long fight.

A mere two days drifted by and the 661st M.P. Company was told to cut their losses and leave. Their job as soldiers was done. Each person was honorably discharged back into the National Guard. Although it should have been a time of celebration, most drove away with their heads spinning. Only months earlier, America's defenders of democracy proudly answered their country's call. With honor, they helped free Kuwait from the forces of oppression. Now, suffering from a wide variety of debilitating symptoms, they were never diagnosed or treated for any.

Together, they were fighting again. The veterans of Operation Desert Storm were fighting for the truth — the truth about what the government quickly labeled the "Persian Gulf Syndrome," or "Mystery Illness."

Leaving Fort Devens, Steve knew that for the government he swore to uphold and defend, there was no mystery. The real issues were liability and compensation. The almighty dollar was going to dictate the outcome. It didn't look promising.

The long ride home was driven in silence. Filled with a bitter anger toward the government and the anticipation of finally going home, his emotions danced between good and evil. Breaking his harsh train of thought, Monica said, "Your parents want us to go over for lunch."

He cringed. He longed to be with them, too, but he also wanted to sit on his own couch.

"Okay," he said and took the detour.

Everyone was at the table when they arrived. His mom had made a big spread and they all sat to eat. There was silence. Everyone waited for Steve to speak. He didn't. He ate. His mom began.

"I don't know if this is the right time to tell you this, but . . . ."

"Go ahead," he told her.

"I had some very strange feelings the day that you got into the accident over there. I didn't say anything to anyone, but said a prayer for you and finally went to sleep . . . ." She stopped. She was already crying. ". . . Your grandmother came to me in a dream and told me, 'Don't worry about Stevie. He's going to be okay. There was someone there to hold his head . . . .'"

Goose bumps covered his body and the dike blew wide open. Everyone cried. Steve looked up. Everyone was crying but Monica. She looked uncomfortable. It scared him.

Cutting the visit short, he grabbed her and headed home. Turning onto his street, his heart jumped into his throat. Before he reached his driveway, he saw that his house had been lovingly prepared for a hero's homecoming.

There were hundreds of tiny yellow ribbons offsetting the red, white and blue. He drew in a deep breath and looked over at his smiling wife.

"Welcome home, Babe!" she said, hugging him.

He pulled in slowly, trying to remember what it once felt like. He couldn't. That was a different lifetime. Stepping out of the car, he yelled, "McGruff!"

The dog let out a wailing howl, announcing to the whole neighborhood that his master finally returned.

Starting toward the back yard, he ran to see his old friend. Monica laughed at the playful meeting. He unhooked his loyal companion from the long runner and the three headed for the house.

Stepping over the threshold, he waited for the warm and wonderful feeling of being home. It didn't come. With each step up the staircase, he expected to be overcome with the relief of returning to the comfort of his real life. It never came. There was something different. Walking from one room into the next, he toured every inch of the house. Besides being heavily decorated for The Dream Team's homecoming party, it was exactly as he had left it. He suddenly realized what he was feeling. He had hoped that once he made it home, all of his pain would disappear. Instead, there was a disappointing sadness. He felt like a stranger in his own home.

Grabbing a cold brew from the stocked refrigerator, he noticed one of the photos stuck to the door by a magnet. It was an old picture of the smiling Dream Team, proof that life was once carefree and fun. Emptying both duffel bags onto the floor, he found a similar group photo that had been taken just weeks earlier in the Gulf. The smiles were still there, but comparing the two, his heart sank with understanding. He could see what he had missed in the mirror. He could now see why his mother had cried so mournfully. They hadn't grown up. They had grown old. Shaking his head, he stepped out onto the deck.

He took a seat on one of the colorful patio chairs and McGruff flopped down beside him. He chuckled. Petting the dog with one hand, he used the other to take small sips from the shiny can. It was a beautiful day, and he listened to the sounds of spring. One neighbor, while sunbathing, blasted her radio. Another wrestled with his beat-up lawn mower. Before long, the frustrated gardener got the mower started. The noise made him take notice of his own yard. The grass needed a trim. Lounging back, he had no desire to cut it. It was then, without warning, that the past jumped out at him. Only two weeks before, he was trying to save the life of a child. Now, the grass needed cutting. Priorities had changed. Yet, he wasn't ready to change with them. Things that were so important before, now meant relatively nothing. It wasn't going to be a smooth transition.

He and Monica spent the next several hours talking on the deck. Holding hands, they knew there was a need to renew their relationship. The scant 100-hour war had been quite an interruption. As they talked, he sensed a new independence in his wife. All alone, she had held down the fort while he was gone. She had gotten used to doing things her way. The war had taken its toll on her, too. In many respects, she had been stripped of her own innocence, and was now as different as he. They both needed to adapt.

Monica never asked him any questions about his trials and tribulations in the Gulf. Knowing her fears and insecurities, he never offered the information. He felt it better to protect her from the nightmares. Regretfully, time proved him wrong. Keeping the pain inside made it fester like a cancerous sore. No matter how much it hurt, he needed to open the floodgates. He didn't. Instead, they spoke of other problems that needed attention, such as the burden of outstanding debts. There was no denying it. They were in an incredible financial dilemma.

The Soldiers and Sailors Relief Act was a federal law protecting the job security and credit status of servicemen during combat service. It also prohibited any creditor from foreclosure, but that protection was lifted as soon as they returned. Steve and Monica now faced a pack of hungry wolves, each snapping at any penny they could collect. She had only recently returned to work, and his army pay wasn't half of what his civilian salary had been. He felt as if they would drown in unpaid bills. It was going to be years to catch up. The pressure was sure to place an enormous strain on the marriage. They agreed they were in big trouble.

Sickened by the depressing conversation, he told her, "I need a few hours alone. I haven't been completely by himself in months and I really need to sort out my thoughts. The next few days will be consumed with parties and parades. I just have to have some solitude . . . ."

Though she hated to see him go anywhere, she waved as he drove off to the beach. He yearned for the tranquility of the ocean, but breathing through an oncoming panic attack, he wondered if it could be found.

Heading due east, the anxiety surged throughout his body. His palpitating heart raced faster, and his mouth felt like he had eaten a pillow. Then, the speeding car was stopped by a red light. Waiting for the green, every second that passed seemed like forever. He was dizzy from the million jumbled thoughts rushing through his mind. He had the sudden urge to punch out the windshield. He couldn't breath and had to get out of the car. Throwing the shifter into park, he leapt out and tried to calm himself down. Pacing back and forth, he thought about going to the hospital, but knew that it was just another powerful panic attack. His only option was to suffer through it. Tingling from the surge of released adrenaline, he ignored the honking horns behind him. Slowly, he took his seat behind the steering wheel. Scared and confused, he forged on.

While trying to swallow the lump that had formed in his throat, he attempted to direct his thinking away from the past and focus on the future. These thoughts scared him even more. Feeling the way he did, he was afraid to face the next day, never mind look any further. It was agonizing. He could understand feeling anxiety while he was in the Gulf, but he was home now. He was safe. It was terrifying. For months, every second of his life, he had felt his heart was going to break from depression, or explode from the severe anxiety. Now, it didn't look like anything was going to change. Wiping the cold sweat from his brow, he pulled the car into his favorite spot and shut off the ignition.

Stepping out of the suffocating interior, he walked around the front and jumped up on the hood. His sneakers kicked some sand into the air. The fine powder made his skin crawl. Pulling his knees up to his chest, he watched as the tide ran in and out. Desperately hoping to feel the smallest sense of serenity, the inner torture only increased. The anxiety grew stronger. He felt worse than the night he had mourned the death of his best friend, only now he didn't know what to grieve over. Sticking it out for better than an hour, he finally gave in. It was a losing battle. There was no peace to be found at the old safe haven. That hurt even more. He understood that it was only going to get worse. There was no question about it. Each day was going to be more difficult than the one before it. He needed answers and, jumping back into the car, he didn't have the slightest idea where to start. Turning the key, he looked down at the floor and noticed the small mound of sand. He shook his head, screaming, "Will I ever get away from it? Will it ever be over?"

He steered toward home, knowing only one thing. He knew that, for the rest of his life, he never wanted to see another grain of sand.

Returning to his house, he found Monica visibly upset. After his quick dash to the beach, there was no need to ask why. Although there was no way she could understand everything that churned inside him, he had no

alternative but to try to explain. Reluctantly, he began, avoiding each grotesque detail of his experiences in the Gulf.

Her frightened face scared him more. It was clear. There was no room
for his pain. There were just too many problems on the home front. Feeling
very much alone, he stopped talking. That brought relief to his wife's eyes.
Wrapping her limp arms around him, she whispered, "Before you know
it, everything will be back to normal. You'll see!"

She was speaking blindly. For him, normal was no where in sight. The
termite of miscommunication had taken its first bite of many.

He reported to the armory the following morning. After a brief formation, the company was transported back to the bus depot from where
they had departed. On the way up, he watched as the parade route filled in
with thousands of spectators. In a hurried fashion, the boys were dropped
off. They quickly lined themselves into their respective positions. For the
last time, The Dream Team marched together as one unit.

The Army band struck up a tune and the soldiers of Operation Desert
Storm began the final leg of their journey home. With each step of the victory celebration, Steve's heart pounded to the drummer's beat. The cheers
of a proud and grateful nation echoed through the crowded street. There were
screams and whistles. People broke through the flimsy barriers to shake the hands of their hometown heroes. It was
the grandest welcome ever. There was no order and the
soldiers followed the mood of the crowd. Steve waved and
shook hands. Like his friends, he even broke ranks to touch
those who were out of his reach. The cries of patriotism
lasted the entire two miles. Through it all, he felt alive.

Once halted, he noticed his family gathered beneath the
flagpole. They stood together, wiping their eyes and posi-
tioning themselves to watch the emotional ceremony. The

Along a parade route, The Dream Team makes
their final leg of the journey home. Steve
marches in the foreground.

The Dream Team snaps a stiff salute — just before receiving the Liberation of Kuwait and Southwest Asia Service medals.

National Anthem called out to its sons and daughters. Instinctively, he snapped a stiff salute. After paying respect to America's song, the boys listened to the words of several familiar speakers. One person after the other spoke of duty, honor and country. They also spoke of valor, which Steve had learned was usually inspired by fear. At the conclusion, each soldier was decorated for their service in the Persian Gulf. They were awarded with the National Defense, the Liberation of Kuwait and Southwest Asia Service medals. Looking down at his breast pocket, Steve was overcome with pride. Then, looking up at his own cheering section, that feeling was replaced by love. With a closing prayer, the company was released into the massive celebration. It was a day that would never be forgotten.

The following morning ushered in the first homecoming party. It was hosted at Steve's house. The boys joked that it was just another stop on The Dream Team's world tour, and were grateful that the Manchester family had pulled out all the stops. Poking fun at Saddam Hussein, the gala was quickly labeled the mother of all parties. There were more people than Steve could count. Everyone he ever loved was in attendance. The entire Dream Team was there — his family, his friends, everybody. From late morning until early into the next, they celebrated their successful mission and safe return home. There was barbecued food, kegs of beer and music that blared into the sultry night.

Dancing with his sisters, Steve noticed several of his friends personally include his Uncle Brian in the homecoming. With tearful eyes, the veteran of jungle warfare accepted and took his rightful place as one of the guests of honor. Drinking the night away, Steve discovered that the alcohol numbed his anxiety, but it was only a bandage. This awareness made him vow that, no matter how much the booze eased his pain, it wouldn't become a habit. Looking back at his uncle, a man who continued to drown his sorrows, he was reminded to keep that promise. To his surprise, Steve thought about being shunned by the U.S. government. Glancing back at his drunken uncle, his own self-pity led to shame. He and his friends were experiencing only a fraction of this man's pain. At least they had the support of the people. Uncle Brian never did.

On the fourth day of civilian life, Steve moped around the house in his underwear. It was a perfect opportunity to get caught up on recent events. Fumbling through some video tapes, he discovered that Monica had captured the entire war in a neat, little collection. Making an early lunch, he threw in the first tape and watched. It was a running account of Operation Desert Storm. Certain news stations had televised the war from beginning to end. As a result, their ratings and stock values had skyrocketed. Reflecting back on his army pay and the financial dilemma that he and Monica were in, he thought it was quite ironic that some people had made money off of the war. Snickering, he ate his sandwich and watched.

He realized that he had missed so much of the war by being there in person. The historical videos showed a truly different war than he remembered. There were no faces of the innocent children who were pushed over the threshold of death. Instead, he viewed a sanitized version, which concentrated on the true enemies — groups of barbaric animals that he and the boys had never encountered.

He also learned that the analytical reports were far too revealing. Considering that the Iraqi Army monitored the rapid broadcasts and relied on them for a good part of their intelligence, he decided that certain members of the news profession should have been tried for treason. The American public had a right to know what was happening, but they didn't have to know about it *as* it was happening. Every armchair warrior and military expert in the nation got in on the action. It was mostly rambling bullshit and it made him nauseous. As one more analyst began talking about America's disadvantage of fighting in the desert, he had seen enough. He shut the tape off and swore to never view the sensationalized reports again.

He despised the media. It was just like the time the marathon runner was suffocated by their exhaust fumes years earlier, the media's philosophies hadn't changed. No matter the price, just get the story. In the case of

Desert Storm, there were thousands of lives at stake. It didn't matter. As long as the story got out, they had done their job. He put the tapes in their rightful place. He threw them into the trash.

That evening, he sat in his basement with his four high school chums. They had decided to throw a poker game as a private celebration of his return. Scott brought the bottle of vodka. No sooner had they taken their respective seats around the table, when George asked, "So Steve, you've seemed a little preoccupied. What in the hell happened over there that's got you so wired?"

Steve looked around the table. With an honest concern, they waited for his response. He didn't know if they could truly understand, but it was his third opportunity to get some of the heavy weight off of his constricted chest. He took a sip from his vodka and soda, and started.

"There was a kid, a small, innocent girl who was rushed into camp by her screaming father. She had lost both an arm and leg to a land mine, but it was her eyes that told us she was close to death. By the time we started C.P.R., her gurgling lungs were struggling for air, so . . . ."

He stopped. George stood and nervously excused himself. Matt closely followed behind and the two headed for the bathroom. Although it hurt, he understood. The gruesome details of a real war experience were too much to handle. Searching Scott's avoiding eyes, he realized that it was even too painful to listen to. The truth was better left unsaid.

George returned to the table and offered the universal answer to all problems.

"You'll get over it, Steve,"

Steve felt even more alone. The mention of the war had driven a wedge between the old friends. Now, he was different. Things had drastically changed. He felt an awkward responsibility for it. He was just on a different level in life. In such a short period of time, he had gained a harsh maturity. Maintaining a false smile, he gave his friends the benefit of the doubt. Remembering the tape he had thrown into the trash just hours before, reality left its sting again. The glorious battle scenes, viewed by his friends and the rest of the world, never reflected his experience. There was no way they could ever understand the chaotic disaster, the painful conflicts, or the cruel deaths. Besides, Hollywood's unreal version of the war was over for them once the media stopped following it. It was less personal that way. He never judged them for it. On the contrary, he envied them.

His mind floated back to a time of great suffering. He tried, once again, to make sense of his inner struggles. To him, the war would have made more sense, been strangely easier, had he met the enemy face to face. Instead, they remained invisible. They planted their land mines, murdered sinless children and vanished into the shadows of the shifting sands. No threat was seen, yet it was still felt deep within. The constant anticipation was like speeding 200 miles per hour, only to smash into a brick wall each time. Like a man restrained, witnessing the slaughter of pure innocence, he was forced to watch helplessly. There were no means to displace the anger, nor any outlet for the aggression. There was only the frustration of seeing constant victimization. Operation Desert Storm was certainly a war like no other, where the same philosophy had stood strong for centuries: Kill or be killed. This time, soldiers were trained to fight, sent to strike, yet watched as technology did the job. In a sick sense, had he been shot at, then returned fire, all of the hatred and horrifying death would have made better sense. All the rage, which was fueled by fear, would have been unleashed and not been stored deep within, where it multiplied and silently destroyed.

It was well past midnight when his mind staggered back into the present. With a stack of poker chips sitting in front of him and the help of a smooth bottle of vodka, it turned out to be a pretty good night. Walking his intoxicated guests to the door, he stood back to watch George shove his foot in his mouth one last time.

"Steve, did you have to kill anyone?"

Although he expected it sooner, the ignorant question made him smile. It was the alcohol that gave George the courage to ask the question everyone else was wondering. Their eager faces awaited a reply.

His smile widened. It was a lose-lose situation. If he answered yes, then he was a murderer and would be labeled forever. If he answered no, then he went off to war and experienced nothing. He told the truth. "No, George, not yet." The tension was broken by a nervous laughter. They finally staggered down the driveway.

As he closed the front door, he noticed something sparkle from beneath Scott's jacket. It was the empty vodka bottle. His smile turned sincere. Scott, his dearest friend of them all, had decided to keep the souvenir. The gesture touched him and allowed him to hope that, in time, they would all be close again. The old friendships were worth the extra effort.

The following morning, he awoke with a heavy head, but quickly dressed in his desert camouflaged uniform. He wanted to personally thank the students of Darlene's elementary school for their unwavering support during the war. Pulling up to the large, brick schoolhouse, he checked his watch. He was right on time to meet the most honest people alive — children.

Starting with the Kindergarten, he dramatically expressed his appreciation and explained to the young children just how much their letters and packages meant. Their reactions were both cute and touching. With open mouths and wide eyes, each little person was overwhelmed by the presence of an American soldier in uniform. He slowly made his rounds through each class, finding that with each visit, Darlene was quickly gaining popularity. Starting from the bottom, one hour later, he finally reached the fifth grade class. The grinning teacher placed a small, wooden chair in the front of the class for his comfort. The chair had the opposite effect and made him squirm with anxiety. A map of the Middle East was pulled down over the chalkboard and the questions started flying. The kids wanted answers. He was astounded by how educated on the war they already were. By the time it was over, even he had learned a thing or two.

With the permission of an equally interested teacher, he fielded one good question after the other. He answered the children as honestly as possible, sensing that they would have seen straight through anything else. Through the bombardment, their strong infatuation with death was amazing. He knew they were not alone. Like most other adults, the teacher was just as curious. The children were just more straight forward in asking. He liked that. He liked the intelligent questions so much that he decided to speak to them like adults.

Though the increasing distress made him want to crawl out of his skin, he stood and addressed the class in a soft tone. "War is the most terrible thing there is, but unfortunately, sometimes it's a necessary evil. With men like Saddam Hussein walking the earth and threatening mankind, sometimes there's no choice!" Pausing, he cautiously continued, "If you never remember this day or never remember me, that's okay, but try to remember what I'm about to tell you." Every set of youthful eyes were glued on him. "As you grow up, you may have to stand up for something you believe in. Those beliefs may end up causing you a great deal of sacrifice and pain, but trust me today — stand up! Do whatever it takes because if you don't, I promise, it'll cost you alot more later on in your lives!"

Finishing the spontaneous speech, he looked around the room to find unexpected understanding in most of their eyes. The deep words shocked him more than the children. It was as if they were waiting for something so strong. The room echoed with the clapping of tiny hands.

Grabbing for the doorknob, it was time to leave. He had taught them all he could. Through history books, they'd learn that war only produced four things: Wealth and power for those who waged it, and suffering and death for those who fought it. He looked back one last time at the beauty of their innocent faces. He prayed that not one of them would ever experience it first hand.

With sorrow, his mind drifted back to his own experience. He thought of war as nothing more than a killing machine — a machine that got rolling and didn't stop until it was done exterminating, mutilating or destroying lives. It never discriminated or felt anything. It only maimed physically, scarred mentally or killed and kept killing.

The grateful teacher patted his arm and startled him. Blushing from being caught in a terrible daydream, he waved goodbye and left.

Returning home, he was surprised to find Scott waiting in the driveway. Reaching the steps, Steve extended his hand in friendship. Instead of his own hand, Scott handed him a bottle. It was a full bottle of very expensive vodka. With a confused shrug of his shoulders, he accepted the gift.

Scott said, "Steve, we should never have drank that bottle last night. That was supposed to be saved for when you got home, but you're not home, are you?"

He never answered, but waited to hear more.

"I have no idea what kind of hell you went through, but at least I understand that you're in pain. I'm here, Steve. For whatever that's worth, I'm here for you!"

Steve hugged his friend. In a life that was getting foggier by the day, the first ray of hope had arrived. The long hug sealed more than a friendship, it bonded them together as brothers. When everyone else was tired of hearing it, Scott would still be there to listen.

Leaving, his friend yelled, "Steve, you call me when it's over. Then, we'll kill that bottle together!"

Steve threw him a thumbs-up and headed into the house. He knew it would be some time, but holding the bottle tight, he longed to drink the symbol of inner peace. He was already counting the days until he and Scott would celebrate again. The countdown had begun.

The first week of being home was almost over. He had one more before returning to work. The prison, another bizarre world, was patiently waiting. He was worried.

The isolated and self-contained society functioning behind the giant walls was often violent, primarily negative and always risky for every officer who walked within. For the most part, he remembered a brutal and dreary picture that was painted by cold-blooded murderers and despised child molesters. Not much different from war, survival was the name of the game, and the weak were preyed upon in a shark feeding frenzy. It was another place where horrors became reality and reality continually changed. Behind the thick walls, concealed as well as his own feelings, the dominant emotions were fear and anger. Within that sub-society, he had witnessed every illicit activity, from drug smuggling and extortion to prostitution, with such heinous crimes as homosexual rape being commonplace. For many of the inmates, the only two exits were escape or suicide. Very often, one or the other path was taken. But the money and benefits were too good. He had to return.

Dreading his re-entry into the grotesque system, he doubted that he was ready. He wasn't even close to healing from one violent experience and was already taking the plunge into another. He needed help. Swallowing whatever pride he had left, he reluctantly called the V.A. hospital. He felt ashamed, but made the appointment. As he hung up the receiver, he decided he had made the right move. It was better to face up to the problem. He had only been home for a week, and already he was a walking powder keg. If he waited ten years, he'd probably be drinking a quart of whiskey a day and beating his wife with the bottle. Writing the time of the appointment on the calendar, he was blinded by the irony. He was looking to the government for help in entering another world full of daily traumas. It was going to take time to clear his mind and see the truth. It was going to take a great deal of time.

With reservation, he and Monica pulled into the huge, brick building complex. In the center, a shadowing water tower stood guard. Its 50-foot letters, V.A., told him that he was in the right place. Filled with even more doubts, he turned off the ignition and hurried to his appointment. No matter how confused, he knew he needed help. Besides, even a bad experience would be child's play compared to the gripping panic attacks that were controlling his every waking moment. Opening the creaky door, he stepped in. In his long and feverish search for answers, it was the first step in the right direction.

The first thing to make an impression on him was a bronze plaque, hanging a tad crooked, in the main foyer. The simple, yet honest words of F.D.R. stopped visitors in their tracks. Each person was granted the opportunity to contemplate its deep meaning. He took that opportunity. It read: Those who have long enjoyed such privileges as we enjoy, forget in time that men have died to win them.

The message spoke to his soul and after bowing his head with understanding, he looked around the hectic corridor. There were veterans lying on gurneys, while others were strapped to wheel chairs. Many were amputees, yet there were a good number who appeared unscathed. Physically, these men looked as healthy as the day they were born, but Steve had learned the hard way. All too often, looks are deceiving. He searched their faces.

They were the more unfortunate warriors. They had lost so much more than sight or limbs. They had lost themselves, and there was no prosthesis for the mind or the spirit. It was those who were physically whole that he could sympathize with. They had suffered, and continued to battle without any acknowledgment for their invisible pain. Their eyes were empty or consumed with torment. He knew their dilemma. He shared it. These men suffered alone, each one fighting on the battlefields within their anguished minds. Whether it was depression, anxiety or a different mental struggle, each veteran continued the search for the right path out of hell. He could tell that many had been on that quest for decades. That scared the hell out of him. Walking among them, reality cut to the core. He was now one of them.

There was never any doubt that he was in for a rough ride, but his greatest fear was triggered by the blank stares of the lost souls who filled the main corridor. Above all else, he didn't want to be left behind. He dreadfully feared being stuck in the past, where the rest of his life would seem anti-climatic. He didn't want his mind to become frozen in Operation Desert Storm, a six-month period of time. He wanted to move forward. He needed to look ahead toward the future. It was a future of trouble and uncertainty, but it was still awaiting his return. Urgently, he grabbed Monica's hand and walked faster.

The long, empty corridors were covered in yellow tile, from the dull floor running halfway up the walls. With the nauseating scent of pine oil and the obnoxious fluorescent bulbs lighting their way, it felt like standing in a recently emptied fish bowl. The desolate hallway had an air of unfeeling about it, which he found was deceptive. More often than not, behind every door, there was a caring and compassionate soul eager to help any suffering veteran. They were the jewels of a totally inefficient system. The Veterans Administration, like any government agency, was a bureaucratic mess, with its miles of red tape and ludicrous obstacles to overcome. It was always the employees, the people, who made the difference.

Wiping his sweaty palms onto his trousers, he knocked on the door of room 206.

A gentle voice answered, "Come in."

He hesitantly opened the door and gestured for his reluctant wife to step in. The genuine smile of a caring and compassionate man beamed from behind a small desk.

His name was Mark Goldstein. He was a clinical psychologist, though in the endless months to follow, he would become a friend. The awkwardness was nipped in the bud and the session began at once. Mark asked only one question, "So, what's eating at you?"

Steve rattled on for the next hour. He couldn't speak fast enough, and, when it was nearly over, he realized that he had barely put a dent in the possible causes of his mental and emotional turmoil. The entire time, Monica looked on in shock, frightened for their future. He dreaded her reaction.

As they concluded, Mark kicked his feet onto the tiny desk, placed his hands behind his head and nearly knocked Steve over with his truthful words.

"Let me see, Monica was injured, making it difficult to meet the mortgage payments. You got sent off to war, responsible for the lives of nine other people. While you were there, you saw countless deaths, a good part being innocent children. You were left for dead after a traumatic accident. Then, at 23, you face your own mortality two more times?" Sitting up straight, he grinned. "I have no idea why you'd have problems with panic or anxiety now?"

Steve stared into his eyes.

The man unloaded a hearty laugh.

He got the message, but before he could say a word, Mark asked another simple question.

"Besides the anxiety, how do you feel about yourself right now?"

Without hesitation, he sincerely responded, "I feel like a coward!"

The candid answer came as a shock, though the therapist wasted no time with the obvious follow-up. He inquired, "Why? Did you ever run from anything or neglect your duties?"

He bowed his head and stumbled through the answer. "No! Never once! But there's more to it. I never had to kill anyone, not one of my friends died and I came out of it basically unharmed, but the entire time I was there, I was paralyzed with fear! I still feel ashamed of that."

The honest answer touched the man. He stood and placed his hand on Steve's shoulder. "Steve, you're harder on yourself than anyone I've met. To be honest with you, I'm glad that we've met, but let me say this — as a result of the accident and other experiences in the Gulf, I can already tell you suffer from Post Traumatic Stress Disorder, P.T.S.D. To what degree, it's still too early to tell. As far as feeling like a coward, get that thought out of your head. It takes great courage to admit fear. You are no coward! You are a man, and a good and decent man at that. Good men feel fear. It's instinctive and quite normal. Decent men detest death, and let's be grateful for that. Unfortunately, like many of us, you've watched too many John Wayne and Audie Murphy movies. We both know that war isn't like that. War is for real. It's permanent!" He smiled kindly, then added, "We'll get through this. I promise. Until Wednesday, it's one day at a time, okay?"

Steve and Monica rose. They shook Mark's hand and left. It was a good start and he was grateful, but the anxiety level had only skyrocketed since his arrival. He had hoped to feel better, but was brutally disappointed. Walking out of the building, he lit a cigarette and looked back. There was an older man sitting on the front steps. He was talking to himself and chuckling at his own responses. Steve desperately hoped it wasn't a sign of things to come. Jumping in the car, he didn't know what to think. He felt powerless over his own life. Then, as he expected, his mind became lightened with an unwelcome dizziness, while the plentiful adrenaline overtook his bloodstream.

Suffering ever so quietly, he listened to the scared, but selfish words of his wife. "Babe, I don't think that you need this therapy. In time, it'll pass." Staring into his watering eyes, she awaited a reply.

He said nothing. There were times when the strongest statement he could make was to remain silent. Besides, the truth about his future was nearly carved in stone. Monica couldn't face reality. Her fragile shoulders couldn't bare the weight. For her, if trouble remained out of sight, then her mind was clear. He felt destroyed. He was totally on his own now — alone to find his way through a long, dark tunnel of pain.

He returned to the V.A. alone on Wednesday, surprised to find Mark Goldstein sitting with another doctor. Standing, Mark introduced his colleague, the staff psychiatrist. Together, they talked to him about the need for medication. They explained that the mind and body were connected and for the time being, a small dose of some sedative might take the edge off. They promised it would help him through each immeasurable day of torment.

He refused. "I'd rather face this thing without drugs. I've seen too many people become addicted to them."

The psychiatrist stood. Considerately, he asked, "Mr. Manchester, if you had diabetes, would you take insulin?"

With a nod, he offered the only response.

The good doctor continued, "Well, you have an anxiety disorder and the only person suffering from your disorder is you. For the time being, we'd like to supplement your therapy with medication. For all we know, it could be a chemical imbalance."

The man was right. He couldn't deny it. He was barely surviving, never mind living. Sadly, all he wanted was to function normally, so that he could return to work and support his worried wife. Taking the prescription, he eventually bounced from Valium to Xanax to others, detesting every sedating pill he popped. He struggled with the medication, but always found that when not taking it, the anxiety was much worse. In the meantime, however, it enabled him to walk through the steel doors of the prison.

He was welcomed back with open arms, and the administration immediately promoted him to prison investigator. Operation Desert Storm had paid its first dividend. Changing into a different shade of blue, the new uniform brought more respect from the prison's clientele, but it also brought more responsibility. Officer Manchester successfully had made it within his profession. Focusing his energies on the new job, he expected life to return to normal. It didn't. Instead, as part of an intricate team, he was tasked to maintain order within the concrete jungle. It was time to think as the convicts did. From their strong desire for drugs and weapons, to their illicit businesses such as loan sharking, gambling and pimping, the games never ended. He and his partners encountered every con-artist imaginable, but with the frequent assistance of many enthusiastic informants, they continually penetrated the prison's underworld and fought crime behind the walls. No matter what they did, violence was woven into everything.

The first weekend drill in the National Guard since returning from the Middle East started on a bad note. Although his six-year enlistment expired while serving in Iraq, Steve was barely reconsidering a re-enlistment when First Sergeant Kline appeared before the company. After announcing his own return, the coward took roll call.

"From now on, people, you are no longer authorized to wear the desert camouflage uniform. I expect to see you all dressed in the green woodland next drill."

The blood boiled in Steve's veins. Hearing a hum travel through the ranks, he knew his anger was matched by all. Everyone stood furious. The order was given because Kline didn't own a desert camouflaged uniform. The jellyfish didn't have enough nerve to serve his country, yet he still showed his sorry face. To Steve, it was a personal insult.

By mid-morning, Kline waved him over. He asked, "Sergeant Manchester, why is Private Tripp wearing his hat like a cowboy?"

He couldn't take it. Impulsively, he snapped, "Because Private Tripp's earned the right to wear his hat any way he chooses. To be honest, I think he looks quite handsome."

Kline stood speechless. Finally, he screamed, "If you can't stand serving under me, then get the hell out of this unit!"

Masking his own rage, he smiled. Patting the man's shoulder, he softly replied, "I think I'll do just that. Besides, I've completed my job. But of course, you'll never know that feeling, will you?"

Kline stormed off and Steve began his goodbyes. His military days were over. He knew, after Desert Storm, life in the National Guard would never be the same. He was right. Month after month, The Dream Team dwindled down to a handful of die-hards. The tragedy was that they never spoke about their experiences of war again. They reunited at the birth of Ryan's son, Christopher. They also met at the tattoo parlor, where 30 men were branded with The Dream Team's logo, the horned demon holding its shield. There were weddings and funerals, but life went on. Desert Storm became one of those passing phases. Each man wanted the experience so far behind him, that it wouldn't be so easy to look back. Besides squirming at the sight of sand, the smell of diesel fuel, the terror of life-like dreams and other reminders, they did their best to move forward. Their close-knit brotherhood gradually became a memory. It was sad. Although they all shared many of the same problems, and were the only people who could understand what the others were feeling, they each faced the aftermath of Desert Storm alone. Steve was sorry to walk away.

Life got more difficult, but remaining faithful to the therapy and struggling with having to take the medication, he continued his search for answers. He attempted group therapy, but the resentment between generations was bewildering. During the first session, one of the many Vietnam veterans turned to him, disrespectfully snarling, "I would have went to Desert Storm, but I couldn't get the weekend off!"

A Korean War veteran, his own predecessor, quickly countered the man's caustic humor. He was an equally bitter soul and barked, "Quit your crying. You're not the only one who never got any recognition!"

To top it off, the old-timer of the group slapped his knee, calling for everyone's attention. "You boys never saw anything. I fought in the big one!"

That was it for the group therapy. Ironically, whether it was in Europe, Korea, Vietnam or Iraq, each generation shared the same painful tradition. The same government, for which they had risked their lives, had betrayed each of them. From then on, Steve chose to stick with Mark Goldstein, only to find that the healing process took much more time than he could have imagined.

His days were consumed by worry. His nights were split between insomnia and terrifying nightmares. Steve had witnessed the murderous capabilities of men, so he experienced the same recurring dream. Night after night, he pictured himself committing the most hideous acts of violence while walking in his sleep. Shaken by the life-like nightmares, he placed pillows at the foot of the bed. They were obstacles, insuring that if he ever rose while sleeping, he would trip and awaken. There was no escape from it. There was no rest. Every second of his life had evolved into a living hell.

To combat it, he attended classes on meditation and read every book ever written on panic disorders. It helped, but very little. Physically, his body still ached from every joint, his head usually throbbed with a dull pain and the diarrhea lasted for weeks at a time. Looking into a mirror, he hardly recognized the face that stared back at him. It was swollen, and, though he carefully watched his diet and exercised regularly, he grew fatter by the day. His every waking moment was bogged down by tremendous fatigue. The physical problems were only getting worse. Monica stood by him, but only in the physical sense. He never stopped looking for the elusive answers.

Two enduring years elapsed and he found himself sitting in his doctor's office once again. At the risk of being fingered a hypochondriac, he knew his own body, and his problems reached far beyond anxiety. Convincing his doctor, more with his growing appearance than with his words, the man ordered blood work for a careful screening.

One week later, the doctor summoned him into his office.

"Steve, I apologize for not finding it sooner, but I think I now know part of your problem. Your thyroid gland, which regulates your body's metabolism, is barely functioning." Taking a seat across from his obese patient, he continued, "You have a hypothyroid and you've been suffering from a severe chemical imbalance. It's no wonder that you weren't misdiagnosed as a manic-depressive! We never looked in that direction because it doesn't run in your family. I recommend that you see a specialist, an endocrinologist, and I strongly suggest that you do so at the Veterans Administration. God only knows what invaded your body and caused this!"

He left feeling relieved. It was a very likely reason for the anxiety, the depression, even the suicide contemplation. It wasn't the whole answer, but it was a start. He finally held a piece of the puzzle.

He wasted no time and made his appointment with the Veterans Administration's endocrinologist. Expecting to receive a run-around, he was pleasantly surprised to find a female doctor, more concerned with the health of her patients than her own career advancement. He was given a thorough physical exam, followed up by extensive blood work. By the end of a long day of waiting, she called him in and closed the door behind her. It was a sign that the information, she was about to divulge, was off the record.

Fingering through some paperwork, she started.

"Steve, your entire gland system is a mess. Something foreign invaded your body and wreaked havoc! Your prostate is enlarged and will probably cause you problems in the future. Your thyroid is almost non-existent and the pituitary gland appears to be affected as well. The pituitary is an important link between the nervous system and endocrine system. It regulates activity in other glands, to include the fight or flight response. This explains the surges of adrenaline. Your hormones are out of whack."

He sat shocked at the diagnosis.

With no intent to pacify her patient, she continued.

"We can give you medication and monitor your progress, but it looks like you'll be dealing with this for the rest of your life."

Raising his hands, he asked, "Can you tell me what caused this?"

As if she expected the understandable question, she folded her hands and stared into his worried eyes.

"No, unfortunately, I don't have the means, nor the authority to do that. The V.A. has tied our hands with you guys, but let me say this: I've seen hundreds of Desert Storm veterans filter through here and there are thousands, suffering from a wide-range of debilitating symptoms, nation-wide. Believe it or not, you're one of the lucky ones! There have been thousands of young veterans inflicted with cancer, chronic fatigue, spinal problems, rashes, muscle and joint pain, respiratory disease, neurological disorders — the list goes on."

He was amazed. She didn't candy-coat anything.

She finished, "Take the medication and remember that your illness affects both the body and mind. In the meantime, I strongly advise you to file for a service-connected disability. Don't expect any positive results for awhile, but in the long run, the truth about whatever you guys were exposed to may be told."

With two prescriptions and a sympathetic smile, she released him from her honest care.

He returned home and informed Monica of his first major discovery since the beginning of his frantic search.

She replied, simply, "That's great."

Sadly, after all the years of loneliness, anger and resentment, they had already drifted apart. He could have screamed his joyous hopes at the top of his lungs and it would have fallen on deaf ears. To some degree, she had become just as hardened as he.

Rewinding the doctor's words in his head, he researched any available information on the illnesses of Desert Storm veterans. History was repeating itself. Just like the veterans from the Vietnam War, in epidemic proportions Desert Stormers faced their own invisible enemy. The only difference was that, unlike Agent Orange, the younger warriors couldn't even label the cause.

Through research and his own experience, he determined that there were three very likely causes for the crippling ailments. They were exposed to radioactive depleted uranium used by the Allied Forces. There were preventive, or experimental, vaccines administered to all American troops. There was also the possibility that chemical agents were used in the many Iraqi Scud attacks. The government offered other potential causes. They claimed that the puzzling illnesses could have been caused by microwave radiation, petrochemicals, insect bites, parasites, contamination from oil well fires, even the Allied bombing of specific bunkers storing Iraqi chemical agents. The list grew by the month. They pointed fingers in every direction but their own. Ironically, the causes of the physical illnesses didn't really matter. That answer could only come from the same government that realized that some truths were just too big, or too expensive, to tell. The real concerns were treatment and compensation.

The disabling ailments often turned into psychological problems as well. During the long search for answers, many young veterans became afflicted with anxiety or depression. In turn, the Veterans Administration quickly recognized the psychological problems and labeled them as Post Traumatic Stress Disorder. It was the only way for a suffering veteran, who missed work, to be compensated. It was also the government's way of placing blame where it never truly existed to begin with. Many of the psychological problems could have been avoided, were the physical problems solved. Steve had learned the hard way. The mind and body were connected. If one was neglected, the other would surely suffer as well. It was actually quite simple. While some foreign disease was beating the body senseless, gradually, the head was dying, too.

Searching within, he was sure he found another answer. For years, he had known that all war wounds weren't suffered on the battlefield. For many Desert Storm veterans, although the yellow ribbons and flags had been taken down, the shiny medals had lost their gleam and the euphoria of victory had subsided, the war would never be over.

Eventually, he took the doctor's strong advice and filed for the claim. She was right. He faced one denial after the next. It became another drawn-out battle with the government, fraught with controversy. Like veterans of the Vietnam War, he and his suffering comrades would wait years for any decision. He often wondered if he'd still be alive when they decided to reveal the truth. He sincerely doubted it.

Over the next long year, he and Monica strove to revive their failing marriage. He finally took his wife up on her generous offer. They decided to have a child. The decision wasn't as easy for them as it was for another couple their age. There was much to consider.

Statistically, the offspring of Desert Storm veterans were born with a much higher rate of birth defects. It was just another consequence of the war that the U.S. government refused to acknowledge. Although the numbers were staggering, it didn't stop many couples from trying to fulfill their dreams of having a family. He and Monica were no different. Knowing the phenomenal risks, they started at once. After three months of pleasurable practice, the seed was planted. For Monica, it was the beginning of morning sickness. For him, it was a time of great apprehension. Each night, he dropped to his knees and asked the Lord for the blessing of a healthy child, knowing that if his child was born deformed or mentally retarded, his love would be just as strong. Still, with the odds stacked against them, he prayed hard.

The nine months seemed like years, then with little warning, Baby Manchester was ready for its grand entrance. In his usual calm state during crises, Steve drove his panting wife to the hospital. While reassuring her, he thought about the months of preparation. They had taken the child birth classes, read the books, so he figured that they were ready. He didn't realize that there was no preparing for the miracle which was about to change his life forever. With a cool hand, he broke free of Monica's grip and turned the steering wheel into the hospital's parking lot.

Hours passed and he stood by Monica's side, holding her hand and feeling helpless while she bore the incredible torment. Overcome with a deep respect, he watched as she pushed and pushed. She moaned from the agonizing pain, but never once complained.

The head began crowning. With his eyes focused on the birth of his child, his body was overloaded with adrenaline. After witnessing so much death, this new life, a life filled with his own blood, completely swept him away. While his mind was sent reeling into the clouds, his feet were planted firmly for the new arrival of hope. Every freed inch of the baby's head made his heart beat faster. As the entire head broke free, he held his breath while the baby took its first. Through watery eyes, he instantly recognized the face. He swore that the bald, toothless scowl belonged to his late grandfather. A few more pushes from an exhausted mother, and his best friend was born. It was love at first sight. As the doctor lifted the fragile, mucous-covered body into the air, he noticed the swollen plumb between its legs. It was a boy. At a sturdy nine pounds, Evan Steven entered the world angry as hell. He screamed out his rage at the cold air, loud sounds and bright lights. As if he understood his first lesson in life, the baby quietly sobbed. Steve matched the tears of his beautiful son. He vowed that he'd always be there for his boy, no matter what the cruel world offered. It was the first time he had cried in three brutal years. The whole room joined the bawling babies.

He kissed Monica, then proudly strutted over to the heat lamps where Evan was being cleaned up. Bending down, he kissed his son. The baby cried louder. Carefully inspecting the child, his body trembled. He counted ten fingers and ten toes. The nurse noticed the concern and patted him on the back. She promised, "Your son is healthy, Mr. Manchester. Congratulations!"

The tears rolled freely. After nine lingering months of worry, he hadn't passed his service-connected problems onto his son. Looking down into the cradle, he whispered, "Happy Birthday, Evan!" Looking up to heaven, he whispered, "Thank you!" The tears of relief and jubilation continued.

The tiny blessing immediately altered his perspective on life. Evan gave life more meaning, while also helping to heal his daddy's tortured soul. In the months to follow, the boy grew, with Steve as his gentle and loving teacher. The only things promised were Steve's love and time. It was all they ever needed. Together, they both learned.

There were lessons in politeness, sharing, honesty, the reasons not to fight. The list went on. Each informal class was a refresher course for Steve, relearning the simple, yet invaluable lessons of childhood. As the days turned into months, he gave all of himself to his son. In awe, he watched as the boy returned the gifts, ten-fold. It was his second chance to see the world through the eyes of pure goodness, innocence and love. He took full advantage of every opportunity, all the while wondering why every person couldn't love like a child.

Two more trying years passed by and he continued to report to the job he despised. Out of sheer self-preservation, the prison had turned him into a hunter. He felt good only during emergency situations, but when everybody else came down from the fight-or-flight rush of adrenaline, his body still pumped with unfocused energy. The job steadily overlapped into every aspect of his life. It went too far. At home, surrounded by family and friends, he constantly felt the urge to lash out, sensing an unreasonable need to protect himself. It was the most primitive instinct of survival and he couldn't turn it off anymore. Fighting off the constant impulses to fight, his fragile mind struggled for peace. Trying to appear normal became the toughest job of all. He couldn't enjoy his life.

He was burned out and knew it was impossible to heal from the P.T.S.D. when he still faced traumas on a weekly basis. Still, he needed to provide for his family. Although he was in too deep, one very violent inmate had another plan in mind. Physically, their meeting was painful, but mentally, the animal did him the biggest favor ever.

It was an emergency call for assistance. Steve was already running full-steam when he heard the commotion. Upon arrival, he witnessed one of the criminally insane clientele wrestling with an officer. Jumping in, he took over. While attempting to restrain the assaultive man, the skirmish led to the top of a steep staircase. Before he knew it, he was tumbling down the granite stairs, with the crazed inmate in tow. He felt each step pound into his body. They landed at the bottom, with the inmate landing on top. He winced from a piercing pain in his lower back, while the right side of his body throbbed. Gazing up, he saw some officers pull the lunatic off of him. That was the last thing he remembered. Everything went black.

Waking up in the rear of an ambulance, he tried to recall what had happened. It took a moment, but finally his mind began registering. Lying strapped to a gurney, the ambulance cleared the vehicle trap and sped off toward the hospital. An enormous weight was lifted from him. He would flirt with disaster no more. He had finally escaped from the prison, and he knew it. As the siren wailed, he slipped out of the rat race and re-entered the human race. The paramedic questioned his smile. He said nothing. He just closed his eyes, endured the pain and enjoyed the ride to freedom.

Nursing a severe back injury, no different from what his wife had once suffered, he contemplated his future options. Returning to the prison wasn't one. He informed Monica, "I'm never going back, Babe! I sleep better. I'm happier ...."

"And what are you planning to do?" she interrupted.

Without hesitation, he answered, "I'll go back to school for writing. I think it's the answer. I'll finally be able to interact with normal people and ...."

She smirked, but said nothing. Her face said it all. She feared financial insecurity more than anything. The thought of her husband temporarily unemployed scared the hell out of her. Steve, the problem solver, was now creating one of his own. Still, he felt there was no choice. There was enough money saved, and he'd work, but no longer at the prison. His health and happiness depended on it. That had to be more important. His desperate decision sparked a controversy that rocked the foundation of their unity as man and wife. After all of the years of marital wear and tear, it brought everything to a head.

For weeks, they argued about priorities and then, the sensitive issues of Desert Storm arose. He had always felt alone in struggling to get well, and resented Monica for not being there. He knew she was frightened of the truth, but the silent truth had gnawed at him for so very long. From the moment he returned from the war, he had carried the burden of an invisible illness. There were only a handful who could tell. She was one of those few. For years, he stumbled through a dark tunnel. Every day, he hoped she would reach in and pull him out. She never did. Sadly, she never knew how, so he carried the weight alone. Now, it came down to one question. He asked, "If I can only make five dollars an hour and we have to lose the house, will you still be with me?"

In a cool, uncaring tone, she replied, "I don't know."

That was it. It was the beginning of the end.

He spent the night on the couch, though his thoughts remained with his son. The last thing that he wanted was to leave, but he wondered if the boy was better off with unhappily married parents, or a pair who were quietly separated. He knew that pride or stubbornness shouldn't get in the way of the truth, but it wasn't a matter of pride. It was a matter of survival. He felt adamant about his stand. To him, the American dream was nothing more than an illusion. He swore he'd never sell his soul for a price tag again. Throughout his marriage, he had understood that measureless and perpetual bliss was unrealistic. Yet, complete unity was all he ever wanted. His wife had forgotten their vows — for better or for worse, for richer or for poorer, in sickness and in health. When they recited the words, he expected they'd share everything, whether good or bad. The truest test of that unity was at hand. It looked bleak. He cried himself to sleep.

In the morning, he watched the deadly frictions in Bosnia heat up on the television. Monica entered the room, looked at the broadcast and turned it off. Sitting across from him, her tired face showed signs that she was ready to talk. Smirking, he thought about how easy it was for someone to turn off a crises when it didn't affect them personally. Catching her impatient stare, his thoughts quickly focused on his own crises.

They calmly decided on marriage counseling and an appointment was set for that evening. The day drudged by, and, at last, they sat on some overstuffed chairs. They each gave their side of the dilemma. It was cut and dry. He needed peace and she wasn't prepared to lose everything that they had struggled to keep, namely, the house.

The councilor asked, "Mr. and Mrs. Manchester, do you love each other?"

They each concurred that they did.

"So, what's the problem?"

He didn't wait for his wife. "I've heard men tell me that they would give their lives for me and I believed every word." Looking at Monica, he finished, "And my wife wouldn't even give up her way of life?" The angry words cut like a knife.

Shaking his head, the councilor asked, "Mr. Manchester, how do you expect your wife to understand what you've gone through?"

The answer came too easy. He spent years thinking about it. "I don't. I never did. But if, God forbid, my wife was ever raped, how could I understand that? The way I see it, there are only two options. You can either hold someone's hand and help them heal, or stand in the shadows, hoping that someday, they return to you." Standing, he added frigidly, "What ever happened to unconditional love?"

The question left everyone speechless. He and Monica left the office in worse shape than when they arrived.

Days turned into weeks, but eventually they separated. The damage had reached far beyond blame. The cycle of communication had been severed forever. It was, by far, the greatest tragedy Steve ever encountered. He, and the woman he adored with everything inside of him, stood on opposite sides of the world. Though they searched, there was no bridge to connect them. Neither would budge. Monica had her own reasons and he refused to be controlled by material objects another day. He considered Monica the last casualty of the war. In a sad sense, he was relieved. Operation Desert Storm could take nothing more.

Before long, each hired an attorney to represent them in court. Steve sat back, only to watch both mouthpieces destroy whatever goodness or love remained. The lawyers were quite competent at turning beauty into something dirty and vulgar. Even so, while Monica became consumed with a bitter spite, he tried to remain fair.

After losing everything he had, to include his last dime, Monica asked coldly, "So, what is it that you care about?"

He softly replied, "Please kiss my son for me."

Throughout the divorce proceedings, Monica stayed true to form. She fought for every penny she could get. Steve forked it over. In turn, he was criticized a fool and judged to be meek. Most people didn't understand the true loss. While she played her cruel games, he had already learned. Though he'd never witness the retribution, she would have to live with every wrong decision she made, every spiteful action she chose. He was warned that nice guys finished last, but snickered at the advice. He never saw the finish line. Besides, nice guys slept better at night. No matter the price, it was his relationship with his son, Evan, that meant most. Monica would pay. It was inevitable. She refused to accept any responsibility for the failed marriage. That, alone, was going to stop her from ever moving on.

In the end, they lost the house, but much worse, they lost each other. He tried to understand Monica's struggle. She hadn't experienced war, yet she had suffered the full brunt of its effects. While he spent every second looking for the exit out of his dark tunnel, her needs were neglected. Along the way, whether she chose it or not, she was left behind. The war, the prison — it all changed him. His failed marriage was just another statistic of Operation Desert Storm.

He returned to school, spent every minute he could with Evan and continued his search for inner peace.

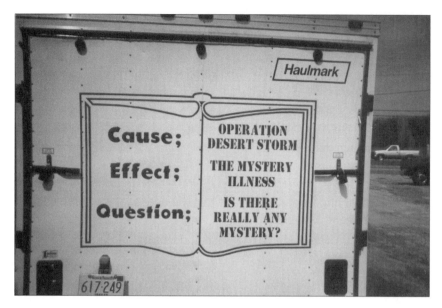

A sign of awareness is displayed on the back of Billy Manchester's #95 Pro Stock race car trailer.

Medals and memorabilia are all that's left to show for the sacrifices made in Operation Desert Storm. The Arabic writing on the MP brassard translates into — Military Police; Manchester. The unit patch on the brassard is that of the 14th MP Brigade — which served under 7th Corps.

Chapter 10

The Quest for Inner Peace

S teve didn't know where to turn until he recalled a famous saying of his late grandfather. The old man would wisely shake his head, saying, "If you help someone dig themselves out of their troubles, you'll always find a place to bury your own." He decided to put that theory to the test. It was the best decision he ever made.

Pulling into the Rose Hawthorne Home, a health care facility for terminally-ill cancer patients, he had second thoughts about volunteering his time. It was where his grandfather spent his last moments on earth, so it seemed like the place to start. His anxiety level, however, was on the rise. He wondered if he could handle any more. The answer awaited him within. Drawing in a deep breath, he stepped into his future.

The head nun was quickly summoned to the humble foyer. Her soft eyes couldn't conceal the tough, no-nonsense character she possessed. She wasted no time.

"What can I do for you, young man?"

He nervously grinned. "No. What can I do for you?" The repetitive answer was meant sincerely and he expected her to smile.

She didn't. Instead, she continued her line of questioning. "Can you cut grass or wash dishes?"

With a genuine nod, he affirmed that he could, but added, "I was thinking that there must be a patient or two who never receive visits. Perhaps, I could sit and talk with them, play cards, maybe just spend some time with them?"

The pious woman smiled. With a stern finger, she gestured for him to follow her into the home. Walking closely behind, he entered with every good intention of lending a compassionate hand. In the short days to follow, however, he discovered an even stronger, steadier hand extended back to him.

The home was segregated into two sections. He was escorted into the men's side. It had been years since his grandfather had passed on, but the initial tour jogged his tired memory. There were beds lined on both sides of the ward, with dying men lying beneath each set of covers. He saw the tubes and wires sticking out of some of them. It was clear, though, that medical technology was merely a last ditch effort at saving what was already gone. He heard the moans of those in pain and smelled the foul odors of raw flesh. This was the end of the line, the last stop before stepping onto the other side. Turning abruptly, the nun searched his face for a reaction. All she saw was his bright smile. He had spent years mastering the art of concealing his true feelings. The old lady had nothing on him. With a wave of her hand, she welcomed him onto the ward. Within seconds, she was gone and he stood alone. The eyes of every suffering man were upon him. It was time to introduce himself. It was time to spread the smile.

For the first hour, he just walked around. He introduced himself to the caring staff first, then to the ward's many patients. The reactions were varying. As he jumped from bed to bed, most of the men were happy to see him. Others were a little more suspicious of his intentions and were far too old or tired to hide it. Their simple honesty made him question himself. He thought maybe he was being selfish in searching for peace amongst those with much bigger problems. Looking around, it was as if they awaited his answer. With a smile, he gave it. He decided to stick with it. While finishing his first rounds, he was surprised to see that the men were more than happy. They were at peace. It was the peace he constantly dreamed of. He tried desperately to put his finger on it.

Standing back, he took in the tranquil surroundings. It was absolutely amazing. Although torment loomed over every bed, and death lurked behind every corner, the entire home was at peace. A hundred green plants filled the ward, while a handful of caged birds chirped in harmony. The sun's rays engulfed the interior of the building and the same sweet song played over and over on a hidden stereo. But there was more, a great deal more. He was sure of it. It felt as if he walked in the company of angels. Looking to his right, he saw his first.

He was a feeble, old man, strapped to an even older wheelchair. He was enjoying the afternoon from the open view of the sun porch, when he began struggling for Steve's attention. The light surrounding his head gave Steve chills. With a labored wave, he gestured Steve toward him.

Steve didn't think. He just floated to the nameless stranger as if being pulled by a magnet. Standing near him, he could tell that the man was close to his death. After speaking with him, he wondered if perhaps he wasn't meeting an angel in disguise.

His name was Nelson Julius. For the remainder of his hours on earth, not only did he become Steve's treasured friend, he became his spiritual guide. The very moment he opened his mouth, years of hard roads and wisdom learned were revealed.

In a surprisingly deep tone, he said, "Hello, young fella. What's a man like yourself doing in a place like this?"

Steve sheepishly grinned and searched for the right answer. It took a few long seconds before he replied, "I've spent a very long time hanging around bad people. I was wondering if there were any good people left." It wasn't the complete truth, but it was no lie. He added, "But, it looks like I've finally found one!"

Nelson smiled at the compliment. From the look on his face, he didn't buy it. Maintaining the smile, he gazed deeply into Steve's eyes. The stare felt uncomfortable. Only his mother ever peered into his eyes that way. Softly patting the chair next to him, he offered a seat. The familiar gesture sent a shiver down Steve's spine. He accepted.

For awhile, there was silence. Then, the man placed his warm hand on Steve's. Shooting the same penetrating stare into his eyes, he gave his first piece of priceless advice. "Son, I spent the first half of my life filling my mind with things I thought I needed. I spent the second half getting rid of most of it in order to find the truth. Believe me, the only thing worth worrying about is people. Everything else is hog wash!"

Nelson ended his speech on a heated note. The strong words shook Steve down to his bones. He was getting the strange feeling that Nelson Julius already knew about his dilemma. They sat for awhile in silence. Steve pondered the lesson. Nelson just delighted in having the company.

Eventually Steve left, but returned every other day. If there were any other doubts about volunteering his time, Nelson erased them. Each time he visited, he made his rounds, but always ended up on the sun porch. There was an attraction to Nelson's gentle spirit that he had never experienced before. After the first few visits, he finally explained his real suffering.

Nelson only shook his head, giving the impression that he really did have prior knowledge of the pain. He swore, "You never have what you haven't already given away completely. You want respect, then give it away. Love ... give it." Looking hard into Steve's attentive eyes, he concluded, "If you want forgiveness, then give it. If you need it, then that also means yourself!"

For two more weeks, the odd lessons continued, though Steve cherished one very special one. Nelson said, "Steve, life's not about what you want, it's learning to be happy with what you get. Life is about acceptance!" The last sentence rang inside of Steve's head.

Without debt, he was given two enormous pieces to the puzzle of life. He learned that the key to joy was acceptance, but not before there was forgiveness. He stood among men who were dying, yet they knew a peace like no others. They were finished with the denial, negotiating with God and the anger. They now accepted their fate and experienced a beautiful serenity. He had finally learned. It was time to let go. It was time to accept what had happened to him, to forgive others, as well as himself. It was time to move on. The self-destruction — his mental and emotional war could be stopped. He was ready for a cease fire. He had fought within himself long enough.

On the last afternoon he saw Nelson Julius, though the skies were overcast, the sun porch radiated. He gently held his friend's hand. Nelson was weak. He had reached the end. Looking up, in a faint voice, he asked, "Steve, do you believe in God?"

He nodded.

"Then you will find everything you need to know in the book of life, the Bible. It's the manual to a meaningful life. Read it. Study it. Feel it. Then you'll be healed!" They said nothing more.

Steve wished him a goodnight and promised that he'd see him in the morning.

Nelson smiled. He said, "Goodbye, Steve Manchester." Steve pretended he hadn't heard it, and never looked back. He had heard those words in the same firm tone before. He knew what they meant. He kept walking.

The following day, he arrived to find that Nelson had passed away during the early morning hours. It came as no shock. He stepped out onto the dim porch and thought about his wise friend. Mr. Nelson Julius had changed the world, or at least his world. He felt grief, though he knew it was a selfish feeling. Nelson had suffered for a long time, probably an extra two weeks for his sake. He so desperately needed the man's wisdom. Nelson's work was done and he hated to let him go.

As he solemnly walked out, one of the nurses stopped him. "Steve, Mr. Julius left this for you," she said and handed him a book. It was his Bible.

He sat in the parking lot for a few minutes. He was amazed that strangers like Nelson Julius and Jason Matthews could just breeze into his life, touch it in such a permanent way, then leave just as quickly. Both men had swooped in and placed his life back on the right track. At one of his lowest points, Jason Matthews, the combat medic, renewed his faith in mankind. Nelson Julius, also descending out of the blue, gave him an equally valuable gift. For the first time in years, there was a light at the end of the dark tunnel. Both strangers had offered a most profound and lasting gift. They offered hope. All the while, that hope was just a tear drop away. He smiled. Perhaps there are angels sent to help, he thought, and opened the Bible.

There was a small plastic card separating the Old Testament from the New. He plucked it out. It was a prayer that read: God, Grant me the serenity to accept the things that I cannot change, the courage to change the things that I can and the wisdom to know the difference. It was one last act of kindness from Nelson. The prayer said it all. It was the answer.

Returning to his parent's home, he read parts of the Bible and pondered every word. The cleansing scriptures provided a great sense of comfort. It didn't take long to find many truths. As if it were a treasure found, he opened up his heart and soul and believed. As an innocent child believes in Santa Claus, with the same effortless strength, he believed. His mother had been right. It was so easy, so very simple. All he ever needed to do was keep the faith.

He also pondered the last few years of his life. Most of what he'd experienced happened for no logical reason, at least not to him. But there had to be reasons for it. Just believing in that made it easier. So, he believed. Faith was such a simple way to lighten the load. As long as he did his best with the gifts God gave him, the rest was out of his hands. He felt lighter already.

Spiritually, he had found his way. His spirit wasn't crushed and left to die in the sand. It only needed mending. For every closed door, another one opened. He only needed the faith to walk through. There was still the physical pain and anxious suffering, but now he leaned on the pillar of hope. After drawing comfort from the Good Book, as well as the kindness of strangers, he decided it was time to forgive those who had caused him pain. It was time to accept everything that had happened. The wounds would take time to heal, but sitting on his parent's quiet patio, he knew in his heart that the time to forgive was way overdue.

With a piercing pain, he thought about the soldier who left him for dead in the desert. He recalled his paunchy face, his terrified eyes. He remembered everything about him. The memory had haunted him for years. It was time to let it go. He simply pictured the man one last time and said aloud, "I'll never understand why you abandoned me, but I forgive you." It was no more than a verbal acknowledgement, yet he felt the relief. There was an incredible freedom in forgiveness. He could feel the years of anger and rage pour from his soul. From then on, it would be up to the stranger to carry the burden. He had learned the hard way. He'd never allow another person's feelings or actions to dictate his own, or again fall victim to an endless and uncontrollable misery. He cast away the throbbing pain, and, instantly, it lightened his restless spirit.

Looking at his reflection in the patio's sliding door, his eyes watered. It was time to forgive the person who was the hardest on him. He needed to forgive himself. This took a little more effort. As he sat under the open skies, warm sprinkling showers washed his body, while the forgiveness cleansed his soul. Left drenched, he gradually came to terms with his own worse fears. He accepted that he was human, a sensitive man who cared deeply about others. That was where most of his pain originated. His healing heart — the same heart that forced him to stand up and fight for his beliefs — also caused him to cry. There was no more shame in feeling.

He also thought about his mistakes and accepted that he'd make many more. Contemplating his ruthless self-perceptions, he vowed that he'd be less severe in judging himself in the future.

The afternoon whisked by, leaving him refreshed, both inside and out. There were still problems to solve and the physical dilemmas of Operation Desert Storm to deal with. Yet, mentally, emotionally and spiritually, he had made it. He persevered. It made him smile. He had come so very far.

The storm finally passed and he decided to call Scott. "Hey, buddy," he said, "I've got a full bottle of vodka that I need a hand wrestling with!"

With joy, Scott yelped, "I'll be right over!" A dial tone announced that he was already on his way.

For the remainder of the night, Steve and his supportive friend shared the vodka, but both knew they shared much more. Together, they celebrated a triumph of a human spirit. There were very few words spoken. There were very few needed. From a short distance, Scott had followed his long search for inner peace. By the end of the victorious celebration, Scott, the intoxicated math whiz, had figured out the equation. In an attempt at seriousness, he slurred, "It's easy. Your struggles plus your determination equal victory!"

That was the last thing Steve remembered.

He awoke in agony. The stinging reminder of the vodka throbbed inside his head. He grinned at the pain. It was worth it. Sitting up, he grabbed for his cigarettes. He thought about the long-term effects and crumpled up the pack. It was about time he kicked the deadly habit. There was too much to look forward to. He didn't want to cut himself short. Instead, without complaint, he took his pills for a malfunctioning thyroid, an anxiety disorder and a swollen prostate. He lazily slid out of bed and walked to the window. Opening the dark shade, he was immediately faced with the gloomy sky. It didn't matter. He stared out onto the fresh new day, when again, he caught his reflection in the glass. For the first time in years, he liked what he saw.

As he peered into his own eyes, he thought about the heavy price he had paid. Everything he had worked so hard for before Desert Storm was gone. His law enforcement career was finished, the house was foreclosed on, and most tragically, his marriage was destroyed. He never wanted it that way, a clean sweep. It was just the way everything turned out. He had lost everything, but through it all, he had found himself.

He was beginning a second life and being at the bottom, there was only one place to go. He had learned to believe in himself, so focusing on the day ahead, he decided to enjoy tomorrow when it came. For today, he thought it would be nice to rediscover the simple joys of the beach.

The calendar read 1996, and a tardy spring gave way to the searing heat of the summer's sun. After removing the top from his new convertible, he slowly ventured up the coastal highway. While the radio blasted a tune from a decade past, a warm, gentle breeze massaged his short-haired scalp. The tingling sensation immediately brought him back to his days of careless youth. He always loved driving under the open skies. The precious memory made him smile, but there was more. It was déjà vu. His life had come full circle. After all of the tears of pain, all of the tears of suffering, his life had been given back to him.

"Thank God I didn't give up," he said aloud. Through misty eyes, he silently gave thanks and savored his freedom.

A short distance up the highway, his battered lungs inhaled the clean air. That fresh air produced a strong feeling. It was as if a terrible storm just passed over, leaving behind a total calmness. He was sure of it. It was the kind of peace that only follows the worst of storms. Peering in the rear view mirror, he smiled again. The entire sky behind him was threatening the world with black, dreary clouds. The stormy skies were completely behind him. Staring harder, he noticed something else. It was clear they'd never be so far that he wouldn't remember.

Breaking the trance, he turned back toward the east, toward whatever lay before him. The powder blue canvas warmed his entire being. He felt the simple beauty right down to his healing soul. As his smile brightened, he took a quick right.

Hypnotized by the white, puffy pillows floating above, the new rag-top came to a halt. Ironically, he had reached another cross road. Looking left, then right, he decided that it didn't really matter which direction he turned. After all of the sacrifices, through all of the harsh and troubled times, he had learned. There were no wrong roads. It never once made a difference where he ended up. The only thing that ever truly mattered was what he learned along the way. There were reasons for everything. These truths kept him on the back roads.

Though the freshly paved freeways were quicker and the trip was smoother, there was nothing to see, barely anything to learn. The bumpy roads, however, allowed him to take it all in. They were normally the harder paths to follow, with one difficult obstacle after another to overcome. In the end, however, there was always growth, understanding, experience, and if he paid close attention, a taste of wisdom. Each conquered maze made him a better person. Remembering some of the rough routes he tackled, he steered a hard left. It was a winding trail and one very indirect way to the beach.

At a leisurely pace, he kept his eyes glued on the blue skies ahead. Tasting the salt air on his tongue, he knew he was close. The trip was almost over. The thought made him shudder with equal amounts of excitement and relief. For the first time since leaving the highway, he looked back in the rear view. The dark clouds had all but vanished into the past. He remembered traveling under them, but no longer felt their despair.

The salty taste became stronger and the sea winds picked up. He dropped his gaze. There was no need to look back any longer. It was time to relax beneath the warm sun. Life was good. With nothing but hope and determination, he had learned to love it all over again. Jumping out of the car, he stopped to decide his next move. The cool sparkling ocean shimmered invitingly, but, as if he were a child, he ran into the dunes.

Ice Cream Cone
(for Evan)

Minimum wage and all out of luck,
in sofa cushions, some change was stuck.
Enough to buy one ice cream cone,
we shared it on the long walk home.

And on the trip, the questions flew,
"Why just one cone? And why not two?"
So looking deep within his eyes,
I chose the truth, no need for lies.

Explaining that, while life was tough,
with just one cone, we had enough.
He shook his head, took one last taste,
then gave it back and wiped his face.

The pride I felt to watch him share!
At four years old, he didn't care.
As long as we had time to play,
for him, it was a perfect day.

For all the dreams that I had built,
to watch them fall, I'd felt the guilt.
But being poor was not a crime . . .
for on my son, I'd spent my time.

Steven Manchester
(One year later)

Author Steven Manchester and son Evan.

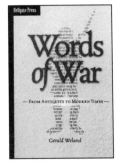

WORDS OF WAR
From Antiquity to Modern Times   ISBN: 1-55571-491-9
by Gerald Weland   176 pages, Paperback: $13.95

Words of War is a delightful romp through military history. Lively writing leads the reader to an understanding of a number of soldierly quotes. The result of years of haunting dusty libraries, searching obscure journals, and reviewing microfilm files, this unique approach promises to inspire many casual readers to delve further into the circumstances surrounding the birth of many quoted phrases.

ARMY MUSEUMS
West of the Mississippi   ISBN: 1-55571-395-5
by Fred L. Bell, SFC, Retired 318 pages, Paperback: $17.95

A guide book for travelers through 23 museums of the west. Army Museums contains detailed information about the contents of each museum and the famous soldiers stationed at the forts and military reservations where the museums are located. It is a colorful look at our heritage and the settling of the American West.

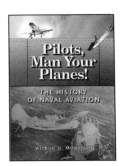

PILOTS, MAN YOUR PLANES!
A History of Naval Aviation   ISBN: 1-55571-466-8
by Wilbur H. Morrison   474 pages, Hardcover: $33.95

An account of naval aviation from Kitty Hawk to the Gulf War, Pilots, Man Your Planes! tells the story of naval air growth from a time when planes were launched from battleships to the major strategic element of naval warfare it is today. This book is filled with rare photographs, detailed maps, and accurate accounts that can be found nowhere else. Ideal for anyone interested in aviation.

ORDER OF BATTLE
Allied Ground Forces of Operation Desert Storm
by Thomas D. Dinackus   ISBN: 1-55571-493-5
407 pages, Paperback: $17.95
Contains photographs of medals, ribbons, and unit patches

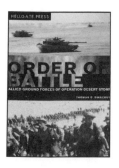

Based on extensive research—containing information not previously available to the public—Order of Battle: Allied Ground Forces of Operation Desert Storm is a detailed study of the Allied ground combat units that served in the conflict in the Persian Gulf.

LEGACY OF LEADERSHIP
Lessons from Admiral Lord Nelson
by Joseph F. Callo   ISBN: 1-55571-510-9
144 pages, Hardcover: $17.95

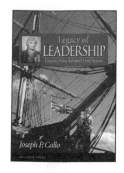

A penetrating view of modern history's most famous naval commander. Legacy of Leadership goes beyond the events of Vice Admiral Lord Nelson's life to illuminate the personal qualities that made him such an exceptional leader—qualities that can be applied to today's military and business leaders.

GULF WAR DEBRIEFING BOOK
An After Action Report   ISBN: 1-55571-396-3
by Andrew Leyden   318 pages, Paperback: $18.95

Available in the George Bush Presidential Library Museum Store. Now you can draw your own conclusion as to what happened during the seven-month period between late 1990 and early 1991. The Gulf War Debriefing Book: An After Action Report provides you with a meticulous review of the events. It includes documentation of all military units deployed, the primary weapons used during the war, and a look at the people, places, and politics behind the military maneuvering.